G000041680

AILA Review

Multilingual, Globalizing Asia
Implications for Policy and Education

VOLUME 22 2009

Guest Editors Lisa Lim
University of Hong Kong

Ee-Ling Low
National Institute of Education, Nanyang
Technological University, Singapore

Editor Susanne Niemeier
University of Koblenz-Landau

Editorial Board Ulrich Ammon
Gerhard-Mercator-Universität, Germany

Jasone Cenoz
University of the Basque Country, Spain

Roy Lyster
McGill University

Tadhg O'hIfearnain
University of Limerick, Ireland

John Benjamins Publishing Company
Amsterdam/Philadelphia

Table of contents

Introduction*

Lisa Lim and Ee-Ling Low

University of Hong Kong / National Institute of Education, Nanyang
Technological University, Singapore

At the end of the first decade of what is often affirmed as the 'Asian Century', we are pleased to have put together this volume with Asia as its focus. It is important to establish from the outset that the basis for this volume stems not from a search for the commonalities that Asia as a whole presents; this is certainly an impossibility. Rather, it is an opportunity for us to turn our focus to the complexity that the multilingual situation in each Asian country, set against the backdrop of the forces of globalization, presents for language planning and education policies.

We begin by briefly deconstructing the three key terms used in conceptualizing this volume: What do we conceive of as 'Asia'? What do we mean by 'multilingualism'? What do we understand by 'globalization' and its particular effects on Asia?

As the largest continent on Earth, bounded by the Arctic, Pacific, and Indian oceans (*Encyclopædia Britannica Online* 2009), and comprising about 4 billion, i.e. 60%, of the world's population, is defining Asia possible, or desireable? A "geographical accident" (*The Economist* 1987 cited in 2009), Asia is often accepted as spanning from Kazakhstan and the Maldives in the west, to Japan and New Zealand in the east (e.g. Kachru 2005:xxiv; *The Economist* 2009); unsurprisingly then, a main characteristic is in fact the diversity that exists on all fronts: geography, climate, race, religion, language, economic wealth, system of government. Even while our collection includes a mere subset of all that can be Asia, namely South Asia (with specific mention of India and Sri Lanka), East Asia (China, Hong Kong, Japan) and Southeast Asia (Malaysia, Singapore, the Philippines), the diversity in ecologies and complexity in challenges are evident.

One element of Asia's diversity is really one of its defining features, namely, how multilingual Asia is, on a number of levels, and how prominent a role language contact has had in Asian ecologies (Ansaldo 2009). The languages of Asia number more than 2,000, comprising some two-thirds of the world's languages (*Ethnologue* 2009; here Asia also includes the Middle East, and excludes Australia and New Zealand), and stem from diverse families, including Austronesian (Malay, Filipino), Dravidian (Tamil), Indo-Aryan (Hindi, Sinhala), Japonic (Japanese), Sinitic (Cantonese, Hokkien, Mandarin), to name just the (more significant) ones figuring in this volume. Heterogeneity within single countries is also widespread, whether already in the original inhabitants or deriving from early historical population movements (e.g. South Asia), or as a consequence of economic immigration or forced population movements in particular during European colonial rule (e.g. Malaysia, Singapore); ethnolinguistic diversity should also be recognized in countries normally viewed as homogeneous (e.g. China, Japan) — for it is also there, and not only in the obviously ethnolinguistically heterogeneous countries, that the more marginal, minority communities often fall out of language policy making (as e.g. Feng's paper on China as well as Tupas's paper on the Philippines highlight). This is not merely an exercise in numbers: typological diversity of the substrates not only make for nativized Englishes which are quite distinct from 'standard' varieties (see e.g. Lim and Gisborne 2009) and which thus find no place in official discourses (e.g. seen in Lim's paper on Singapore); the typological differences between the vernaculars and the official languages can also have significant

AILA Review 22 (2009), 1–4. DOI 10.1075/aila.22.01lim
ISSN 1461–0213 / E-ISSN 1570–5595 © John Benjamins Publishing Company

implications in pedagogy, and mean subsequent success, or lack thereof, of language policies (as e.g. Li's paper on HK shows). In such multilingual, contact ecologies, plurilingual practices (as discussed in Canagarajah's paper on South Asia, and also seen in Lim's paper on Singapore) are thus unsurprising, but again tend not to find a place in official policy.

Globalization, while certainly a buzzword par excellence of the 21st century, is a phenomenon which has existed since pre-modern times, as in the trade links between the Roman Empire, the Parthian Empire and the Han Dynasty, inspiring the development of the Silk Road. We consider the phenomenon in its modern form here, one of its significant elements commonly recognized being the interdependence and interconnectivity of the world's economy, the current world financial crisis being an illustrative case in point. Beyond the economy, the borderlessness of today's world also encompasses the rapid transfer of information through the digital medium in what has become known as the 'knowledge-based economy' of the 21st century. Alongside — and an integral part of — these developments is the undeniable position of English as **the** global language with which the world communicates and operates, which has been increasing significantly in particular in Asia, where the fastest-growing body of English-users is found: the total English-using population of Asia is now more than that of the Inner Circle, and English is the main medium in demand for bi-/multilingualism in the region (Kachru 2005: 15). While the process of globalization should not be too simplistically equated with the dominance of the English language (and indeed many of the papers in this volume examine how Mandarin/Putonghua may become the heavyweight in the region), contemporary geopolitics, coupled with the sociohistorical circumstances of many Asian countries (former British or American colonies), together mean that a consideration of language situations and policies almost always involves a wrangling over the place that English has therein.

In terms of scholarship, it is also timely to turn our lens to Asia, given how it has been felt that Asian Applied Linguistics (AL) research has largely been 'invisible' in the British and North American (BANA) sphere (Pakir 2004: 70) or more generally outside of Asia itself. This in no small part has been simply because a significant proportion of the Asian scholarship in AL has — naturally — been discussed and published in languages relevant to the countries themselves, i.e. the major Asian languages of Chinese, Japanese, Korean, Malay, Thai, Tamil and Hindi, amongst others, and thus has not and still is not read and disseminated in English-dominant global scholarship (Pakir 2004: 70f.). In this respect, a number of the papers in this volume (Canagarajah, Feng, Hino, Li) do well to drink deeply from the precious fount of local scholarship which many outside are not privy to, and remind us too that many insights which gained currency in 'international' (read: English-speaking) scholarship had already been made decades before in local languages. For this reason it was imperative that we called upon scholars ontologically from and intimately familiar with the countries or regions themselves. Turning to the 'younger' voices was also a prerequisite, as we believe it is vital for the views and visions of a new generation of scholars to be reflected who are the ones who will shape ongoing and future research in AL.

This volume thus takes a step towards narrowing the gap between English-dominant discourse and the wealth of research on and in other Asian languages, and has as its basis how Asia maintains and manages its own endonegeous language(s) while at the same time tries to find a place for the English language, either with its own baggage of former colonial language and/or its weight as a most valuable commodity in this age. On the basis of this arise numerous implications for policy and education: What is the medium-of-instruction (MoI) policy implemented, what agenda does it serve, and what are its implications? How is bi/multilingualism defined, and how is bilingual education manifested? How does the status of English as a vital (foreign) language impact on the position of the endogeneous language(s) of the country? Is there tension or complementarity? To what extent or in what way is the teaching and learning of English situated in the context of the country's endogeneous language (s), e.g. in translation studies, cross-linguistic studies, contrastive studies? Will English remain the language universally sought after, or can we already see competition from the major Asian languages, e.g. in terms of the enterprises of teaching Mandarin or Hindi as international languages?

The papers in this volume have taken on the questions above and the collection affords an analysis of myriad contexts, with the first major distinction being between countries where English has been institutionalized, as former British or American colonies (India, Sri Lanka, the Philippines, Malaysia, Singapore, Hong Kong), and countries where English is not (Mainland China, Japan). The concerns and challenges that the two groups of countries face are thus naturally different: the former managing their English language colonial legacy in their independent nationhood, the latter taking on the English language as an international language or foreign language to survive in a globalizing world. A consideration of post-independence language choices further teases forth a range of situations in the former group, with some having English as one of the official languages (Singapore, HK, the Philippines), and others instituting local languages as the official languages but with English in an important position (India, Sri Lanka), and still others relegating English to a much less important position (Malaysia). Cross-cutting official language status, MoI choices are also diverse, either with English being MoI (Singapore), or with English being a possibility amongst one or two other languages (HK, India, the Philippines), or with only the local official language and other regional language(s) as possibilities for MoI, at least at lower levels (Malaysia, Sri Lanka).

Even more, as scholars and insiders of their country or region, the contributors have each highlighted the specific situation and challenges peculiar to their country or region, which at the same time share various themes with each other, such as the reality of plurilingual practices, and the in/exclusion of minority communities, as already mentioned earlier. The collection may thus be grouped in a number of ways; we present but one grouping below, identifying some specific thrusts that emerge from the various contributions.

(i)   Pushing the boundaries of concepts and practices

Canagarah's paper demonstrates how plurilingual practices and ideologies — more than multiple but separate competencies — are deeply rooted in the (South) Asian tradition of communication, and discusses the implications this holds for the language classroom, where what is important is not a focus on the mastery of the rules of any single language but rather the teachers' ability to develop students who are aware of and adept in a repertoire of that might arise in contact situations. Tupas's contribution offers the powerful perspective that, instead of focussing on the language element in language policy development, it is the people and issues related to their social development that require our attention. To do so, it is important to 'dis-engage' from the focus on language policy to that of social policy i.e. on specific social needs of the local communities including grappling with issues like poverty, health care and public safety.

(ii)   Tussling for linguistic supremacy

The contributions by Azirah, Lim and Li have the common theme of the various conflicts and controversies surrounding the language policies adopted by Malaysia, Singapore and Hong Kong respectively. In the case of Malaysia, Azirah's paper underlines how race and religion feature prominently in the shaping of language policies and the selected medium of instruction, with language and education policies swinging constantly between Malay and English and back again to Malay. Lim's paper, highlighting the disjuncture between official language policy and actual linguistic practices in Singapore, describes how the real mother tongues, namely the Chinese 'dialects' and Singlish, the nativized English variety, have been regarded with fear and treated with loathing in the official language policies and accompanying prestige planning, and argues for an enlightened consideration of these varieties as being natural to the multilingual ecology and which should be given the space to thrive. Li's paper discusses the constant tension in Hong Kong language policy between Cantonese, the de facto language of communication and instruction, and both English and Putonghua, involving the struggles various stakeholders face in the increased prominence afforded to these latter two languages in 'Asia's world city' caught between its British past and SAR China present.

(iii) Actively seeking the English language
The last two papers by Feng and Hino on Mainland China and Japan respectively demonstrate the presence and impact that the English language has in countries which were not bequeathed the language by former colonial rulers, but which desire it as necessary capital, both countries having to find a resolution to the tension between the spread of English and their main dominant language Mandarin Chinese and Japanese respectively. More specifically, challenges involve addressing indigenous culture(s): Feng highlights the incongruence in the English language policies adopted in urban vs. rural areas and between different social classes and ethnolinguistic groups; Hino argues for the adoption of de-Anglo-Americanized English as a means of expressing indigenous values in international communication.

The entire collection is then critically discussed in a review article by Bruthiaux, who highlights some of the more fundamental as well as more controversial themes arising in the papers, both methodological and conceptual, as well as geopolitical, and in the latter, drawing richly on facts of economy and demography, e.g. in weighing up China against India — and thus their respective languages Mandarin and Indian English — as likely dominant global player and language. Of the many insightful observations therein, one vital reflection he offers is that the only certainty about the linguistic situation in Asia is its constant state of flux, making it almost impossible to predict what its linguistic future will look like.

That being said, we believe that the collection of articles in this volume will nonetheless stand the test of time, together comprising an authoritative and significant reference work, offering critical views and refreshing takes on the current, diverse, fascinating issues and challenges pertaining to policy and education in multilingual, globalizing Asia.

Note
* We thank Susanne Niemeier, current editor of *AILA Review*, for her support and involvement throughout the creation of this volume — LL also thanks previous editor Jasone Cenoz for the invitation in the first place to edit a volume on Asia — and we are also grateful to Kees Vaes of John Benjamins for being ally and advisor throughout the project. We are especially indebted to our two reviewers for their unrivalled expedient reading of the papers and their positive, constructive comments for the authors. Above all, our heartfelt thanks go to our authors for responding so positively and enthusiastically to our invitation, and for delivering (wonderfully and amiably to our tight deadlines) important and exciting contributions — it has been a most fulfilling collaboration.

References
Ansaldo, U. (2009) *Contact Languages: Ecology and Evolution in Asia*. Cambridge: Cambridge University Press.
Banyan (2009) In the shade of the banyan tree. *The Economist*. 11 April.
Encyclopædia Britannica Online (2009). Asia. *Encyclopædia Britannica*. Retrieved 16 August 2009 from http://www.britannica.com/EBchecked/topic/38479/Asia
Kachru, B. 2005. *Asian Englishes: Beyond the Canon*. Hong Kong: Hong Kong University Press.
Lewis, M.P. (ed.) (2009) *Ethnologue: Languages of the World*, 16th ed. Dallas, TX.: SIL International. Online version retrieved 27 August 2009 from http://www.ethnologue.com/
Lim, L. and N. Gisborne (eds) (2009) *The Typology of Asian Englishes*. Special issue, *English World*-Wide 30(2).
Pakir, A. 2004. Applied linguistics in Asia: Pathways, patterns and predictions. In S.M. Gass and S. Makoni (eds) *World Applied Linguistics*. *AILA Review* 17: 69–76.

The plurilingual tradition and the English language in South Asia

Suresh Canagarajah
Pennsylvania State University

There has been a plurilingual tradition of communication in South Asia since precolonial times. Local scholars consider pluringualism as 'natural' to the ecology of this region. In plurilingualism, proficiency in languages is not conceptualized individually, with separate competencies developed for each language. The different languages constitute an integrated system to constitute a repertoire. After distinguishing plurilingualism from other forms of multilingual communication, the article shows how English has been accommodated in this tradition. What I label Plurilingual English is not an identifiable code or a systematized variety of English. It is a highly fluid and variable form of language practice. Speakers negotiate their different Englishes for intelligibility and effective communication. The article goes on to define plurilingual competence. For communication to work across such radical differences, it is important that acquisition and use go hand and hand. Such a competence is always in a state of becoming and, therefore, acquisition is emergent. Plurilingual communication works because competence does not rely solely on a form of knowledge, but rather, encompasses interaction strategies. In the final section, the article discusses how learner strategy training and language awareness go some way toward facilitating such interactional strategies and repertoire development.

Introduction

Plurilingualism has recently received some attention in the scholarly literature due to the promotion of plurilingual competence by the Language Policy Division of the Council of Europe (2000). The concept has additionally received discussion in the communicative context of late modernity, where languages come into contact in contexts of transnational affiliation, diaspora communities, digital communication, fluid social boundaries, and the blurring of time/space distinctions (see Rampton 1997). However there has been a plurilingual tradition of communication, competence, and pedagogy in South Asia since precolonial times. While plurilingualism is promoted by policy intervention or treated as an effect of atypical social conditions in present times, scholars consider pluringualism as 'natural' to the ecology of South Asia. Bhatia and Ritchie (2004:794) state: "In qualitative and quantitative terms, Indian bilingualism was largely nourished naturally rather than by the forces of prescriptivism". As evidence for this, scholars point to the status of the whole of South Asia as a linguistic area — "that is, an area in which genetically distinct languages show a remarkable level of similarity and diffusion at the level of grammar" (Bhatia and Ritchie 2004:795). This linguistic diffusion they consider extraordinary, relative to other regions of the world. Pattanayak (1984:44) notes: "If one draws a straight line between Kashmir and Kanyakumari and marks, say,

AILA Review 22 (2009), 5–22. DOI 10.1075/aila.22.02can
ISSN 1461–0213 / E-ISSN 1570–5595 © John Benjamins Publishing Company

every five or ten miles, then one will find that there is no break in communication between any two consecutive points". Many scholars attribute this linguistic synergy to language attitudes in the region: i.e., an "accepting attitude, which has brought about the assimilation of features from Dravidian, Indo-Aryan, Islamic, and even Christian and European cultures into a single system, complex, but integrated" (Bright 1984:19). Such features are a testament to the adaptive strategies of the local communities, which develop multilingualism when a new language comes into contact, rather than rejecting or suppressing the language.

The plurilingual tradition is not found in South Asia alone. We are beginning to see descriptions of similar practices from Africa (Makoni 2002), South America (de Souza 2002), and the Polynesian Islands (Dorian 2004), among others. It has also been found in western communities, albeit inadequately acknowledged in mainstream scholarly circles (Gee 2001). It is beginning to be promoted in the European Community nowadays as people here realize the need for transnational communication (Council of Europe 2000). I am not arguing that some communities practise plurilingualism and others do not; it is simply that some communities acknowledge and promote these practices, others do not. There might even be a cyclical process involved in many communities: i.e., plurilingual codes become stable languages over time; stable languages come into contact and become hybrid/plurilingual; at this point, some communities embrace the hybridity (as in South Asia), and others resist further change in favour of upholding the dominance of the stable language. Appreciating the plurilingual tradition in South Asia will help us understand similar practices in other regions in the past or evolving in recent times. It will also help us formulate pedagogical approaches to promote plurilingualism, based on exemplary features in this region.

After defining plurilingualism and comparing it with other manifestations of multilingualism, I will show in the second section how this communicative tradition is sustained by a different orientation to the notions of speech community and language identity. I will then show the unique ways in which English continues to be negotiated and appropriated in this tradition. In the fourth section, I will outline the way South Asian plurilingualism compels us to theorize language competence in new ways. In the final section, I will discuss the changes necessary in pedagogy and educational policy to cultivate plurilingualism in this region and outside.

Defining plurilingualism

The notion of plurilingualism has been emerging gradually through the research of a few scholars in recent years (Silverstein 1996; Khubchandani 1997; Makoni 2002; Canagarajah 2007; Garcia 2009). I highlight the central features emerging from these accounts. In plurilingual competence:

1. Proficiency in languages is not conceptualized individually, with separate competencies developed for each language. What is emphasized is the repertoire — the way the different languages constitute an integrated competence.
2. Equal or advanced proficiency is not expected in all the languages.
3. Using different languages for distinct purposes qualifies as competence. One does not have to use all the languages involved as all-purpose languages.
4. Language competence is not treated in isolation but as a form of social practice and intercultural competence.
5. There is a recognition that speakers develop plurilingual competence by themselves (intuitively and through social practice) more than through schools or formal means.

We have to distinguish this communicative practice from certain other well known practices of language contact. How is plurilingual competence different from multilingualism? Societal multilingualism refers to languages having their separate identities in (sometimes) separate areas of a geographical location. Individual multilingualism similarly refers to separate, whole, and advanced competence in the different languages one speaks — almost as if it constitutes two or three separate monolingualisms. In both forms, multilingualism keeps languages distinct. Plurilingualism allows for the interaction and mutual influence of the languages in a more dynamic way. The difference can be clarified through the following diagram. Multilingual competence (including bilingualism) can be presented as follows:

L1   L2

This is a case of one language being added to another (in additive bilingualism), or supplanting another (in subtractive bilingualism). However, in plurilingual competence, the directionality of influence is much more diverse. Also, the languages may influence each other's development. More importantly, the competence in the languages is integrated, not separated, as in the following diagram (adapted from Garcia 2009:119):

In plurilingual communication, English may find accommodation in the repertoire of a South Asian, combining with his or her proficiency in one or more local languages. The person may not have advanced proficiency in English, and yet mix English words and grammatical structures into syntax from other languages (for examples see below). The English tokens may consist of borrowings, reduced forms (as in pidgins), and creative new constructions that might show the influence of other languages. The type of mixing will differ from speaker to speaker according to their levels of proficiency in English and according to their language backgrounds. So, speakers of language A and language B may speak to each other in a form of English mixed with their own first languages and marked by the influence of these languages. Without accommodating to a single uniform code, the speakers will be able to negotiate their different Englishes for intelligibility and effective communication. In this sense, plurilingual English (PE hereafter) is not an identifiable code or a systematized variety of English. It is a highly fluid and variable form of language practice. It is an intersubjective construct, in the manner similar to lingua franca English (LFE) as I have defined it elsewhere (see Canagarajah 2007).

This way of looking at the use of English is different from the now-familiar concept of World Englishes (WE). WE deals with a highly systematized and stable variety of English in postcolonial communities. Although borrowings from local languages may be included in WE, there is a long tradition of using these borrowings to the point where they become systematized and part of the local English variety. However, in PE, English and local languages may be combined in idiosyncratic ways as it befits the speaker, context, and purpose. In this sense, while WE is a language of its own, PE is not. PE is a form of communicative practice, not a stable variety.

PE may be marked by extreme deviation in phonology, grammar, and semantics from the metropolitan or WE varieties. Often, versions of PE have been called 'uneducated' Indian or Sri Lankan English to distinguish them from 'standardized' forms of local English (see Kandiah 1979). In the South Asian region, they have also been called 'Englishized Tamil' or 'Englishized Hindi' to indicate their status as hybrid forms of language practice (see Canagarajah 1995a), different from WE varieties. A few linguists have already drawn attention to the exclusion of these popular forms of English mixing from the WE paradigm (see Parakrama 1995; Canagarajah 1999). Blommaert (2005) treats these forms of mixing in Tanzania as 'globalization from below', where the spread of elite languages is appropriated at the grassroots level. Consider an example from Bhatia and Ritchie (2004:801), a printed warning in tobacco products in India: "Legal Warning: Chewing of tobacco is injorious to health." Although this example appears in a printed text in a very public domain, the spelling of "injorious" will be negotiated by readers and interpreted in context without a prescriptive tendency of treating it as an error or letting it affect intelligibility. This form of spelling may occur only in this one context and never be repeated again to become a stable form.

In some respects, PE is similar to pidgin. Annamalai (2001), the Indian linguist, points out, "It is similar to incipient pidgin in its indeterminacy. The words taken from the English language differ from speaker to speaker and even in the same speaker from time to time. Even the same sentence repeated after a few seconds may not have the same words from English" (2001:173). And yet, plurilingualism should be separated from other contact varieties. While pidgin is considered a functionally reduced language with a reduced grammar and semantic range, PE is not so. It has the full range of expression for all possible contexts desired by the speaker. It cannot be treated as a reduced language. As for creole, it might be considered as a stabilized form of PE. Although a creole is more developed than a pidgin, it is also different from PE. PE does not have an identity as a separate language, as a creole does. As we discussed earlier, it is a form of practice, not a language with a stabilized system or structure. Also, while a creole has native speakers of its own, PE does not.

PE also has to be distinguished from codeswitching and borrowing. Codeswitching assumes bilingual competence, displaying considerable rhetorical control by the speaker (see Romaine 1989); however, PE can be practised by those without bilingual competence. Furthermore, codeswitching assumes situationally significant switches with different rhetorical implications. However, Annamalai (2001:176) gives the following examples from Tamil to show that the switches do not have different meanings or, rather, more than one structure can be used to convey the same meaning:

(1)   nii ade reach-paNNa muDiymaa?
      'Can you reach it?'

(2)   Onakku adu eTTumma?
      'Is it reachable to you? i.e., Is it within your reach?'

Though (1) involves a mixing and both versions involve different syntactic structures, Annamalai argues they will be used interchangeably in the local context. The switches are automatic and do not add anything significant to the referential or rhetorical meaning. Annamalai (2001:177) argues:

"The mixing described here is not codeswitching, since the mixing takes place when [the variables] are constant". More importantly, in codeswitching there is an assumption that there are two languages involved in this discourse strategy. For locals, however, the languages involved in the mixing form a single continuum.

PE is also different from borrowing. Borrowing assumes that the words from English have been nativized in the borrowing language. Borrowing assumes a prior history of usage in a specific context with a specific meaning. However, in PE, the items from English can be used randomly and spontaneously. More importantly, the (borrowed) English words can be given totally new meanings as constructed by the interlocutors in a particular context. Annamalai (2001: 178) says: "The extremely high percentage of foreign words and the high degree of indeterminacy in their use from speaker to speaker make the mixing a special kind of borrowing, if at all it can be considered borrowing". This hints also at the possibility that the languages involved are not treated as separate by the speakers, but as a single system from which they can draw at will. Furthermore, the borrowed items can take variable and fluid forms. Annamalai argues: "the integrated loans from the source language and the proper names in the base language are pronounced as they are in the source language or as they are in the base language, thus introducing variation in the phonological system of the mixed language. For example, coffee may be pronounced either as *kaafi* or *kaapi*" (2001: 174–175). The first pronunciation is closer to English, and the latter is closer to Tamil.

Nor is PE an interlanguage. PE speakers are not moving toward someone else's target; they are constructing their own norms. It is therefore meaningless to measure the distance of PE from the language of 'native speakers' (i.e. Anglo-American speakers). In PE, each contact situation is a unique context, with a different mix of speakers and languages, raising its own challenges for negotiation. It may not be the case that one communicative act contributes to the other and so on, leading to a cumulative line of progression. Since the contexts are so variable and unpredictable, it is not possible to say that a target can be reached for perfect or competent plurilingual proficiency. If at all, we can speak of achieving a type of language awareness and competence that can help one handle diverse contact situations. However, it is possible that multilinguals already come with a plurilingual competence and do not wait for their interactions in English to develop that. Based on her findings of the creative and complex negotiation strategies of multilinguals in LFE situations, House (2003: 559) argues: "All these strategies seem to show that [LFE] users are competent enough to be able to monitor each others' moves at a high level of awareness". In a similar way, the plurilingual's proficiency has to be granted relatively greater agency, at least analogous to the agency attributed to the development in one's first language in certain generativist models. The PE speaker also comes with the competence — in many respects, more advanced than that of the child because of the years of multilingual practice enjoyed in their local communities — which is then honed through actual interactions. This development does not have to be marked by miscommunication or deficient usage, and should not be treated as such.

The plurilingual communicative tradition

PE is not just a communicative practice. It is sustained by a particular orientation to the speech community, language identity, and cultural orientation. We will turn below to considering the social and cultural background that makes this communicative practice possible.

Linguistic diversity is at the heart of South Asian communities. There is constant interaction between language groups, and they overlap, interpenetrate, and mesh in fascinating ways. Not only do people have multiple memberships, they also hold in tension their affiliations with local and global language groups as the situation demands. Khubchandani (1997), who has reconstructed the plurilingual tradition in his scholarship, uses an indigenous metaphor, *Kshetra*, to capture this sense of community. *Kshetras* "can be visualized as a rainbow; here different dimensions interflow symbiotically into one another, responsive to differences of density as in an osmosis" (1997:84). The unity that develops out of this diversity and continuity of affiliations Khubchandani calls a "super-consensus" (1997:84). Unlike other communities where individual differences have to be sacrificed for group identity, South Asian communities preserve their group differences while also developing an overarching community identity with other groups.

Individuals and communities are so radically multilingual that it is difficult to identify one's mother tongue or native language. People develop simultaneous childhood multilingualism, making it difficult to say which language comes first. Khubchandani (1997:173) points out, "Identification through a particular language label is very much a matter of individual social awareness". Language identity is relative to the communities and languages one considers salient in different contexts. Therefore, the label is applied in a shifting and inconsistent manner.

Because of such intense contact, languages themselves are influenced by each other, losing their 'purity' and separateness. Many local languages serve as contact languages, and develop features suitable for such purposes — that is, hybridity of grammar and variability of form. Khubchandani says: "Many Indian languages belonging to different families show parallel trends of development... [They] exhibit many phonological, grammatical and lexical similarities and are greatly susceptible to borrowing from the languages of contact" (1997:80). He goes on to say that differences "between Punjabi and Hindi, Urdu and Hindi, Dogri and Punjabi, and Konkani and Marathi can be explained only through a pluralistic view of language" (1997:91). Sri Lankan linguist Suseendirarajah (see Balasubramaniam et al. 1999:272–280) makes a similar case for Sinhalese (belonging to the Indo-Aryan family) and Tamil (belonging to the Dravidian language family). Having been in close contact in Sri Lanka, these languages have adopted many lexical and grammatical structures from each other, losing their respective family differences. This "pluralistic view of language", as Khubchandani calls it, departs from many of the assumptions of modernist linguistics, posing questions like the following: How do we classify and label languages when there is such mixing? How do we describe languages without treating them as self-contained systems? How do we define the system of a language without the autonomy, closure, and tightness that would preclude openness to other languages?

Communities are so multilingual that in a specific speech situation one might see the mixing of diverse languages, literacies, and discourses. It might be difficult to categorize the interaction as belonging to a single language. Khubchandani explains: "The edifice of linguistic plurality in the Indian subcontinent is traditionally based upon the **complementary** use of more than one language and more than one writing system for the same language in one 'space'" (1997:96; emphasis in original). If social spaces feature complementary — not exclusive — use of languages, mixing of languages and literacies in each situation is the norm, not the exception. To consider an example from literacy, the Tamil community in India and Sri Lanka has practised the well-known *manipralava* textuality (see Viswanathan 1993). When Sanskrit was considered the elite language for religious and philosophical purposes, local scholars mixed Sanskrit with Tamil in their writing. In this way, they both elevated the respectability of the vernacular and democratized Sanskrit. Nowadays Tamils mix mostly English in their writing, with similar social implications.

It is clear that this linguistic pluralism has to be actively negotiated to construct meaning. In these communities, meaning and intelligibility are intersubjective. The participants in an interaction produce meaning and accomplish their communicative objectives in relation to their purposes and interests. In this sense, meaning is socially constructed. Meaning does not reside in the language; it is produced in practice. As a result, "individuals in such societies acquire more **synergy** (i.e. putting forth one's own efforts) and serendipity (i.e. accepting the other on his/her own terms, being open to unexpectedness), and develop positive attitudes to variations in speech (to the extent of even appropriating deviations as the norm in the lingua franca), in the process of 'coming out' from their own language-codes to a neutral ground" (Khubchandani 1997: 94; emphasis in original). "Synergy" captures the creative agency subjects must exert in order to work jointly with the other participant to accomplish intersubjective meaning. "Serendipity" involves an attitudinal transformation. To accept "deviations as the norm" one must display "positive attitudes to variation" and be "open to unexpectedness". Subjects have to be radically other-centred. They have to be imaginative and alert to make on-the-spot decisions in relation to the forms and conventions employed by the other (as House 2003 observes in lingua franca encounters). It is clear that communication in multilingual communities involves a different mindset and practices from those in monolingual communities. The South Asian orientation to language departs from the Saussurean tradition of modernist linguistics which treats languages as separate, sui generis, products rather than fluid and hybrid social practices (see Lantolf and Thorne 2006).

Plurilingual English
There is evidence that local communities began to appropriate and mix English with their other languages very early in the colonial period. This realization is sometimes missing in the WE scholarship which makes it appear that the appropriation of English is a postcolonial development. The WE perspective is a natural outcome of its focus on stabilized forms of English. However, there were occasions of very spontaneous borrowing and mixing much earlier. Such practices occurred despite efforts by the British to keep the language from mixing and (from their perspective) impurity. We have records of English education in the region where students were kept in boarding schools so that their acquisition of English (and presumably British culture and knowledge) would be preserved from contact with the home culture and language of the students (see Chelliah 1922). Students were also fined for each occasion of non-English language usage. However, we see references to some "unruly" students who were dismissed from the school for escaping from their boarding at nights to attend Hindu temple festivals, maintaining secret miniature shrines for Hindu deities in their cupboards or desks, and surreptitiously practising what are called "heathen" songs and dances (Chelliah 1922). It is clear that students continued contact with the vernacular despite their isolation. That mixing of languages occurred and that students retained their vernacular and plurilingual competencies at that time is also evident from oral history and narratives (as I recount in Canagarajah 2000).

M. Gunasekera (2005) notes that soon the British administration itself began to acknowledge this mixing of languages. It appears as if locals constructed texts in the *manipralava* tradition, mixing English and Tamil or Sinhala in their official writing. The administration soon started publishing guidelines on the appropriate usage and spelling convention for local languages used in English texts. In 1869 the British administration published a *Glossary of Native and Foreign Words Occurring in Official Correspondence and Other Documents* (see B. Gunasekera 1893). Since then, there have been revised and updated glossaries to ensure a uniform policy on the spelling and meaning of Sinhalese and Tamil words in officialese in English. Through these glossaries, even the British administration implicitly recognized the fact that language mixing was an indigenous phenomenon. PE had its origins in that time.

Such tradition of mixing languages in written texts continues in newspapers and creative literature today. M. Gunasekara gives examples from contemporary English language newspapers in Sri Lanka where words from Sinhala or Tamil are used freely. These are not well-established borrowings, but random uses of new words. Consider the title of a news report from the *Daily Mirror* (2004: 1): "Anandasangaree appeals to 'My Dear Thambi'". The report refers to a senior Tamil politician appealing to a young Tamil militant leader to lay down arms and enter the democratic process.

However, the word *Thambi* (i.e. younger brother) is not translated anywhere in the news report. Nor is it italicized to flag its alien status. While bilingual Tamil/English readers can be expected to understand the word, the newspaper editors assume that the majority people in the country (i.e. the Sinhalese) can also understand the reference. The assumption here is that readers are trilingual and can understand the reference. This expectation of trilingual competence derives from the plurilingual tradition.

M. Gunasekera also provides an example in the reverse direction, where a Sinhala insertion in the English language newspaper is expected to be understood by Tamil speakers. Consider the following report (*Daily Mirror* 2004: 1):

(3) Sole-burning kattadiya hauled to court
     A kattadiya who allegedly burnt the legs of a girl during a 'pooja' conducted to cast away a spell, was produced in a Colombo court yesterday.

It is interesting that while the word *kattadiya* ('exorcist') is not flagged, there are quotation marks around the word *pooja*. Gunasekera suggests that *kattadiya* is assumed to be an English word, while *pooja* is not. However, it is *pooja* that is most often used as a borrowing in English. An alternate explanation is that while *kattadiya* is indispensable in the cultural lexicon, *pooja* is not. One might easily use an English word for *pooja*. The editor might be signalling the fact that *pooja* is consciously used in the report for a rhetorical purpose. What the *kattadiya* performed was not a *pooja* in the real sense of the term. *Pooja* is part of the orthodox Hindu or Buddhist religious tradition. What the exorcist does in his unorthodox tradition is a '*pooja*' only in a metaphorical sense. Therefore *pooja* is treated as a metaphorical codeswitch, while *kattadiya* is considered a borrowing. Part of the trilinguality of this text is the fact that *pooja* is a word used in both Sinhala and Tamil, unlike *kattadiya*, which is used only in Sinhala.

Local literature continues this plurilingual tradition of multiliteracies. Analyzing postcolonial English literature, M. Gunasekera makes the telling point that PE is used by less educated speakers, while those of a higher caste or class use standard Sri Lankan English (with less mixing and more stable forms). Consider the difference in the following excerpt:

(4) "And crab?" I said, already imagining half a teaspoon of black pepper, a pinch of ground cinnamon and fresh, chopped green coriander. Lemon and a dash of brandy from the bottle Mister Salgado got at Christmas from Professor Dunstable would make it exceptional and, I was sure, better than she had ever had at some stuffy hotel restaurant. "Yes, can do. No problem. Tomorrow?" Deep inside the stuffing I would bury a seeded slice of green chilli steeped in virgin coconut oil. She looked at me and smiled sweetly. "Not tomorrow, Triton. There is a party tomorrow night. We will be out." I shrugged. "Any time, say please." (R. Gunesekera 1994: 130).

Triton's sentences are not fully formed. They are pidgin-like in their functionality. Also, they are unidiomatic in English and show influences from Sinhala syntax. They are thus marked as less educated, suiting his status as a cook or domestic helper, whereas the language of the lady of the house is syntactically well constructed. Similarly, the authorial prose is distinct from Triton's. Ironically, the narrative voice is that of Triton. However, the author makes a distinction between Triton's speech and the prose adopted to reflect his consciousness.

Bhatt (2008) helps us understand the PE/WE distinction in another way. Analyzing some examples from Hindi/English mixing from recent Indian newspapers, Bhatt argues that they show an advance from the practice of stable forms of WE. He observes: "It represents a discursive change where bilingualism — as opposed to double monolingualism — is increasingly valued and commodified.

The double monolingualism was mainly manifest in the elite English bilingualism in India, where each language was spoken in its homogeneous monolingual expression" (2008: 193). As discussed in the first section, plurilingualism is a more dynamic interaction between languages, unlike "double monolingualism" which assumes equal proficiency in both languages. In saying this, Bhatt is treating some of the examples he provides as a distinctly non-elite practice. This is a more grassroots level and popular form of mixing. However, considering the history of writing practices such as *manipralava* writing, I do not consider such practices as postmodern, as Bhatt attempts to present them. Bhatt's examples are useful, however, in illustrating the distinction between WE (which is associated with the educated and upper middle class) and PE (which is associated with ordinary people). Though WE is used mostly by educated speakers, I am not arguing they do not use PE. I will give examples below where educated speakers also use PE in certain contexts (examples of unguarded communication or where the plurilingual ethos shared with the wider community is mutually invoked).

Whereas the instances of mixing above involve transliterating local languages into English, we also have texts that mix the graphological medium to represent English or Tamil words. Such instances might be considered *manipralava* writing in the classic sense. It is common in India or Sri Lanka to find chunks of quotation in English in the middle of a Tamil book. The script will be different for both languages. For example, it is quite common for academic texts in Sri Lanka and India to involve a prominent mixing of English and Tamil. Sri Lankan scholar Sivatamby's writing is a good example of such practice. In Sivatamby (1992), for example, quotations from primary sources are in English, while the commentary is in Tamil. In other cases, foreign words are inserted into Tamil syntax as he changes the script mid-sentence to accommodate English technical terms or scholarly phrases. He never translates or transliterates these marked codes. Such writing invites readers to perform a veritable bilingual reading. Nor is this a form of elite literacy. Even popular literature now involves English/Tamil mixing. Short stories written by Tamil refugees in the West (in journals like *kaalam* or *eksil*) feature such graphological mixing. Even less educated or non-academic readers are expected to engage in this plurilingual reading — shuttling between scripts and languages to make sense of the text. As in conversational/oral interactions, in writing too South Asian writers expect readers to negotiate the text through context, guesswork, and reading between the lines. Furthermore, plurilingual writing can extend to discourse features. Writers might mix genre conventions and rhetorical traditions in the body of the same text. I have analyzed the writing practice of Sivatamby (1984, 1990, 1992) in this regard and attributed his hybrid writing to the *manipralava* tradition (see Canagarajah 2006). Not only does he shuttle between English and Tamil academic discourses fluidly, he also draws from both rhetorical traditions to construct hybrid texts.

A more problematic feature of plurilingual accommodation of English is the way English grammatical or syntactic structures are combined with Tamil to construct hybrid syntax. Even new words might be coined creatively to express the ideas of the authors. For readers/scholars outside the region, these are interference problems from the writer's first language, and constitute errors. However, for local readers and writers, this is part of the creativity of plurilingual competence. Even educated writers in carefully edited pieces would adopt such novel or peculiar structures. They do so without inhibition as they do not consider them to be errors. Local readers would guess the meanings from context if they have not encountered the usage before. They rarely complain of intelligibility problems or make grammaticality judgments based on native speaker norms. In an article titled "Bilingualism in the Jaffna society", Suseendirarajah uses some unusual sentence structures:

> Bilingualism in English helped speakers earn some kind of esteem in the society particularly among monolinguals. In certain social situations people spoke English in common or public places

intentionally to assert superiority over monolinguals. **People, especially those who were in the lower hierarchy in the society, took pride and pleasure in exhibiting their fluency in English in contexts where they felt that others thought them to be totally ignorant of English. That was a time when it was considered shame not to know English!** Even a beggar who spoke English got more than one who spoke Tamil. People thus used English because it gave a more educated impression of the speaker. (Suseendirarajah 1992:4; emphasis mine).

The two highlighted sentences might be considered to follow local norms of usage. The first sentence shows the influence of Tamil sentence structure in its topic fronting. The second sentence is also unconventional as it translates an idiomatic usage in Tamil. Interestingly, the quotation is from a published article on the decline of English proficiency in the postcolonial period. However, the local editors did not feel compelled to correct these sentences. There is a broad tolerance towards grammatical appropriations of this nature. Although authors and editors can easily get help to approximate native speaker norms, they do not consider it necessary in the light of the plurilingual tradition.

Concerning examples of creativity in vocabulary, consider Sivatamby's usage in one of his articles published in a local bilingual journal: "The quantitative and qualitative changes that have taken place in the evolution of Tamilian nationalism, should be seen in the perspectivity of the liberal Youth Congress tradition. That would provide the nationalist ideology with a continuity and possibility of development on social democratic lines" (Sivatamby 1984:56). Though "perspectivity" is a novel coinage, the editors did not correct this word. They — and local readers — work around it to infer the meaning from the context. Such creativity in constructing new English words is not limited to writing or to the communicative practices of the educated. This practice is found in other social domains as well. In war-torn Sri Lanka, as new military equipment and technology came in, ordinary people started using their coinage to refer to them (see Canagarajah 1995a for a detailed discussion). *Heli* (rather than *chopper*) is the abbreviation for *helicopter*. *Sel* (from *shell*) can refer to grenades or missiles from rocket launchers. *Bommer* stands for jets that carry out bombing raids. These words have been constructed from English. Such appropriations are quite widespread in the South Asian community. Other media, such as advertisements and street signs, also display such appropriations (see Bhatia and Richie 2004 for more examples). Such examples illustrate Khubchandani's point that displaying "positive attitudes to variation" and being "open to unexpectedness", local communities transform "deviations as the norm".

To move from written texts to conversational interactions, we do see some fascinating forms of negotiating diverse languages. Even in formal professional contexts of communication, where English is the unmarked code, local people will mix and switch languages. In the following conversation (that I recorded for a study on language choice in Sri Lanka, see Canagarajah 1995a), L — a candidate for a faculty position — is able to reduce the distance from P — a bilingual senior professor who interviews him for a faculty position — by effectively codeswitching and changing the conversation to a PE medium, away from the conventional English medium for this context:

(5) 1 P: So you have done a masters in sociology? What is your area of research?
     2 L: Naan **sociology of religion**-ilai taan **interested**. enTai **thesis topic** vantu **the rise of local deities in the Jaffna peninsula.**
             '*It is in the* **sociology of religion** *that I am* **interested.** *My* **thesis topic** *was* The **rise of local deities in the Jaffna peninsula.**'
     3 P: Did this involve a field work?
     4 L: oom, oru **ethnographic study**-aai taan itay ceitanaan. kiTTattaTTa **four years**-aai **field work** ceitanaan.

> '*Yes, I did this as an* **ethnographic study**. *I did* **field work** *for roughly* **four years**.'
> 5   P: appa kooTa **qualitative research** taan ceiyiraniir?
> '*So you do mostly* **qualitative research**?'

The senior professor, who is comfortable with prestige varieties of English (having done his graduate work in the UK), begins the interview in the unmarked code. The junior lecturer is locally trained and lacks advanced proficiency in English. However, he draws from the plurilingual tradition to negotiate the conversation in his favour. He is able to understand P's questions and continues the interaction confidently because of his receptive multilingualism (Braunmüller 2006). The term refers to the ability multilingual people have to understand diverse languages, though they cannot always speak them. Furthermore, the mostly technical or scholarly vocabulary that P uses in his utterances can be considered part of the common academic discourse that scholars in different language communities share. L strategically uses the English tokens at his disposal to shift the conversation in his favour. Although L lacks the ability to form complete sentences in English, his mixing is effective. The English phrases he uses are not frequently used loans in the wider society; they are specialized vocabulary. The phrases are well formed, although in being the clichés of academia these would not have demanded much competence from the speaker. This mixing of languages is better than using Tamil only, as Annamalai (2001: 174) points out: "The mixed language, particularly its vocabulary, conceals the social and regional identity of the speaker and thus has a standardizing (i.e. neutralizing) function". Although initially P continues to speak English and maintains a certain amount of distance (perhaps deliberately, as English provides him power and confirms his identity as a senior scholar), he is eventually forced to take L seriously because of his successful strategies. P finally converges to L's PE (in line 5), after which they speak as equals.

In addition to conversations in language-mixed utterances, plurilingual competence might also enable locals to engage in polyglot dialog (see Posner 1991). The term refers to the possibility that a group of multilinguals can conduct a conversation in multiple languages, each sticking to their own language. I have been in situations where a conversation took place trilingually, with each speaker adopting their own preferred or most proficient language, i.e. Sinhala, English, or Tamil (I discuss many recent examples of such polyglot conversation in the diaspora context in Canagarajah 2008). In recorded data from family conversations, where children have dominant proficiency in English (or German or French in other diaspora contexts) and parents are Tamil-dominant, they carry out their conversation multilingually. Such conversational strategies are everyday reality for such families. This is how family conversation takes place in many diasporic and local multilingual homes. It draws from the plurilingual tradition community members are already socialized into. What is on display are what Khubchandani calls 'serendipidity' to accept others with their own language peculiarities and 'synergy' to work out intelligible communication across differences.

We also find plurilingual communicative practices in educational contexts in South Asia. Teachers and students might move in and out of diverse languages to both negotiate content and also facilitate language acquisition. The following interaction was recorded from an English class in a secondary school in Jaffna, Sri Lanka (see Canagarajah 1995b for a detailed instruction):

(6) 1.   T: Today we are going to study about fruits. What fruits do you usually eat? ( )
            inraikku niinkal viiTTilai enna palankaL caappiTTa niinkaL? Cila peer
            kaalamai caappaaTTikku paLankaL caappiTiravai ello? '
            'What fruits did you eat this morning at home? Don't some people eat fruits for
            breakfast?'

     2.   S1: naan maampaLam caappiTTanaan, **Miss**.
            '*I ate mangoes*, **Miss**.'

3.   T: Good, mangoes, eh? Maampalam enRaal **mangoes**.
          '*Maampalam means* **mangoes**.'
4.   S2:   vaaLappaLam caappitta naan, **Miss**.
          '*I ate bananas*, **Miss**.'
5.   T: Okay, bananas.

Note that while students do not respond to the general question posed in English, there is a torrent of response when the teacher reframes the question more specifically in Tamil and relates it to their home. However, the Tamil statement (in line 1) is not a direct translation of the preceding statement in English. While students would have generally understood the statement in English, the switch provides a local context and personal resonance for the students. The teacher proceeds thereafter to subtly introduce the English vocabulary items related to the lesson by translating the fruits mentioned by the students in Tamil. In this way, teachers and students often discuss culturally relevant anecdotes, explanations or illustrations to clarify the lesson content. Through this process, teachers also relate the lesson content to knowledge gained outside the classroom or, rather, bridge the gap between school and home.

Ramanathan (2005) provides an example from India where the locally produced English language textbook for the class is itself written in both English and Hindi. While the content of the language instruction is in English, the instructions for teachers and students are in Hindi. In this sense, the textbook mimics the *manipralava* style of writing. Ramanathan goes on to describe the interactions in the classroom which are also multilingual. Similarly, Rajan (1993) considers the benefits of using local languages for studying English literature in India. She argues that local languages enable students to defamiliarize the narratives set in alien contexts, reframe them to suit local contexts, develop a critical perspective on the foreign text through a local lens, and appropriate the codes and messages in culturally sensitive ways.

Such plurilingual practices in the English classroom might be disconcerting to teachers influenced by traditional English language teaching methods. They might consider the use of other languages as hampering the acquisition of English by giving students confusing input and leading to interference errors. It is for this reason that students were isolated from vernacular influences of the home and fined for mixing languages during colonial times. However, other scholars have now articulated the benefits of such plurilingual practices in the classroom (see Michael-Luna and Canagarajah 2007; Garcia 2009). These practices lead to the development of a linguistic repertoire and intercultural competence. For those who treat languages as separated from each other, and language competence as distinct for each language, such plurilingual practices may appear dysfunctional.

For South Asians, English and other local languages are not distinct languages that can be mixed only guardedly. These languages are a continuum that can be accessed at will for their purposes. In other words, these are not separate languages; they are part of the same communicative system. A term that captures this activity of plurilinguals is translanguaging (Garcia 2009). Garcia defines translanguaging thus: "Rather than focussing on the language itself and how one or the other might relate to the way in which a monolingual standard is used and has been described, the concept of translanguaging makes obvious that there are no clear cut borders between the languages of bilinguals. What we have is a languaging continuum that is accessed" (2009:47). For plurilingual communities, the multiple languages in their locality (including those imposed from outside) eventually constitute the same system. They are also open to one language influencing the shape and sound of the other. It is for this reason that what appear to be errors for some (blamed on interference from one language or the other) are legitimate uses for those who see the languages as mutually influencing each other.

Implications for theorizing plurilingual competence

How do South Asians make meaning out of idiosyncratic usage, mixed language, and variable structure? How do local people develop proficiency in a form of communication that involves multiple communities and languages in contexts that can thrust an unpredictable mix of forms and conventions? How is harmony achieved out of diversity, synchrony out of differences in form and conventions, alignment in discordant and unpredictable situations?

For communication to work across such radical differences, it is important that acquisition and use go hand and hand. As speakers deal with the creative coinage of each other, unpredictable types of mixing and switching, and idiosyncratic grammars, a lot of learning takes place: i.e., they monitor the form and conventions the other brings; they learn to ascribe meanings to their forms and conventions; they monitor their own forms and conventions to negotiate communication. Meeting different speakers from multilingual backgrounds, one always has to learn a lot — and rapidly — as one decides which receptive and productive resources to adopt for a context. Furthermore, the lessons learnt in one encounter will help to constantly reconstruct the schema to monitor future communications of similar or different participants and contexts. In this sense, learning never stops in plurilingual communication. If there is no language use without learning, there is also no language learning outside of use. Since there is no a priori grammar, the variable language system has to be encountered in actual use. The contexts of multilingual communication are unpredictable, and the mix of participants and purposes has to be encountered in real situations. Also, the strategies that enable negotiation are meaningless as abstract knowledge or theory; they have to be constantly activated for their development. A language based on negotiation can be developed only through and in practice.

Plurilingual communication works because competence does not rely solely on a form of knowledge, but rather, encompasses interaction strategies. Khubchandani argues that the ability to communicate is not dependent on "explicit formulas" such as formal grammars and dictionaries of words. For South Asians, "interpretation [is] dependent on the focus of communication 'field' and the degrees of individual's 'sensitivity' towards it" (1997:40). In other words, participants have to engage with the social context, and responsively orchestrate the contextual cues for alignment. As we have already seen, meaning in language is not a product that can be prescribed objectively. Communication is intersubjective. In addition to knowledge of form, plurilingual competence features an array of interactional strategies that can create meaning. As Khubchandani explains: "Communications in everyday life are based on the synergic relationship between the twin criteria: (a) the reciprocity of language skills among communicators (spread over a speech spectrum comprising one or more languages, dialects, styles, etc.); and (b) the mutuality of focus (that is, sharing the relevance of the setting, commonly attributed to the attitudes, moods, or feelings of the participants)" (1997:49). What Khubchandani highlights are skills and strategies. Mutuality and reciprocity indicate the ways participants align their moves and strategies in relation to their language resources. Synergy is the outcome of this alignment, when participants jointly invoke language resources and collaboratively build coherence. Plurilingual competence is thus a mode of practice, not resident solely in cognition.

Furthermore, plurilingual competence is open to unpredictability. In a sense, each context of communication poses a new and unpredictable mix of languages and conventions. As Khubchandani explains further: "it is often difficult to determine whether a particular discourse belongs to language A or B" (1997:93). Therefore, it is difficult to transfer the forms and conventions of one context to the next. In this sense, learning is non-linear. It is for this reason that when SLA is able to theorize language use and acquisition as based on 'directed effort' (i.e. something predictable, with learners armed with a stock of forms and strategies that can make them competent for successful communication), in the South Asian community speech is "an effortless integral activity; discourse centres around the 'event' with the support of ad hoc 'expression' strategies" (1997: 40). Local people realize that "the 'tradition inspired' standardized nuances of another language or culture" (1997: 93) cannot help them communicate successfully in the mix of languages and dialects they encounter in each situation. It appears as if all that speakers can do is to find a fit — an alignment — between the linguistic resources they bring and the context of communication. Acquisition is not a cumulative process, but an ability to come up with diverse strategies for speech events that need to be addressed for their own sake. The mention of "ad hoc strategies" reminds us that competence does not involve predictability but alertness and impromptu fabrication of forms and conventions to establish alignment in each situation of communication. Thus, acquisition aims towards versatility and agility, not mastery and control.

In theorizing this complex social practice, some scholars have begun to explore how successful communication depends on aligning the linguistic resources one brings to the social, situational, and affective dimensions operative in a context (see Kramsch 2002). In other words, language learning involves an alignment of one's language resources to the needs of a situation, rather than reaching a target level of competence. Atkinson et al. (2007: 171) define alignment as "the means by which human actors **dynamically adapt to** — that is, flexibly depend on, integrate with, and construct — the ever-changing mind-body-world environments posited by sociocognitive theory. In other words, alignment takes place not just between human beings, but also between human beings and their social and physical environments" (emphasis in original). They go on to illustrate alignment through the way both Japanese and English and, sometimes, co-constructed words/meanings of ambiguous linguistic identity are used as cues and effects of successful alignment to facilitate English language learning.

This notion of alignment makes us question another bias in traditional linguistics — i.e. language competence as an individual possession. It is clear that the individual's proficiency is shaped by collective and contextual factors. But there are other implications for assessing an individual's level of proficiency. PE makes sense only as an intersubjective construction, something achieved by two or more people, based on the strategies they bring to the interaction. We have to consider the collaborative nature of communication and linguistic negotiation in assessing the meaning and significance of an interaction. From this perspective, the conduit model of meaning as information transfer has to be questioned as well. In PE, even an ungrammatical usage or inappropriate word choice can be socially functional. They can create a new meaning originally unintended by the speaker, or they may be negotiated by the participants and given new meanings. Participants negotiate the language effectively to ascribe meaning in case of deviation from the norm. A radical implication of this assertion for assessing language proficiency is that errors are also socially constructed. An error occurs when someone fails to ascribe meaning to a linguistic form used by another. In plurilingual communication, such cases rarely occur. A breakdown in plurilingual communication is possible only in rare cases of refusal to negotiate meanings — which is itself a form of communication as it conveys the participant's desire to cut off the conversation. Therefore, if there is a case of failed communication, we cannot blame an individual for their lack of proficiency. This might be a divergence strategy (Giles 1984).

Furthermore, in plurilingual competence, grammar receives reduced significance. In contexts where "deviation is the norm", multilinguals cannot rely on grammar or form. Grammar is a hybrid and variable one, even if it can be described *a priori*. To further reduce the importance of grammar, Khubchandani says that speech process is "regarded as a non-autonomous device, communicating in symphony with other non-linguistic devices; its full significance can be explicated only from the imperatives of context and communicative tasks" (1997: 40). In other words, communication is multimodal. Meaning does not reside in language alone. Readers or listeners guess the meaning of idiosyncratic language tokens in relation to diverse symbol systems (icons, space, colour, gesture, or other representational systems) and modalities of communication (writing, sound, visuals, touch, and body), not to speak of diverse languages. This orientation differs from the structuralist tradition that proceeds further inwards into autonomous language to find the rules of linguistic meaning making.

Such a competence is always in a state of development and, therefore, acquisition is emergent. There is no end point to learning, where one can say a person has mastered all the peculiarities that shape communication in diverse contact situations. First of all, there is no limit to the diversity, hybridity, and variability that can characterize a communicative medium. Furthermore, each interaction, with its own set of participants, interests, and dynamics features new requirements of form and convention. As a result, plurilingual competence is treated as always evolving and creative. Khubchandani explains that the "total verbal repertoire is malleable, responsive to contextual expediencies resulting in uninhibited convergences between speech varieties with the contact pressures of pidginization, hybridization, code-switching etc." (1997: 40–41). In other words, one's competence is based on the repertoire that grows as the contexts of interaction increase. Also, plurilingual competence is more than the sum of its parts, constituting a qualitatively different whole.

Implications for policy and education

There is a general recognition in many communities nowadays that it is important for citizens of late-modernity to shuttle between languages and develop plurilingual competence. However, some of the assumptions of traditional linguistics and education stifle efforts to develop this competence in language classrooms. In mainstream educational curricula and policy, models of subtractive or additive bilingualism are promoted. As we saw in the first section, these models develop language competence one at a time, in isolation from other languages, and sometimes at the cost of the others. This is especially evident in Western communities which treat multilingualism as a problem rather than a resource (see Ruiz 1984; Horner and Trimbur 2002). Other policies, such as treating the native speaker as the target for proficiency and treating additional languages as interferences in developing proficiency (which Phillipson 1992 identifies as the native speaker fallacy and monolingual fallacy, respectively), also militate against plurilingual education.

Nor is this a problem only for countries in the Northern hemisphere. South Asia itself finds it difficult to implement plurilingual policies in the aftermath of colonization and modernity. Ajit Mohanty (2006) feels that the modernist approach based on centralized languages and/or a hierarchy of difference, such as the Three-Language Formula in India, are alien to the South Asian tradition. He argues that Indian pluralism works most effectively through functional distribution of languages, not hierarchies. What is conducive to the region is how individuals, families, and communities assign different languages for different domains of communication without treating one as better than the other. He also argues that the imposition of English in colonial times and its glorified current status as the global language have also upset the plurilingual balance in South Asia. They have led to social and educational policies based on a hierarchical relationship of languages, resulting in the denigration of minority languages, language attrition, and even language death. These postcolonial developments he finds damaging to the language ecology of South Asia. Drawing an analogy from his personal life to illustrate the complementary relationship between languages, Mohanty says: "These languages fit in a mutually complementary and non-competing relationship in my life. Under such conditions of multilingual functioning individuals naturally need and use different languages because no language is sufficient or suitable for meeting all the communicative requirements across different situations and social activities" (2006: 263). Mohanty argues that such patterns of individual and community bilingualism at the local or regional level constitute "the first incremental step towards concentric layers of societal multilingualism" (2006:263).

To some extent, certain non-Western communities (India, Singapore, Hong Kong, Brunei, and some countries in the Middle East and North Africa) have adopted forms of education that provide a complementary relationship to languages. Garcia (2009) calls this 'multiple multilingual education'. These programmes "use more than two languages in education and often have moveable parts — that is, languages are weaved in and out of the curriculum as needed. Multilingualism is considered a resource for all children in the society. As a result of the inclusion of all children, there is considerable variation in bilingual proficiency; translanguaging is therefore a common feature of this education. Transculturalism is promoted, as not only languages, but also cultures, are blended" (2009:283). We can see how the practices promoted in this form of education go against dominant policies. Students may learn different subjects in different languages. The goal is not to develop parity of competence in all languages. Switching and mixing languages in classrooms is permitted. Language awareness is combined with intercultural competence.

We have to also consider the implications of plurilingualism for language teaching. Already communities in Europe are promoting plurilingual competence. The Council of Europe defines its goal as developing "the ability to use several languages to varying degrees and for distinct purposes... This ability is concretized in a repertoire of languages a speaker can use. The goal of teaching is to develop this competence (hence the expression: plurilingualism as a competence)" (Council of Europe 2000, cited in Garcia 2009:54). There are mixed reviews on the effectiveness of this pedagogy in Europe (for a critical review, see Garcia 2009:197–216). The problems include lack of training for teachers who have not transitioned from traditional pedagogical practices; lack of new teaching materials that promote plurilingulism; and the de facto dominance of certain languages and communities which stifle the development of proficiency in less prestigious languages.

The more pressing question is whether the type of spontaneous negotiation of languages that we see in face to face conversations can be taught in the somewhat constrained context of the classroom. What we need is a paradigm shift in language teaching. Pedagogy should be refashioned to accommodate the modes of communication and acquisition seen outside the classroom (see Canagarajah 2005 for a more elaborate pedagogical discussion). Rather than focussing on a single language or dialect as the target of learning, teachers have to develop in students a readiness to engage with a repertoire of codes in transnational contact situations. While joining a new speech community was the objective of traditional pedagogy, now we have to train students to shuttle between communities by negotiating the relevant codes. To this end, we have to focus more on communicative strategies rather than on form. Students would develop language awareness (to cope with the multiple languages and emergent grammars of contact situations) rather than focus only on mastering the grammar rules of a single variety. In a context of plural forms and conventions, it is important for students to be sensitive to the relativity of norms. Therefore, students have to understand communication as performative, not just constitutive. That is, going beyond the notion of constructing prefabricated meanings through words, they will consider **shaping** meaning in actual interactions and even **reconstructing** the rules and conventions to represent their interests, values, and identities. In other words, it is not so much what we know but the versatility with which we can do things with words that defines proficiency. Pedagogical movements such as learner strategy training and language awareness go some way toward facilitating such interactional strategies and repertoire development.

Plurilingual competence does not mean that students cannot produce 'standard' language for formal production when the context requires it (as I have argued elsewhere, see Canagarajah 2006). The heightened language awareness and multilingual proficiency can create a keen awareness of language norms and contextual appropriateness of usage. In other words, plurilingual competence does not mean a disrespect for norms and conventions, but the ability to critically and creatively engage with them.

References

Annamalai, E. (2001) *Managing Multilingualism in India*. New Delhi: Sage.

Atkinson, D., E. Churchill, T. Nishino and H. Okada (2007) Alignment and interaction in a sociocognitive approach in second language acquisition. *Modern Language Journal* 91: 169–188.

Balasubramaniam, A., K. Ratnamalar and R. Subathini (eds) (1999) *Studies in Sri Lankan Tamil Linguistics and Culture: Selected Papers of Professor Suseendirarajah*. Chennai, India: Students' Offset Services.

Bhatia, T.K. and W. Ritchie (2004) Bilingualism in South Asia. In T.K. Bhatia and W.C. Ritchie (eds), *The Handbook of Bilingualism*, pp. 780–807. Oxford: Blackwell.

Bhatt, R. (2008) In other words: Language mixing, identity representations, and third space. *Journal of Sociolinguistics* 12(2): 177–200.

Blommaert, J. (2005) Situating language rights: English and Swahili in Tanzania revisited. *Journal of Sociolinguistics* 9(3): 390–417.

Braunmüller, K. (2006) On the relevance of receptive multilingualism in a globalised world: Theory, history and evidence from today's Scandinavia. 1st Conference on Language Contact in Times of Globalization, University of Groningen, 28 September 2006.

Bright, W. (1984) *American Indian Linguistics and Literature*. The Hague: Mouton.

Canagarajah, A.S. (1995a) The political-economy of code choice in a revolutionary society: Tamil/English bilingualism in Jaffna. *Language in Society* 24(2): 187–212.

Canagarajah, A.S. (1995b) Functions of code switching in the ESL classroom: Socialising bilingualism in Jaffna. *Journal of Multilingual and Multicultural Development* 16: 173–196.

Canagarajah, A.S. (1999) *Resisting Linguistic Imperialism in English Teaching*. Oxford: Oxford University Press.

Canagarajah, A.S. (2000) Negotiating ideologies through English: Strategies from the periphery. In T. Ricento (ed.), *Ideology, Politics and Language Policies: Focus on English*, pp. 107–120. Amsterdam, Philadelphia: John Benjamins.

Canagarajah, A.S. (2005) Introduction. In A.S. Canagarajah (ed.), *Reclaiming the Local in Language Policy and Practice*, pp. xiii–xxx. Mahwah, NJ: Lawrence Erlbaum.

Canagarajah, A.S. (2006) Toward a writing pedagogy of shuttling between languages: Learning from multilingual writers. *College English* 68(6): 589–604.

Canagarajah, A.S. (2007) Lingua Franca English, multilingual communities, and language acquisition. *Modern Language Journal* 91(5): 921–937.

Canagarajah, A.S. (2008) Language shift and the family: Questions from the Sri Lankan Tamil diaspora. *Journal of Sociolinguistics* 12(2): 1–34.

Chelliah, J. (1922) *A Century of English Education*. Vaddukoddai: Jaffna College.

Council of Europe (2000) *Common European Framework of Reference for Languages: Learning, Teaching, Assessment*. Strasbourg: Language Policy Division. http://www.coe.int/t/dg4/linguistic/CADRE_EN.asp

Daily Mirror (2004, 13 October) Sole-burning kattadiya hauled to court, p. 1.

Daily Mirror (2004, 16 October) Anandasangaree appeals to 'My Dear Thambi', p. 1.

de Souza, L.M. (2002) A case among cases, a world among worlds: The ecology of writing among the Kashinawa in Brazil. *Journal of Language, Identity, and Education* 1(4): 261–278.

Dorian, N. (2004) Minority and endangered languages. In T.K. Bhatia and W.C. Ritchie (eds), *The Handbook of Bilingualism*, pp. 437–459. Oxford: Blackwell.

Garcia, O. (2009) *Bilingual Education in the 21st Century: A Global Perspective*. Oxford: Wiley-Blackwell.

Gee, J.P. (2001) Educational linguistics. In M. Aronoff and J. Rees-Miller (eds), *The Handbook of Linguistics*, pp. 647–663. Oxford: Blackwell.

Giles, H. (ed.) (1984) *The Dynamics of Speech Accommodation*. Special Issue. *International Journal of the Sociology of Language* 46.

Gunasekera, B. (1893) *Glossary of Native and Foreign Words Occurring in Official Correspondence and Other Documents*. Colombo: The Government Printer.

Gunasekera, M. (2005) *The Postcolonial Identity of Sri Lankan English*. Colombo: Katha Publishers.

Gunasekera, R. (1994) *Reef*. London: Granta Books.

Horner, B. and J. Trimbur (2002) English only and U.S. college composition. *College Composition and Communication* 53: 594–630.

House, J. (2003) English as a lingua franca: A threat to multilingualism? *Journal of Sociolinguistics* 7(4): 556–578.

Kandiah, T. (1979) Disinherited Englishes: The case of Lankan English. *Navasilu* 3: 75–89.

Khubchandani, L.M. (1997) *Revisualizing Boundaries: A Plurilingual Ethos*. New Delhi: Sage.

Kramsch, C. (2002) Introduction: How can we tell the dancer from the dance? In C. Kramsch (ed.), *Language Acquisition and Language Socialization: Ecological Perspectives*, pp. 1–30. London, New York: Continuum.

Lantolf J.P. and S.F. Thorne (2006) *Sociocultural Theory and the Genesis of Second Language Development*. New York: Oxford University Press.

Makoni, S. (2002) From misinvention to disinvention: An approach to multilingualism. In G. Smitherman, A. Spears and A. Ball (eds), *Black Linguistics: Language, Society and Politics in Africa and the Americas*, pp. 132–153. London: Routledge.

Michael-Luna, S. and A.S. Canagarajah (2007) Multilingual academic literacies: Pedagogical foundations for code meshing in primary and higher education. *Journal of Applied Linguistics* 4(1): 55–77.

Mohanty, A. (2006) Multilingualism of the unequals and the predicaments of education in India: Mother tongue or other tongue? In O. Garcia, T. Skuttnab-Kangas and M. Torres-Guzman (eds), *Imagining Multilingual Schools*, pp. 262–283. Clevedon: Multilingual Matters.

Parakrama, A. (1995) *De-hegemonizing Language Standards*. Basingstoke: Macmillan.

Pattanayak, D.P. (1984) Language policies in multilingual states. In A. Gonzalez (ed.), *Panagani: Language Planning, Implementation and Evaluation*, pp. 75–92. Manila: Linguistic Society of the Philippines.

Phillipson, R. (1992) *Linguistic Imperialism*. Oxford: Oxford University Press.

Posner, R. (1991) Der polyglotte Dialog. *Der Sprachreport* 3(91): 6–10.

Rajan, R.S. (1993) Fixing English: Nation, language, subject. In R.S. Rajan (ed.), *The Lie of the Land: English Literary Studies in India*, pp. 7–28. Oxford: Oxford University Press.

Ramanathan, V. (2005) Seepages, contact zones and amalgam: Internationalizing TESOL. *TESOL Quarterly* 39(1): 119–123.

Rampton, B. (1997) Second language research in late modernity: A response to Firth and Wagner. *The Modern Language Journal* 81: 329–333.

Romaine, S. (1989) *Bilingualism*. Oxford: Blackwell.

Ruiz, R. (1984) Orientations to language planning. *NABE Journal* 8(2): 15–34.

Silverstein, M. (1996) Monoglot 'standard' in America: Standardization and metaphors of linguistic hegemony. In D. Brenneis and R. Macaulay (eds), *The Matrix of Language: Contemporary Linguistic Anthropology*, pp. 284–306. Boulder: Westview Press.

Sivatamby, K. (1984) Towards an understanding of the culture and ideology of the Tamils of Sri Lanka. In K. Nesiah (ed.), *Commemmorative Souvenir: Jaffna Public Library*, pp. 49–56. Jaffna: Catholic Press.

Sivatamby, K. (1990) The ideology of Saiva-Tamil integrality: Its sociohistorical significance in the study of Yalppanam Tamil society. *Lanka* 5: 176–182.

Sivatamby, K. (1992) YaaLpaaNa camuukaTai viLanki koLLal — aTan uruvaakkam asaiviyakkam paRRiya oru piraarampa usaaval [Understanding Jaffna society: A preliminary inquiry into its 'formation' and 'dynamics']. Mimeograph. Prof. S. Selvanayagam Memorial Lecture 8, University of Jaffna, Sri Lanka.

Suseendirarajah, S. (1992) English in our Tamil society: A sociolinguistic appraisal. Mimeograph. Academic Forum, University of Jaffna, Sri Lanka.

Viswanathan, G. (1993) English in a literate society. In R.S. Rajan (ed.), *The Lie of the Land: English Literary Studies in India*, pp. 29–41. Oxford: Oxford University Press.

Language as a problem of development:

Ideological debates and comprehensive education in the Philippines

T. Ruanni F. Tupas
National University of Singapore

Fixation on language in language policy debates is not a natural given. In fact, it has to be re-examined. This paper argues that another effective way to look at language policy is to suspend talk on language, and instead first engage with social development issues where people are at the heart of the social landscape. It discusses three ways of engagement with language policy as seen in the landscape of the politics of language, education and social development in the Philippines. The first way is **engaging** language policy which means debating the key features of the existing language policy usually based on ideological concerns. The second way is **re-engaging** language policy which highlights previously sidelined provisions of the policy such as those concerning local languages in education. The third way is **disengaging** from language policy which primarily sees language policy as part of a general social development framework, i.e. the imperative to focus on specific needs of local communities from which the roles of language emerge. The key point to note is that language does not seem to figure as a fundamental problem that needs to be addressed.

> ...none of the major problems of the country (e.g. massive poverty, land-holding inequality, inadequate access to modern agricultural technology) can be solved by literacy and education.
>
> Canieso-Doronila (2001: 279)

Introduction

When people — academics, politicians, and men and women on the street — discuss language policy, the debate expectedly focusses on the problem of language. That is, language becomes the centre around which all other problems in society revolve. The more nuanced discussions situate language in broad political and social contexts (May and Hornberger 2008), especially because there is now a growing awareness of the fact that "language issues are at the core of political and military conflict in a range of settings worldwide" (Tollefson 2008: 7). But these perspectives usually do not find their way into public and popular debates in the media or the parliament, and consequently into the policy-making process. Similarly, these discussions also still tend to start and end with the question of language, thus it reconfigures the social landscape at the heart of which is language. There is then perhaps much common sense in thinking that the core business of language policy is to talk about language.

AILA Review 22 (2009), 23–35. DOI 10.1075/aila.22.03tup
ISSN 1461–0213 / E-ISSN 1570–5595 © John Benjamins Publishing Company

But fixation on language in language policy debates is not a natural given. In fact, it has to be re-examined. This paper argues that another effective way to look at language policy is to suspend any talk about language, and instead highlight the need to engage with social development issues where people, grounded in the real and messy realities of daily life, are at the heart of the social landscape. To **not** talk about language is not to diminish the importance of language policy; in fact, it strengthens it, except that it starts and ends with the users of language. The point is to go back to where people live and (help) make them map out their own social development strategies. What is needed is not just an ethnography of language policy (Johnson 2009), but an ethnography of social development (Canieso-Doronila and Acuña 1994) within which issues of language emerge against the backdrop of fundamental problems of community life such as poverty and nutrition. The key point here is that the role of language emerges from, and is not imposed upon, the development process. This approach initially makes language "'invisible' in the development process" (Aikman 2001:113) but, as will be shown in this paper, in so doing it makes language visible as well.

Three ways of engagement with language policy

This paper discusses three ways of engagement with language policy as seen in the landscape of the politics of language, education and social development in the Philippines. The first way is **engaging** language policy. This means debating the key features of the existing language policy (e.g. English and/or Filipino as medium of instruction?) usually based on ideological concerns. Stakeholders take on differing ideological positions vis-à-vis the role of languages in the country, specifically in the educational system. These positions have been labelled in many ways, for example as pragmatic, nationalist, colonial and postcolonial (Gonzales 1980, 1982; Sibayan and Gonzalez 1996; Sta. Maria 1999). Direct engagements with language policy in the Philippines have dominated the discussion on languages in political and public discourses for the most part of the 20th century.

The second way is **re-engaging** language policy. The approach continues to work within the same framework of the current language policy, but this time it highlights previously sidelined provisions of the policy. These specific provisions recognize the role of the mother tongues in education and society. Successive Philippine constitutions since the 1930s have clearly articulated the important role of the mother tongues in the literacy development of Filipinos, but in reality not much has been done to put this recognition in practice especially after the current bilingual policy was promulgated in the early 1970s. Re-engaging language policy uses evidence-based arguments for the use of local languages in education (such as their positive effect on children's cognitive development) (Dekker and Young 2005; Walter and Dekker 2008) in order to help change the policy itself but it simultaneously works with specific communities to put into action mother tongue education frameworks in the schools.

The third way is **disengaging** from language policy. It primarily sees language policy as social policy and, as such, it is part of a general social development framework. It does not start the discussion with language policy, but with social development needs of specific communities in the Philippines. To improve education, it has to improve the general well-being of the people; thus issues in nutrition, health, taxation, literacy, mortality rates and political maturity, among other things, are brought together to formulate a general framework of social development. There is heavy reliance on research on the communities involved based on multi-sectoral consultations and ethnographic descriptions of the people's daily struggles. The educational curriculum, therefore, is a unified curriculum because, while it is anchored essentially on the demands of the core requirements of the national curriculum, the content is made much more relevant to the specific needs of the students. It is here where a re-configured language policy 'emerges' without much ideological debate. The roles of languages in education and society are not couched in worn-out positions which essentially have not changed since the American colonial times (Bernardo 2007; Tupas 2007, 2008a). Rather, these roles are seen from the lived experiences of particular groups of people whose basic concerns are poverty, livelihood, health and education.

In these practices of disengagement from language policy, the key point to note is that in the transformation of education on the ground, "where human development — or the process of widening the range of people's choices — is severely constrained by poverty and neglect" (Bautista 2005: xv), the problem of language does not seem to figure as a fundamental problem that needs to be addressed. But in decentring language in social development, fresh configurations of language uses emerge as part of the solution to the myriad problems of education and development. These strategies of disengagement, in other words, ironically pose the greatest challenge to language policy itself because they make the policy appear somewhat irrelevant, unfair and unsophisticated.

Engaging language policy

Officially, a bilingual education policy has been in place in the country since 1974, the time when a new Philippine constitution was ratified under Ferdinand Marcos's martial law. This policy — highly a product of deep ideological and ethnolinguistic rivalries among members of the Philippine congress — states that English should be the medium of instruction in the teaching of science and mathematics, while Filipino should be used in the teaching of all other subjects. Thus, direct engagement with language policy meant debates on these key features of the bilingual policy: English and/ or Filipino as medium of instruction? Filipino as the national language?

The name 'Filipino' itself is replete with political and ideological meaning (Tupas 2007), also a product of direct ideological engagements with the problem of language. Its history goes back to the 1930s when Tagalog, the language spoken by the political elite of Manila and neighbouring provinces in Luzon, was named the national language of the Philippines, then a political necessity among the (Tagalog-dominant) nationalists (including then Philippine President Manuel Quezon) who were posturing against American colonial governance (Gonzalez 1991) which privileged English in society and education over the local languages. The choice of Tagalog angered other ethnolinguistic groups, especially those who spoke Cebuano, the language of the South, which was then spoken by more people than Tagalog, but was perhaps less powerful politically. In 1949, Tagalog was renamed Pilipino, a move to 'de-ethnicize' the national language and make it a more inclusive term. It continued to be the national language in the 1950s and 1960 around which anti-colonial and nationalist politics revolved because of the perceived 'mis-education of the Filipino people' through English (Constantino 1970).

However, when the language problem was once again tackled in the early 1970s, the same old ethnolinguistic wounds surfaced in the debates (Gonzalez 1980). In what would become a cunning political compromise, 'Pilipino' was dropped as the national language, but 'Filipino' (then actually a non-existent language) was named as the future national language that was to be developed by the State. 'Filipino' was to evolve from Pilipino and other local languages, thus making it even more inclusive because its very existence was dependent on the contribution of all languages in the country.

The bilingual compromise partly emerged from this decision to drop Pilipino as the national language. 'Filipino', not Pilipino (which was really Tagalog in structure), was to become one of the languages of instruction alongside English, the preferred language of non-Tagalog speaking politicians. In reality, however, the mandate to develop a national language that was yet to exist would start with Tagalog as the core language because it was already firmly entrenched in the educational system, it having been the national language since the 1930s. The Tagalog core of 'Filipino' would then be expanded to include syntactic structures and lexicons from other Philippine languages. In other words, although 'Tagalog', 'Pilipino' and 'Filipino' are conceptually different from each other,

practically speaking the 1974 constitution reaffirmed Tagalog as the national language without it being officially called such. More importantly, it paved the way for a bilingual education policy which
was theoretically sophisticated (if viewed by scholars in the field), politically ingenious (if viewed
from the way it was used to pacify all warring groups in congress), pragmatic (if viewed from the
position of 'global English'), and nationalist (if viewed as anti-colonial rhetoric) (Gonzalez 1980).

When the 1987 Philippine Constitution was written in the midst of the nationalist euphoria
of People Power during which Marcos was ousted from office in 1986 and replaced by Corazon
C. Aquino, the hugely popular widow of the assassinated opposition Senator Benigno Aquino Jr.,
'Filipino' became the official national language of the country. More than a decade of bilingual education helped establish Tagalog as a medium of instruction without it being called the national
language, and when the time came that a national language was needed to rally Filipinos around
a new vision of the Philippines, 'Filipino', conceptually an amalgam of many Philippine languages,
but whose base form as mentioned earlier is essentially Tagalog, was perhaps the most practical
choice. Whereas 'Filipino' was a linguistic fiction (Gonzalez 1980) at the time the 1974 constitution
was promulgated, in 1987 it was already a sociolinguistic reality because it had been in use in the
schools through Tagalog. Nevertheless, direct engagement with language policy meant debates on
similar key features of the policy: English and/or Filipino as medium of instruction, and Filipino as
the national language?

Bilingual education in effect was responsible for the spread of Tagalog-based Filipino across
erstwhile non-Tagalog-speaking regions. This was also helped in no small measure both by Manila-
based, thus Tagalog-dominant, Philippine media, as well as by the rapid urbanization of rural areas
through which the establishment of huge commercial centres necessitated the recruitment of a much
bigger workforce from neighbouring provinces and regions, thus requiring the use of Filipino as the
lingua franca. Since the 1990s therefore, while resistance against Filipino as a national language
could still be heard in public debates, research on the ground has shown that the national language
has become the de facto lingua franca among ethnolinguistic regional groups in the country. Consequently, even in Cebu, the political centre of resistance against "Tagalog imperialism", Filipino has
been gradually accepted as the national language of the country (Espiritu 1999; Fuentes and Mojica
1999; Kobari 1999; Sibayan 1999).

What remains highly controversial, however, is the use of Filipino as the medium of instruction in most subjects in the schools, except science and mathematics which are taught in English. In
fact, there is reason to believe that the continued resistance against Filipino as the national language
partly emanates from people's resentment against it as a medium of instruction. In the debates,
there is no delineation between Filipino as national language and Filipino as medium of instruction,
thus further muddling any potentially nuanced dialogue concerning the problem of language in the
country. Proponents of Filipino as a medium of instruction position their arguments against the
dominance of English in Philippine life. Those who are pro-English not only use "globalization" as a
major rationale for the sole use of English as medium of instruction (globalization here sometimes
reduced simply to the rapid growth of call centres in the country), but they also use "Tagalog imperialism" as an important reason for their rejection of Filipino (Espiritu 1999).

The key question, then, is this: how much have past and recent direct engagements with language policy changed the way languages in the country have been viewed? Indeed, if viewed historically, nothing much. Perspectives on English, Filipino and mother tongues have remained essentially
the same, although recently they have been "rehashed in ways that appropriate new jargon related
to globalization" (Bernardo 2007: 2). The bilingual education policy of the 1970s has not diminished
the role of English in education and society. While Filipino has spread across most sections and regions of Philippine society, the symbolic power of English has remained strong (San Juan 1998; Hau

and Tinio 2003; Bernardo 2007). Ethnolinguistic animosity emanating from the institutionalization of Tagalog as national language in the 1930s remains strong as well, and regionalistic sentiments against it continue to favour English over the local languages as medium of instruction. Direct engagements with language policy, in other words, have not altered the ideological structure of the entire debate (Tupas 2007, 2008a) and, therefore, have not resulted in new or alternative ways of looking at the roles of languages in society in such a way that languages in education are re-distributed to account for the changing realities and needs of the country and the world (Bernardo 2007).

This does not mean that direct engagements with language policy are futile attempts at understanding the politics of language in the country. The reality is that (1) it is politicians who create laws in congress so their sometimes erratic positions on language and education hold sway, and (2) public debates on language are important because they reflect as well as change people's sentiments which are crucial in the legitimization of policies. The point simply is that language ideological debates, especially in relation to language policy, are usually couched in similar discourses which have polarized Filipinos for decades and have been found to be problematic. Here is a simple example: the 'English-only bill' currently in the Philippine Congress carries with it, using the words of Blommaert (2008: 195), a "heavy ideological load" as "the language of upward globalised mobility", but really this load is "not matched by actual resources". As can be seen in the latter part of this paper, the shape of a viable, realistic and fair language policy can and should emerge from realities on the 'ground', especially from the development needs and aspirations of local communities.

Re-engaging language policy

There are currently two opposing bills in the Philippine congress which deal squarely with the problem of language in the country. The consolidated Gullas, Villafuerte and Del Mar Bill (or the 'English-only' Medium of Instruction Bill) proposes a 'return' to English as the mandatory medium of instruction from pre-school to college. The other bill, the Gunigundo or the Multilingual Education and Literacy Bill, proposes the use of the mother tongues as the medium of instruction from pre-school to elementary school, with English and Filipino to be introduced at latter stages once the foundations of literacy, science and mathematics have been put in place. The Gunigundo Bill has received support from a wide range of institutions and stakeholders in Philippine education, including the Linguistic Society of the Philippines, the Department of Education, the National Economic Development Authority, Department of Foreign Affairs and UNESCO Philippines, and the Philippine Business for Education. The 'English-only' Bill, however, is co-authored by the majority of the legislators and, in the words of its main proponent, Cebu 1st district Rep. Eduardo Gullas, is "as good as approved" (Llanto 2009).

According to Juan Miguel Luz, president of the International Institute of Rural Reconstruction and a former education undersecretary, the 'English-only' Bill "ignores world experience on learning by prescribing a solution that misses the problem completely: Why are Philippine schoolchildren not learning?" (Luz 2007: n.p.). In other words, English is not an isolated problem. It is part of the much larger problem of education in the Philippines. The entire education system is the problem. And because there is indeed a tendency to treat language as a unique and separate problem, there is reason to believe that, more than a solution to the country's problems, the 'English-only' Bill may in fact contribute to the worsening results of Philippine education. However, there is currently "a certain amount of fatigue surrounding the discussion of medium of instruction" (Licuanan 2007); thus non-governmental organizations, international donor agencies and particular government agencies in education have explored alternative ways of addressing the country's educational problems by directly working with communities and people 'on the ground', instead of waiting for new, more sympathetic legislation to be passed. They are, nevertheless, working within the same broad framework of the current language policy in the country, except that they choose to focus on the much less articulated provisions on the role of the mother tongues in education, as in the highlighted sections of Article XIV (Language) of the 1987 Philippine Constitution below:

> Article XIV (Language) of the 1987 Philippine Constitution
>
> Section 6. The national language of the Philippines is Filipino. As it evolves, it shall be further developed and enriched on the basis of existing Philippine and other languages.
>
> Subject to provisions of law and as the Congress may deem appropriate, the Government shall take steps to initiate and sustain the use of Filipino as a medium of official communication and as language of instruction in the educational system.
>
> Section 7. For purposes of communication and instruction, the official languages of the Philippines are Filipino and, until otherwise provided by law, English.
>
> **The regional languages are the auxiliary official languages in the regions and shall serve as auxiliary media of instruction therein.**
>
> Spanish and Arabic shall be promoted on a voluntary and optional basis.
>
> Section 8. This Constitution shall be promulgated in Filipino and English and shall be translated into major regional languages, Arabic, and Spanish.
>
> Section 9. The Congress shall establish a national language commission composed of representatives of various regions and disciplines which shall **undertake, coordinate, and promote researches for the development, propagation, and preservation of Filipino and other languages.**

Thus, advocates of mother tongue education have in recent years worked with the schools to try out the use of local languages in literacy development. One successful project has been the Lubuagan Kalinga First Language Component project which explored the use of innovative approaches to literacy and education for minority language users in the Philippines based on a broad multilingual pedagogical framework (Dekker and Young 2005; Walter and Dekker 2008). Lubuagan is a small town centre situated in a sloping valley belonging to the Province of Kalinga in Northern Philippines. The specific aim of the project, initiated in 1998, was to explore the feasibility of using the local language in a structured method in order to transition students into English and Filipino, the two mandatory languages of formal instruction. Through community consultations and mobilization, teacher training and orthography development, a localized curriculum was developed to bring its content closer to the cultural milieu of the learners, with the local language, Lilubuagen, as the main medium of instruction, and Filipino and English taught as subjects (see Table 1 for a sample section of the curriculum). A cognitive argument underpinned the framework of the entire project; that is, the project was based on the assumption that the primacy of community languages in early literacy development is necessary to exploit the full potential of learners' cognitive and academic development.

The success of the project became the basis of a longitudinal study in Lubuagan to explore empirically the educational benefits of a multilingual approach to education. This was spearheaded by the Summer Institute of Linguistics and supported by the Department of Education and other educational agencies. The key question that arose from the initial phase of the project was: "Will the introduction of first language literacy and interactive instructional strategies in the Lubuagan educational system improve educational outcomes for Lubuagan students?" (Dekker and Young 2005: 196). Based on results from control and experimental groups, research has shown that the use of the mother tongue in early education does not compromise the pupils' educational achievement and that performance in math correlates positively with instruction in the local language (Walter and Dekker 2008).

Table 1. Lubuagan Kalinga First Language Component curriculum (Dekker and Young 2005: 192)

	Lilubuagen 4½ hours per day	Filipino 1 hour per day	English 1 hour per day
First semester	Language development through study of grammar, vocabulary, concept development integrated into reading, writing, culture study	Listening skills in Filipino taught through TPR — 6 weeks	Listening skills in English taught through TPR — 6 weeks
	Reading 80 minutes per day	Oral Filipino continued through listening comprehension, vocabulary building, and conversational skills	Oral English continued through listening comprehension, vocabulary building, and conversational skills
	Writing 45 minutes per day		
	Study of indigenous culture including arts, music, oral language styles, etc. 1 hr weekly	Oral Filipino through grammatical comparison between Lubuagan sentence structure and Filipino	
	Math 45 minutes per day	Bridging to reading Filipino at end of semester	
	Science 45 minutes 3 days a week		
	Social studies 45 minutes twice a week		

The Lubuagan experiment figures prominently in the current conflicted discourses on language and education in the Philippines brought about partly by the contending bills in the Philippine congress (Nolasco 2008). To be sure, the 20th century has seen intermittent efforts to bring vernacular education into mainstream formal education in the Philippines (Saleeby 1924). There were already attempts at vernacularization (1903–1909) at the start of American colonial rule in the country, and the vernacular experiments in Iloilo in the Visayan region (1948–1954) during the early postcolonial years revealed results that would later serve as good justification for the use of local languages in the schools (Dekker and Young 2005: 186). There have been at least ten major research projects carried out since the Iloilo experiments attesting to the validity of mother tongue education in the early grades (Castillo 2009). However, as mentioned earlier, such evidence-based argument has been overshadowed by language ideological debates on English and Tagalog/Pilipino/Filipino.

Nevertheless, in recent years have vigorous efforts been exerted to push for mother tongue education in the country, with a multisectoral support base from the academe, business, non-governmental organizations, regional ethnolinguistic groups and government agencies. Training of local teachers in the use of local languages in the schools in different regions has started, while academics have forcefully argued the case for mother tongue education in national newspapers with an intensity perhaps unmatched by most efforts in the past. Graduate curricula in bilingual education such as those in the University of the Philippines and the Philippine Normal University have also been recently revisited to incorporate a multilingual/mother tongue framework. A primer on mother tongue education has recently been written in easily accessible language in order to gain support from the general public (Nolasco 2009).

The current state of the two bills in Congress, however, demonstrates how the symbolic power of English remains essentially uncontested. One of the main proponents of mother tongue education in the Philippines concedes:

> International and local research studies in the use of language in education are conclusive — when the mother tongue is the medium in primary instruction, learners end up being better thinkers and better learners in both their first AND second language(s). Sadly, legislators at the House of Representatives continue to ignore the studies and are in fact set to approve a bill "strengthening" English as the medium of instruction (MOI) from the elementary grades to the tertiary level (Nolasco 2009: 2, emphasis as original).

The positive features of recent re-engagements with language policy in the country include using empirical evidence to demonstrate the cognitive advantages of local languages as media of instruction and working with local schools to address their specific concerns and needs. The focus is on how the local languages can be incorporated into the school curriculum because of their perceived cognitive advantages over English and Filipino (which is not a local language in most communities in the country). There is sustained work with local communities to work out appropriate syllabi. However, the cognitive dimension seems to be given much prominence with little work on how the local languages relate to the social development needs of the community. Such re-engagements, in other words, attempt to change the educational landscape from below through a reconfiguration of the role of languages in the schools, thus putting these languages (explicitly or implicitly) at the centre of community life. In other words, if strategies of re-engagement are to become more effective, especially in articulating alternative voices in language ideological debates, local languages must not only be seen as pedagogically superior because of their cognitive potential for faster learning. More importantly, they must also be seen as useful elements in the development process.

Disengaging from language policy

Another way of dealing with language policy in the Philippines is to locate it within the broadest possible framework of social and community development. That is, language policy as social policy (see Tsui and Tollefson 2004) is treated as part of a much bigger problem of development in the country. As such, development needs of communities are considered **basic** concerns; thus the languages of education are issues related to poverty, health, public safety and so on.

In the late 1990s, an emergent structure of Philippine education paved the way for a new official definition of literacy in the country. Ideologically aligned with the nationalist, anti-colonial politics of the 1960s and the decades thereafter (Constantino 1970), this definition no longer sees literacy simply as a set of skills to be learned, but as a social practice that is "anchored in the overall development of communities and nation" (Canieso-Doronila 1998: 83). This means that education and community development are inextricably linked, with education seen as support for the social development of communities. What is needed then is a comprehensive education framework which integrates the development needs of a community, thus its appropriate name, Comprehensive Education and Community Development or CECD. What this particular approach to education does is to develop the framework through substantive and organized ways of doing research and consulting the various stakeholders in the community. It assumes that to address the problem of education, it has to address the problem of community development as a whole. To initiate reform in the schools, it must attempt to reform the social landscape of the community in general (Canieso-Doronila and Acuña 1994; Canieso-Doronila 1996, 1998, 2001).

Table 2. A Sample CECD Programme (adapted from Canieso-Doronila 1998:88)

Social Reform Agenda		CECD Programme of Valencia, Negros Occidental	
Agenda 1	Components	Components	Activities
Access to quality basic services	1. Food and nutrition 2. Health 3. Water and sanitation 4. Clothing 5. Shelter and socialized housing 6. Peace and order /Public safety 7. Basic education and functional literacy 8. Family care/psycho-social	1. Social Services Programme	a. Health services and other social services delivered by the Municipal Social Welfare Office, such as free caskets for indigents, and nutrition programme b. Bloodtyping for the whole municipality to easily access blood from potential donors for emergency purposes c. ID Card to facilitate access to these social services
		2. Literacy and Education	a. Early Childhood Education/Daycare b. Basic Literacy and Numeracy c. Functional Literacy

Let us look at a small section of sample CECD program in Valencia, Negros Oriental, a low-class municipality in Central Philippines. This is a project initiated by the University of the Philippines Centre for Integrative and Development Studies (UP-CIDS) (Canieso-Doronila 1998).

First of all, what we see is that CECD locates its work within the Social Reform Agenda (SRA) of the government, a major policy of development in the country. It then concretizes the SRA in terms of specific activities for a particular community. The example represented in Table 2 is one section that addresses the first agenda of SRA: Access to quality basic services. (The two others are Sustainable development of productive resources and providing access to economic opportunities and Enhancing institution-building and effective participation in governance.) It can be seen that this particular agenda has eight components which the CECD framework then repackages into two major components: (1) Social Services Program and (2) Literacy and Education. Out of these components emerge various specific activities and needs that concretize the main objectives.

It is in the literacy and education component that the question of appropriate curriculum becomes apparent. First, if a comprehensive education is necessary to help develop a community, it is therefore necessary to develop an educational curriculum that takes into account the development needs of the community. According to Canieso-Doronila, "literacy and education are strong elements of the development process but not the major defining elements" (2001:278) because "none of the major problems of the country (e.g. massive poverty, landholding inequality, inadequate access to modern agricultural technology), can be solved by literacy and education" (2001:279). Thus, an appropriate curriculum in a comprehensive education must address the real, **material** conditions of learning; in the words of one unnamed professor dedicated to addressing problems of illiteracy in the country, "We only wanted to teach them literacy but they asked us to provide piglets to raise as well" (quoted in Canieso-Doronila 1996:4).

Second, an appropriate curriculum will be one which treats "local cultures as **sources** (not **targets**) of knowledge which can only be understood in its own terms" (Arinto 1996:13, emphasis as original). Nevertheless, at the same time, it is also an expansive curriculum because it taps into the core requirements of national education. Therefore, in both requirements of a suitable curriculum for local communities, the important role of local languages in basic literacy and elementary education emerges almost 'naturally'. This is a different take on the primacy of local languages in education because it deploys an argument which assesses a more realistic valuation of language in the development process, thus able to identify both its possibilities and limitations in educational and social change. The more 'cognitive' argument which focusses on the pedagogical superiority of local languages in education usually misses this point, thus focussing simply on the role of language for educational change.

Interestingly, this view does not close off the possibility of English to be part of the entire educational process, especially as a subject to be taught at all levels and as the medium of instruction in science and mathematics at the secondary level (if students opt for it) except that its role becomes more prominent in the latter grades and secondary levels where pupils and students develop skills needed to interact with communities outside their own. English continues to be seen as an important language which will serve as a bridge between local communities and the global community within which those who are able to continue their education beyond the primary grades may eventually work. The local languages, though, are the necessary medium through which children and adults alike are taught ways to help them make sense of their local environment and see the connection between formal education and daily life (Tupas 2008b). This is one way to address "the unevenness in educational provision (or educational quality) as well as in cultural practice and competence in English [which] continues to exacerbate the difference and distinction between the elite and the masses in the Philippines" (Canieso-Doronila 1998:66).

The CECD framework of education has produced positive results in the development of communities as a whole. In Valencia, for example, the following changes have been observed (Canieso-Doronila 1998:93–94):

- Increase in municipal income, thus transformation of Valencia from a fifth to a third class municipality within three years
- Improved tax collection: access to basic social services through an ID System requires people to pay their taxes first
- Increase in the level of community organization through CECD programmes which were conceptualized by the people themselves
- More participation in community programmes because people understood what these programmes were about
- More participation in literacy, education, teacher training and translation programmes resulting in 79% of Grade One pupils in all grade schools to read and write within six months

A comprehensive education framework, therefore, assumes broad involvement of all sectors in the community. It assumes that education can transform an entire community if, in the first place, the development of the community plays a primary role. Thus, if one has to grapple with the problem of language in Philippine education, one has to disengage from it and instead look at the problem of development at the community level first and foremost. Through this, language becomes part of the problem of development and not just of education. Consequently, past and present dominant language policy-making practices in the Philippines (which take place at the national and/or ideological level) can be seen as inappropriate and inadequate because they rarely tackle the issue from 'below' or from a development perspective (Tupas 2008b). Current initiatives to promote the local languages as primary media of instruction in early education are, of course, commendable and must be supported, but they need to generate a much more inclusive political discourse which includes the imperative to use such languages for social development purposes. Otherwise, such initiatives may suffer the same fate as earlier well-intentioned literacy projects discussed in the earlier sections of this paper and clearly captured by the quote: "It is not easy to say 'This is our land' when one has no land" (in Canieso-Doronila 2001:271).

CECD has produced what Canieso-Doronila (1998) calls 'schools of the people' which function within the framework of comprehensive education as discussed in this section. They draw on the energies of entire communities. Local languages are used not simply because children learn faster through them than through unfamiliar languages, but also because the local development needs of the people require that local languages be used. But English, too, is deemed an important language. While its use as language of instruction is considered flawed because it is not the language of community development, "greater attention to good English instruction will have to be made to ensure that the country's edge in this area is not dulled" (1998:79). This means sustained English instruction as a subject from elementary school to college. All languages have a place in the schools of the people only that their distribution responds to local, and **then** global, needs, and not to global needs only at the expense of the local ones.

Conclusion: Schools of the people and transformative education

The CECD framework of education has become part of the basis of a huge project of the Department of Education funded by the World Bank, called the Third Elementary Education Project (TEEP). In particular, TEEP schools implemented a School-Based Management (SBM) framework which ceded power to local principals and teachers in the management of their schools in order to improve the quality of basic education in the country. The SBM, "the institutional expression of decentralization of education at the grassroots level" (Department of Education 2005b:323), has resulted in improved academic performance among the participating schools around the country and, therefore, has foregrounded "a movement to place education at the centre of a development process that is ultimately sustained by the communities" (Quijano 2005:ix).

These schools of the people have shown that "opportunities can be equalized in the highly unequal setting of this country" (Bautista 2005:xxii), thus "defying probabilistic predictions of school achievements based primarily on social class" (2005:xxiii). Interestingly though, while a whole range of problems has been identified as basic challenges to the implementation of SBM (from leadership styles to dire poverty of the community), in research on 50 of the most successful schools of the people, not one has identified the problem of language as a basic problem that needs to be solved (see Department of Education 2005a). It may as well be that language is indeed a critical component in academic performance, but what is important to emphasize again (as it has been pointed out many times in this paper) is that the problem of language is ultimately a problem of development. Language policy becomes more useful and fair if it re-views languages in education from the point of view of the schools of the people. These schools have disengaged from language policy in order to transform education on the ground.

References

Aikman, S. (2001) Literacies, languages and developments in Peruvian Amazonia. In B.V. Street (ed.), *Literacy and Development: Ethnographic Perspectives*, pp. 103–120. London, New York: Routledge.

Arinto, P.B. (1996) *Reconstructing Educational Knowledge: Incorporating Community Knowledge in Functional Literacy Programs*, Vol. 1. Philippines: ERP-CIDS-UP & BNFE-DECS.

Bautista, M.C.R.B. (2005) Schools of the people: Transforming education on the ground. In M.C.R.B. Bautista (ed.) *Fifty Studies of School-Based Management under the Third Elementary Education Project (TEEP)*, pp. xi–xxix. Philippines: Department of Education.

Bernardo, A.B.I. (2007) Language in Philippine education: Rethinking old fallacies, exploring new alternatives amidst globalization. In T.R.F. Tupas (ed.), *(Re)making Society: The Politics of Language, Discourse and Identity in the Philippines*, pp. 1–26. Quezon City: University of the Philippines Press.

Blommaert, J. (2008) *Grassroots Literacy — Writing, Identity and Voice in Central Africa.* London, New York: Routledge.

Canieso-Doronila, M.L. (1994) *Learning from Life: An Ethnographic Study of Functional Literacy in Fourteen Philippine Communities,* Vol. 2: Main Report — Abridged version. Abridged by P.B. Arinto and P. Flores. Philippines: UP-ERP-CIDS, LCCP & DECS-BNFE.

Canieso-Doronila, M.L. (1996) *Landscapes of Literacy: An Ethnographic Study of Functional Literacy in Marginal Philippine Communities.* Hamburg, London: UNESCO & Luzac Oriental.

Canieso-Doronila, M.L. (1998) The emergence of schools of the people and the transformation of the Philippine educational system. *UP-CIDS Chronicle* 3(1): 63–97.

Canieso-Doronila, M.L. (2001) Developing a literate tradition in six marginal communities in the Philippines: Interrelations of literacy, education, and social development. In D.R. Olson and N. Torrance (eds), *The Making of Literate Societies,* pp. 248–283. Malden, MA: Blackwell.

Canieso-Doronila, M.L. and J.E. Acuña (1994) *Learning from Life: An Ethnographic Study of Functional Literacy in Marginal Philippine Communities,* Vol. 1: Main Report. Philippines: Literacy Coordinating Council of the Philippines & Department of Education, Culture and Sports, Bureau of Non-Formal Education.

Castillo, E.S. (2009) Mother tongue education in Philippine schools. Retrieved 18 June 2009 from http://www.pssc.org.ph/Downloads/nssc/MotherTongue.pdf.

Constantino, R. (1970) The mis-education of the Filipino. *Journal of Contemporary Asia* 1(1): 20–36.

Department of Education (2005a) *Fifty Studies of School-Based Management under the Third Elementary Education Project (TEEP),* pp. xi–xxix. Philippines: Department of Education.

Department of Education (2005b) A primer on School-Based Management and its support systems (Appendix A). In Department of Education, *Fifty Studies of School-Based Management under the Third Elementary Education Project (TEEP),* pp. 321–367. Philippines: Department of Education.

Dekker, D. and C. Young (2005) Bridging the gap: The development of appropriate educational strategies for minority language communities in the Philippines. *Current Issues in Language Planning* 6(2): 182–199.

Espiritu, C.C. (1999) The Cebuano response to the language controversy in the Philippines: Implications for the intellectualization of Filipino. In M.L.S. Bautista and G.O. Tan (eds), *The Filipino Bilingual: A Multidisciplinary Perspective (Festschrift in Honor of Emy M. Pascasio),* pp. 65–69. Manila: Linguistic Society of the Philippines.

Fuentes, G.G. and L.A. Mojica (1999) A study of the language attitudes of selected Filipino bilingual students toward Filipino and English. In M.L.S. Bautista and G.O. Tan (eds), *The Filipino Bilingual: A Multidisciplinary Perspective (Festschrift in Honor of Emy M. Pascasio),* pp. 50–64. Manila: Linguistic Society of the Philippines.

Gonzalez, A.B. (1980) *Language and Nationalism: The Philippine Experience Thus Far.* Quezon City: Ateneo de Manila.

Gonzalez, A. (1982) Language dilemma in Philippine academia: Nationalism or modernization? In J. Pride (ed.), *Language for the Third World Universities,* pp. 23–38. New Delhi: Bahri.

Gonzalez, A. (1991) Cebuano and Tagalog: Ethnic rivalry redivivus. In J.R. Dow (ed.), *Focus on Language and Ethnicity (Essays in Honor of Joshua A. Fishman),* pp. 111–130. Amsterdam, Philadelphia: John Benjamins.

Hau, C.S. and V.L. Tinio (2003) Language policy and ethnic relations in the Philippines. In M. Brown and S. Ganguly (eds), *Fighting Words: Language Policy and Ethnic Relations in Asia,* pp. 319–352. Cambridge, MA: The Massachusetts Institute of Technology Press.

Johnson, D.C. (2009) Ethnography of language policy. *Language Policy* 8: 139–159.

Kobari, Y. (1999) Reassessment after 15 years: Attitudes of the students of Cebu Institute of Technology towards Filipino in tertiary education. In M.L.S. Bautista and G.O. Tan (eds), *The Filipino Bilingual: A Multidisciplinary Perspective (Festschrift in Honor of Emy M. Pascasio),* pp. 56–64. Manila: Linguistic Society of the Philippines.

Licuanan, P.B. (2007) Language and learning. *Sawikaan*, Filipinas Institute of Translation. Retrieved 1 June 2009 from http://www.sawikaan.net/language_and_learning.html

Llanto, J.F. (2009) Language experts, educators nix House bill for all-English teaching. *ABS-CBN News*. Retrieved 12 June 2009 from http://www.abs-cbnnews.com/nation/01/15/09/language-experts-educators-nix-house-bill-all-english-teaching

Luz, J.M. (2007) 'English First' policy will hurt learning. *Inquirer Politics*. Retrieved 27 May 2009 from http://archive.inquirer.net/view.php?db=1&story_id=44752

May, S. and N. Hornberger (eds) (2008) *Encyclopedia of Language and Education*, 2nd ed. *Language Policy and Political Issues in Education*, Vol. 1. USA: Springer.

Miclat, M.I. (2006) *Beyond the Great Wall: A Family Journal*. Manila: Anvil Publishing, Inc.

Nolasco, R.M.D. (2008) The prospects of multilingual education and literacy in the Philippines. The 2nd International Conference on Language Development, Language Revitalization, and Multilingual Education in Ethnolinguistic Communities, Bangkok, 1–3 July 2008. Retrieved 17 June 2009 from http://www.seameo.org/_ld2008/doucments/Presentation_document/NolascoTHE_PROSPECTS_OF_MULTI-LINGUAL_EDUCATION.pdf

Nolasco, R.M.D. (2009) 21 Reasons why Filipino children learn better while using their mother tongue. A primer on mother tongue-based multilingual education (MLE) and other issues on language and learning in the Philippines. *Mother Tongue Based Multilingual Education (MLE) — Philippines*. Retrieved 16 June 2009 from http://mothertongue-based.blogspot.com/2009/01/mle-primer.html

Quijano, Y.S. (2005) Preface — The story of SBM, as told by TEEP. Transforming education on the ground. *Fifty Studies of School-Based Management under the Third Elementary Education Project (TEEP)*, p. ix. Philippines: Department of Education.

Saleeby, N.M. (1924) *The Language Education of the Philippine Islands*. Manila: Filipina Book Guild.

San Juan, E. Jr. (1998) One hundred years of producing and reproducing the 'Filipino'. *Amerasia Journal* 24(2): 1–35.

Sibayan, B.P. (1999) *The Intellectualization of Filipino and Other Essays on Education and Sociolinguistics*. Manila: The Linguistic Society of the Philippines.

Sibayan, B. and A. Gonzalez (1996) Post-imperial English in the Philippines. In J. Fishman, A. Conrad and A. Rubal-Lopez (eds), *Post-Imperial English — Status Change in Former British and American Colonies, 1940–1990*, pp. 139–172. Berlin, New York: Mouton de Gruyter.

Sta. Maria, F. (1999) On the teaching of English. *Journal of Asian English Studies* 29(1): 84–89.

Tollefson, J.W. (2008) Language planning in education. In May and Hornberger (eds), pp. 3–14.

Tsui, A.B.M. and J.W. Tollefson (2004) The centrality of medium-of-instruction policy in sociopolitical processes. In J.W. Tollefson and A.B.M. Tsui (eds), *Medium of Instruction Policies — Which Agenda? Whose Agenda?*, pp. 1–18. Mahwah, NJ, London: Lawrence Erlbaum Associates.

Tupas, T.R.F. (2007) Go back to class: The medium of instruction debate in the Philippines. In H.G. Lee and L. Suryadinata (eds), *Language, Nation and Development in Southeast Asia*, pp. 17–38. Singapore: Institute of Southeast Asian Studies.

Tupas, T.R.F. (2008a) Bourdieu, historical forgetting and the problem of English in the Philippines. *Philippine Studies* 56(1): 47–67.

Tupas, T.R.F. (2008b) Kalayagan, tawid-buhay and other uses of language in a marginal Philippine community: The place of language in literacy and social development. *International Journal of Bilingual Education and Bilingualism* 11(2): 226–245.

UNESCO (1953) *The Use of Vernacular Languages in Education*. Paris: UNESCO.

UNESCO (2003) *Education in a Multilingual World*. Paris: UNESCO.

Walter, S.L. and D. Dekker (2008) The Lubuagan Mother Tongue Education Experiment (FLC) — A report of comparative test results. Report presented to the Committee on Basic Education and Culture, Committee on Higher and Technical Education, House of Representatives. Quezon City, Philippines.

Not plain sailing

Malaysia's language choice in policy and education*

Azirah Hashim
University of Malaya

This paper focusses on language and education issues in Malaysia as they have unfolded in the context of nation building, societal multilingualism and globalization from independence to the present day. The paper first examines the origin and nature of language and medium-of-instruction policies in Malaysia and the rationale for them. Secondly, it discusses the conflicts and controversies pertaining to language and education analyzing the domains of contestation. The next part of the paper reflects on the various shifts in language policy over the decades, from the early institutionalization of Malay to the growing importance of English amidst globalization trends, and finally the recent shift back to Malay, also examining the positioning of the Chinese and Tamil languages in the country. This is followed by a discussion of the emergence of an indigenized variety of English and English as a lingua franca in the region. The paper ends with a critical evaluation of the impact of the language and medium-of-instruction policies, and the constraints of alternative policies, with suggestions for a possible way forward.

Introduction

Language has often been seen to have a significant role to play in promoting national identity, and the use of a common language across ethnic groups has been useful in uniting the different groups. The selection of a language as the designated national language or the medium of instruction in a multiethnic country, however, is not a straightforward matter, and a number of issues concerning the justification for the choice made are often raised. Additionally, the presence of multiple languages in a population has often been seen to be an obstacle to the development of a desired national identity. Formerly colonized nations have had to make a conscious effort to develop a language in order to make it suitable for adoption in all domains, thus making it a national language. This has inevitably led to less attention being paid to other languages as attempts are made to assimilate the different ethnic groups for the purpose of achieving a national identity.

Linguistic complexity is further enhanced by the fact that the pragmatic value of English has not just been maintained in the region and has become increasingly more important as a result of globalization. The preferred use of English in some domains has posed some challenges to the success of national languages, and the use of English as a second or foreign language has given rise to indigenized varieties and the concomitant emphasis on English as a lingua franca. It is important that in any multilingual population, the government has to ensure that some fundamental obligations are fulfilled. In the case of Malaysia, while Malay is the national language, Malaysia's other languages must also be preserved even as English proficiency is emphasized.

AILA Review 22 (2009), 36–51. DOI 10.1075/aila.22.04has
ISSN 1461–0213 / E-ISSN 1570–5595 © John Benjamins Publishing Company

This paper focusses on language and education issues in Malaysia as they have unfolded in the context of nation building, societal multilingualism and globalization from independence to the present day. Firstly, the paper examines the origin and nature of language and medium-of-instruction policies in Malaysia and the rationale for them. Secondly, it discusses the conflicts and controversies pertaining to language and education analyzing the domains of contestation. The next part of the paper reflects on the various shifts in language policy over the decades, from the early institutionalization of Malay to the growing importance of English amidst globalization trends, and finally the recent shift back to Malay, also examining the positioning of the Chinese and Tamil languages in the country. This is followed by a discussion of the emergence of an indigenized variety of English and English as a lingua franca in the region. The paper ends with a critical evaluation of the impact of the language and medium-of-instruction policies, and the constraints of alternative policies, with suggestions for a possible way forward.

Background to the country

Malaysia consists of two parts separated from each other by the South China Sea: Peninsular Malaysia (or West Malaysia), and Sabah and Sarawak on the island of Borneo (East Malaysia). The population is about 26 million, comprising Malays (about 60%), Chinese (about 25%), Indians (about 7%) and the remainder consisting of other ethnic and indigenous communities in West and East Malaysia. The Chinese come from different dialect groups such as the Hokkien, Cantonese, Khek, Teochew and Hainanese and other smaller groups. The Indians include those from northern and southern India and also the Pakistanis, the Bangladeshis and the Sri Lankans (Asmah 2007: 337). In terms of religion, 60.4% are Muslims, 19.2% are Buddhists, 9.1% Christian, 6.3% Hindu and the rest are of various minority faiths (Department of Statistics 2002).

The Malay Archipelago already had their own system of governance when the first Europeans (first the Portuguese, then the Dutch, and finally the British) arrived. The Malay language was the lingua franca, the language of diplomacy, the language used in the ports as well as the language that the Europeans used with the rulers in the region. It was only when the British came that there was an attempt to introduce English as the language to be used in schools. Schools using Malay as well as English as the medium of instruction were subsequently established, and the Roman script was added to the Jawi script that was already in use at that time.

While Chinese and Indians had been in Malaya (where 'Malaya' then included a loose set of states on the Malay Peninsular colonized by the British, also including Singapore) since the 14th century, they began to arrive in large numbers only towards the end of the 19th century to make a living from tin mining and rubber industries. This led to a change in the demography, with the three different ethnic groups tending to be located in different parts of the Peninsula. The Malays were found mainly in rural areas in the traditional sectors of rice and fruit farming, the Chinese in the tin mining and urban areas, and the Indians in the rubber estates and near railway stations where they worked as labourers. Each ethnic community had their own languages, cultures and economic domains which were encouraged by the British through their divide-and-rule policy (Asmah 2007: 341).

The Malays are generally homogeneous in terms of language, religion and culture. They all speak Malay although various dialects are found in the different states, they are all Muslims and practise the Malay way of life. The Chinese are homogeneous as a race (this term is widely used in Malaysia to denote an officially designated ethnic group and thus does not carry the negative connotation it does elsewhere) but are divided according to the Chinese dialect groups they belong to. They are not homogeneous where religion is concerned, with some being Buddhists, some Christians and some Muslims. The Indians come from different subgroups and castes, speak a number of different languages such as Tamil and Malayalam, and are generally either Hindus, Christians or Muslims.

The language situation is diverse with at least 80 languages spoken in the country (Asmah 1992:1). Malay was made the national language in 1957, initially termed *Bahasa Melayu* ('Malay language'), but in 1969 it was renamed *Bahasa Malaysia* ('Malaysian language') to enable all ethnic groups to identify with and be emotionally attached to it. English was termed the 'second most important language', and between 1957 and 1967, both Bahasa Melayu and English enjoyed almost equal status. Chinese and Tamil were taught in government schools. In Sabah, English and Bahasa Malaysia (henceforth referred to as 'Malay') continued to be the official languages until 1973, and in Sarawak, English was the official language until 1985.

Origin and evolution of language policies in the colonial period

Since the colonial period, various preferences in the choice of language in policy and as medium of instruction have emerged. Prior to independence, although Malaya had become a country with a multilingual population, policies for language and education did not do much to assimilate the different ethnic groups and, in fact, did not help to facilitate a common national identity. Three factors influenced the colonial state's choice of approach towards education. Firstly, the designation of the Malays as the indigenous group and the Chinese as 'alien residents' gave rise to different language and educational policies for the different ethnic groups. Secondly, economic considerations which included the cost of education and the demand for educated people in the job market had a role to play in determining language and education policies. Thirdly, the preference for education in the vernacular languages rather than an English-medium one contributed towards shaping the education policy (Lee 2007:119).

Under British colonial rule, where the national, vernacular schools were concerned, three languages served as media of instruction: Malay, Chinese and Tamil (while English was used in the minority English school system). The Cheesemen Committee of 1945–9 recommended that the various vernaculars be used at the primary level, to which there were conflicting responses. The Barnes Report (1951) favoured Malay-English bilingualism, stating: "We have given prolonged thought to the language question. It has been clear throughout that two languages, and only two languages should be taught in the National schools, and that these two must be official languages of the country, namely, Melayu (Malay) and English" (Barnes Report 1951, Article 7). This was met with resistance from both the Indians and the Chinese who, although they were willing to accept Malay as the sole national language, were not accepting of the choice of Malay and English as the only official languages nor the establishment of a bilingual national education system (Lee 2007:125). The Fenn-Wu report (1951), prepared by a committee set up to review Chinese education in the country, supported the establishment of a multilingual national education system with English, Malay, Chinese and Tamil. This report was the complete opposite of the Barnes report, and therefore at the end of 1951, another committee was set up to review the two reports. This committee was more in favour of the Barnes proposal, and as a result, in 1952, the Education Ordinance proposed the establishment of the bilingual national school system where either Malay or English was used with the view of establishing a Malay-medium system in the long run. As a form of compromise, it was decided that Mandarin and Tamil would be provided to the Chinese and Indian students. This decision was argued against by the Chinese educationist movement, the *Dongjiaozong*, which persistently called for the Chinese language to be given official status and for Chinese schools to be included in the national education system. The Razak Report of 1956 then proposed the establishment of two types of primary schools, the 'national school' using Malay as the medium and the 'national-type' school which could use either English, Chinese or Tamil as the medium. At the secondary level, a single system, that of the national school, was recommended, but at the same time, Chinese schools could still continue, provided that they adopt the common syllabus and examinations.

As the country emerged from being a colonial state, linguistic nationalism became part of nation building. The issue of the medium of instruction has been a subject of debate for the last fifty years, focussing primarily on whether English should be replaced by Malay or other languages.

In 1957, upon independence, the Reid Commission adopted many of the recommendations of the 1956 Razak Report, resulting in Malay-medium national schools, and English, Chinese and Tamil national-type schools where Malay was a compulsory subject. At secondary schools, public examinations could only be done in either Malay or English. Eventually a compromise was reached, with Article 152 of the Constitution stating that Malay be given the status of sole national and official language, and English the status of an official language for ten years after independence; further "non-Malays would not be prohibited or prevented from using (otherwise than for official purposes), or from teaching or learning their mother tongues" (Lee 2007:128). The Language Act of 1967, however, removed the official role of English, and relegated it to the status of second language; English nonetheless continued to be used widely, with an unwritten rule observed by the government sector and institutions such as universities that, besides the master version which is in Bahasa Malaysia, every official document or report has to have an English version (Asmah 1992:92).

The reasons why Malay was chosen as the national language are many. Firstly, it was the language of the indigenous ethnic group, the Malays, who make up the majority of the population. Secondly, Malay had been the language used between members of different ethnic groups from before independence. Thirdly, Malay had been the language of administration in the Malay states and the Malay archipelago for centuries (Asmah 1979, 1987). According to Asmah (2007:348), "independence and the offer of citizenship by birth for recognition of the central place of the Malay language in Malay reflected a critical way of thinking in the minds of the Malays: that language was their soul and the soul of the nation as contained in the slogan *Bahasa Jiwa Bangsa* (language is the soul of the nation)". The Dewan Bahasa dan Pustaka, the Institute of National Language, was established in 1956 to implement policies concerned with the development, use and usage of the national language.

Medium-of-instruction policy in independence
In the early years of independence, there was apparently no hurry for accelerating Malay into the system, but to ensure that Malay was used in education, the Education Act of 1961 made Malay the only medium of instruction in national secondary schools. The 1967 National Language Act then stipulated the conversion to Malay of all English-medium primary and secondary schools by 1976 and 1982 respectively. After the racial riots of 1969, efforts were made to expedite this conversion, and in 1971, the Education Act was revised to extend the shift to Malay to tertiary education. The development of the Malay language became a priority in order to consolidate its status as the sole national and official language and as the main medium of instruction. Strict and rapid implementation of the national language policy took place. English as a medium of instruction was slowly phased out over a period of 14 years. The process of replacing English with Malay was done subject by subject, and the whole process was completed by 1980 (Asmah 1982:89). All English-medium schools were converted to national schools in Peninsular Malaysia by 1982, and in Sabah and Sarawak by 1985. The national-type schools, i.e. the Chinese and Tamil primary schools, continued to use Mandarin and Tamil respectively as their media of instruction, with Malay taught as a compulsory language.

However, in national schools, English was retained as a compulsory school subject, though it was no longer a requirement to obtain a pass in it to be awarded a school certificate. Instead, Malay became the subject that students had to pass to get a grade one in the school leaving exam. What in effect took place was an abandonment of a bilingual school system for a monolingual one. This contrasts with the decisions of other former British colonies, with Brunei adopting a bilingual education system (*Dwibahasa*) fully implemented by 1973, and Singapore as well (Ozog 1993:67). As a consequence of the conversion of national schools to Malay medium, the number of students enrolled in Chinese primary schools surged and an increasing demand for more Chinese schools especially in the urban areas could be observed.

Language and education in Malaysia have always been closely linked to ethnicity. The continuation of the Mandarin- and Tamil-medium schools alongside the national schools indicates this trend. Some years ago, it was reported that more than 24% of the Malaysian school population was currently enrolled in Chinese and Tamil vernacular schools, with a close relationship between ethnicity and type of school selected. 90% of the Chinese were in Chinese primary schools, while 90% of the Malays were in national schools. Furthermore, 88% of the Indian children studied in Tamil vernacular schools (David and Govindasamy 2003).

In the national schools, Malay was the medium of instruction until the implementation of English for science and maths in 2002. English is taught from Primary One, and the teaching of Mandarin and Tamil is also made available. The introduction of Malay as a medium of instruction saw an increase in Chinese and Tamil schools catering to the demands of these ethnic groups, who believe that these schools are more culturally and linguistically suited to their communities. The segregation that this inevitably brought about appears to have contributed to racial polarization, with national schools having mostly Malay children, and Chinese schools mostly Chinese and Tamil schools all Indian children.

The focus was mainly on the educational and government sectors, and allowances were made for the use of English in the law courts in the interest of justice, because many judges and lawyers had been trained in the United Kingdom and were therefore more adept at conducting trials in English rather than in Malay. It was much later, in 1982, that the Lower Courts began conducting trials in Malay and interpreters had to be used when English was not understood. The 1983 National Language amendment applied the new policy to the High and Federal Courts, requiring Malay for all proceedings other than for oral testimonies with an option for English to be used "in the interest of justice" (Powell 2008:21).

As in other parts of the world, English has now made a comeback from the postcolonial era, when its use tended to suggest the values of the colonizers. Now it is seen as a tool of international communication and the motivation for its use is mainly instrumental. With globalization, English is seen as the key to success, and the question as to what languages should be the media of instruction has been raised again. The constant struggle between the linguistic pragmatic approach — what needs to be done for the development of the nation — and the emotional relationship with the language continues to take place. This is discussed in the next section.

Forces of change: English

In Malaysia, as in other countries that were colonized, there has been the constant need to promote national languages for national and ethnic unity, and at the same time the need to have English for communication in a globalized world. In the 1990s, the challenges of globalization and internationalization brought about the pressure to be competent in English, which is seen as the language needed for functioning in a global marketplace. A conflict arose between what was important for national interest and what was required for internationalization; given the multiethnicity of the population, certain challenges were inevitable.

Today, three groups of speakers of English can generally be found, although not always identified, as a consequence of language policies and language education. The first group of speakers are those who went through an English-medium education and are generally proficient in the English language. The second group of speakers comprises those who went through both the English and

Malay media of education, and are in general quite proficient in English although not as proficient as the first group. Finally, the third group comprises those who had their education completely in Malay, and this is the group that is suffering the consequences, especially in their lack of ability to land themselves lucrative jobs. With the implementation of English as the medium of instruction for science and maths, it is expected that we should soon be seeing a group who are better off than this third group in terms of English language proficiency.

Due to internationalization and globalization, linguistic complexities are manifest in higher education. There has been an increasing need to place greater emphasis on English. It has often been stressed that emphasizing English does not mean the decline of other languages, especially Malay. The former Prime Minister Tun Dr Mahathir often stated that speaking in English in no way shows disrespect towards the status of Malay, and that promoting the use and increased proficiency in English is actually in the interest of the Malay community, who is in many ways at a disadvantage on the job market. According to Asmah (2007: 356), "if in the past the Malay slogan was *Hidup Bahasa, Hidup Bangsa* (If the language thrives, so will the nation), Mahathir's solution was *Hidup Bangsa, Hidup Bahasa* (If the nation thrives, so will the language)".

McKay and Bokhorst-Heng (2008: 10–17) very aptly mention the three main incentives for learning English. The first incentive is economic, and two growing areas of globalization can be said to be the use of English in transnational corporations and in outsourcing. To obtain jobs in either, proficiency in English is absolutely necessary. A rapid increase in businesses, multinational companies and media expansion in recent years has brought about the spread of English all over Asia. These entities all run their businesses using English as the language of communication. Graduates who have a good command of English are usually employed immediately upon graduation, while the ones who do not have a good command of English are generally rejected by these companies. Graduates from private universities or universities abroad are usually favoured by employers mainly because of their competency in English. This has had an impact on the national languages in countries in the region and has brought about a reemphasis on English.

The second incentive is educational. There appears to be an increasing trend for universities to offer courses in English. Many local universities are recruiting students from other countries, and therefore English has to be the medium of instruction in the programmes that accept these students. Furthermore, there is also the pressure to publish in English to compete in the international arena. In Malaysia, a reform of the education act was implemented, allowing the private institutions to conduct their programmes in English. Since the 1990s, there has been an expansion of private education in the country. Malaysia liberalized its education policies in a bid to become a regional centre for education. The government realized that, for the education sector to flourish, there had to be some freedom for the choice of medium of instruction, just as in the business sector.

Transnational education started being encouraged, with foreign universities allowed to set up branch campuses in the country, with "the number of private tertiary education increas[ing] from 280 in 1995 to 611 in 1999, local private universities and university colleges from none in 1995 to nineteen in 1999, and five foreign universities [having] established branch campuses in Malaysia since 1999" (Lee 2007: 137). English has always been the medium of instruction in these universities, some of which have twinning programmes with British, Australian and American universities, so it was inevitable that English would gain a lot of importance in education. As a result, higher education has become divided into either Malay-medium or English-medium, with the government universities using the former and the private universities the latter, entailing that graduates of private universities became more sought after because of their competency in English.

Finally, the media provide a strong motivation for learning English as the general public is exposed to films, music, advertising and electronic communication. Many advertisements in Malay use English either in the entire advertisement or in code switching with other languages (Azirah fc). In addition, with the internet dominating our lives, electronic communication has encouraged the use of English, although most of the English used there is colloquial and mixed with other languages. Code switching is used to either express solidarity, to express a meaning that is hard to express in the other language or to exclude others (see e.g. David 2000; Morais 2000; Ooi 2001).

Measures that were taken to address the decline in English language proficiency initially did not affect the use of Malay as the medium of instruction. From around 1980, students were sent abroad to do a degree in English in order to increase the number of qualified English teaching personnel for schools and universities. Teachers and trainers were brought over from the United Kingdom to assist in improving the standard of English. English language campaigns were initiated as well. The former Prime Minister Dr Mahathir constantly reiterated the need to master English in his speeches and underlined the fact that to become a fully industrialized nation by the year 2020 (Vision 2020 created by Dr Mahathir), Malaysia should not just be a consumer of technology but also a provider. In 1993, he announced the Cabinet's decision to allow the teaching of maths and science and science-based courses in English in universities, providing the following reasons for reinstating English as the medium of instruction, namely because competence in English is necessary (Mohamad 1993: 2, cited in Gill 2004: 144):

- For Malaysians to remain competitive at an international level.
- To prevent the efficiency and capability of our people from being lower than those in other countries.
- Because the pace of translation cannot keep up with the generation of knowledge and information in the field of Science and Technology.

The government's proposal did not get the support that was needed to enable the change to take place effectively, largely due to resistance from Malay intellectuals who wanted Malay to remain the medium of instruction. The year 2002 can be considered significant in Malaysian education when a change in policy was once again announced and this time effected, with science and maths to be taught in English, starting with Primary One, Secondary One and Lower Six. This was 40 years after the implementation of Malay in the education system and after all the efforts to modernize it.

The reasons for the change in policy had to do with the impact of Science and Technology on the nation, with economic considerations and with the non-marketability of graduates who are not proficient in English. While Malay as the national language had been implemented rather successfully, there had been a decline in English language proficiency. University graduates were found to be unable to communicate in English when they attended job interviews and multinational companies were reluctant to employ such graduates. Gill (2005: 250) identifies the major challenges that the nation faces: "The first is the challenge of ensuring that the nation possesses the necessary human resource capacity, whether the existing quality of language capacity meets the needs of the nation. The second challenge arises out of the knowledge and information explosion and its implications for language policy". Access to knowledge in Science and Technology is crucial, and although Malay has been successfully implemented over a period of 30 years, translation work of materials from English to Malay has not been all that successful.

Another reason was the use of English in the business domain. Language policy has never affected this domain, indicating that economic considerations had priority. Restricting language use to Malay would only have had a negative impact on business in the country and discourage foreign investors. Tan's (2005) study of the medium-of-instruction debate in the press and news agency reports further found that much of the debate centred around the international status of English and that many of the arguments for reinstating English as a medium of instruction had to do with the notion of English as the main language of knowledge and for information and communication technology. Key items picked out from the quantitative study show that words like *globalization* and *information technology* were commonly found in the debate and that English was described as the lingua franca of business, science, technology and research (Tan 2005: 56). The study also shows that references are made to how English helps job seekers become employable and that with English, the country will be more competitive.

Unlike the implementation of Malay as the medium of instruction which took place over a 14-year period, the implementation of English for science and maths was drastic and happened without much prior warning. Teachers had to find ways to cope with this sudden change and support came in the form of trainers from overseas as well as locally. With this change in policy, the Malaysian education system has now gone back to a system that is bilingual, or trilingual in the national-type schools. The proposal met with opposition from various groups of all ethnic communities. Some Malays viewed it as a threat to Malay: they claimed that the Malay language would be sidelined and the position of the Malays threatened. This change in policy went against what they had fought for from the time prior to independence until when efforts were made to develop the Malay language as a suitable medium of instruction in schools and universities. Many Malays, however, were supportive of the move, realizing that it would bring about an improvement in their socioeconomic status, which would ensure their survival in the competitive climate.

Chinese groups strongly protested against this proposal, claiming that the quality of the Chinese schools would be affected, and that they wanted to preserve the characteristics of the Chinese schools. There was also the constant claim that the Chinese culture would be eroded. The initial proposal was subsequently altered to allow for the teaching of science and maths still to be carried out in Mandarin as long as English is also given priority. A similar agreement was worked out with Tamil schools.

There are two diverging opinions on this issue. The first group of people feels that the majority of the students will be at a disadvantage as they will have to learn through rote learning if they are not proficient in English and will not obtain the knowledge that they would obtain if the subjects were taught in their mother tongue. This would then lead to further failure in school. Since the implementation was sudden, teachers would not have received adequate training to teach the subjects in English, especially if they were educated in the national education system when the medium of instruction was completely in Malay. The second group of people, mainly from urban areas and already proficient in English, feels that learning through Malay will disadvantage students because they will not be able then to access knowledge especially in science and technology which is mostly found in English.

As a result of the change in the medium of instruction, changes in higher education have also been implemented. Universities also started to switch to English as a medium of instruction especially in the Science-based faculties, and in the Arts-based faculties the proportion of courses taught in English has been increased. It can therefore be said that the change in language policy was largely due to the influence from two domains, that of science and technology and that of business.

The rise of Chinese

The opening up of China and its meteoric rise as a major economic force has led to the strengthening of ties between China and Malaysia in recent years. Increased cultural exchanges with a number of memoranda of understanding (MOUs) signed between universities in Malaysia with universities in China and the Institute of China Studies of the University of Malaya have taken place. This increasing need to be competitive in international markets has led to economic policies being deethnicized. The importance of the Chinese language has grown in tandem with this shift since the 1990s.

Although many of the Chinese schools are partially funded by the government, the Chinese community ensures that the schools are well equipped and well run, and that two sessions are conducted, the morning with Mandarin as the medium of instruction, and the afternoon with Malay. Teachers are mostly local Chinese, with many who were teaching in the 1990s and earlier having Mandarin as a second language and who therefore speak it with an accent influenced by their mother tongues, while nowadays many young teachers have Mandarin as their mother tongue (Sim Tze Wei p.c. 21 July 2009). Students in the Chinese schools are therefore bilingual and are prepared for both the Unified Examination Certificate and the Malaysian national examination.

The recognition of the importance of Mandarin and the recognition of China as an economic power as well as a regional partner can be seen in the rising numbers of non-Chinese students who attend Chinese schools. In 2000, more than 60,000 non-Chinese, many of them Malays, were enrolled in Chinese primary schools, and this tendency appears to be gaining popularity (David and Govindasamy 2003). The main reasons for non-Chinese parents to send their children to Chinese schools is to enable them to learn the Chinese language, seen to be an asset these days, the strict discipline and longer hours in these schools, and the reputation of Chinese schools of producing excellent results in maths and science. They also want their children to be able to take advantage of the opportunities in China or Chinese companies (Lee 2007: 140).

In short, while Malay was the sole medium of instruction in national schools over the last 30 years, Mandarin and Tamil continue to be used in national-type schools. Due to the increasing economic value of Mandarin, Mandarin is now offered as the additional subject taught to non-Chinese children in schools, and it is a sought-after language for many for business and trade with China. Mandarin therefore is not likely to suffer from the growing emphasis on English. Chinese dialects may suffer though, as more and more children are taught Mandarin at school, and some parents who went through a Chinese-medium school use Mandarin even at home. The result is often a mixture of Mandarin with other dialects, sometimes code-switched with English and Malay, and an increasing number of younger Chinese for whom Mandarin is the mother tongue.

The Tamil dilemma

The Tamil language, however, is not learnt beyond the Indian community as it is not seen to be of economic value, unlike Mandarin. It is not a language that is needed for conducting business, and business deals with India are often done in English rather than Tamil. Malay and Tamil do not have the economic pull that Mandarin has, but they are seen to be important for in-group interactions and have cultural and literary value.

Tamil-medium education started in 1816 at the Penang Free School (Tate 2008: 160). When Tamil labour was being brought in from 1900 onwards, government schools were set up, and rubber estate companies also opened Tamil primary schools to attract workers. In general, children of the lower-income Indians went to these Tamil schools, and students of the middle-income Indians to the English schools. These English-educated Indians were the ones who were against the switch from English to Malay medium as they were the ones who were generally proficient in English, being English-speaking at home. However, it can be said that over a period of time, Indian students were able to cope with this switch. The 1980 Census indicated that 50% of the Indians could speak Malay in 1970, compared to 86% in 1980, and 35% of them were literate in the language in 1970, as compared to 61% in 1980.

The problems faced by Tamil-medium schools included the lack of teachers for teaching in Malay, with the shortage in the country in the 1980s and the absence of feeder schools after the primary level. Of the 526 Tamil-medium primary schools in the country, 61% of them are classified as being under-enrolled, with a student population of fewer than150 students per school (David and

Govindasamy 2003: 218). This was unlike Chinese schools which had a well developed system from primary to secondary school and even up to university level. And unlike the Chinese community which was able to provide job opportunities for their graduates, the Indians, who were not as successful economically as the Chinese, were not able to do the same. The Tamil language did not and still does not have the economic pull that Chinese has. In comparison to Malays and Chinese, the Indians have been less successful. Tamil primary education for many leads to a dead-end, with no Tamil secondary schools. Schiffman's (2002) bleak conclusion of a study carried out on Malaysian Tamils and their linguistic culture seems to support this. According to him, since Tamil lacks economic value in Malaysia, it is therefore "maintained by the socio-economically destitute as a last vestige of primordial ethnicity" (Schiffman 2002: 168). The ones with an English- or Malay-medium education have generally fared well, while many who went to Tamil primary schools end up in menial jobs, or as factory workers or labourers (Tate 2008: 178).

Nonetheless, although it may appear practicable for Tamil-medium schools to be abandoned, and for all Tamil-speaking Indians to go to national schools, like the Chinese, a number of Indians have a strong belief in preserving the Tamil medium, and wish to have it extended also to the secondary level. The community remains divided, with affluent Indians at one end, and poorer ones at the other. Social and cultural differences have also kept the South Indians, who are mainly Tamil, separate from the other Indian groups who are mainly from Northern India.

Effect of policies

The outcomes for the various language policies introduced still leave much to be desired. While a lot of effort was put into the development of Malay to make it a suitable language as a medium of instruction in schools and tertiary education, inadequate resources may have been the cause of it not being as effective as planned in terms of dealing with terminology in Science and Technology, Law and Medicine. Not only were the non-Malays lacking in proficiency to teach those subjects in Malay, even the Malays faced problems. In terms of establishing national unity and a common identity, it could be said that the implementation of Malay as the medium of instruction has been generally effective, with Malaysians of all ethnic groups generally able to interact in Malay and use Malay in communication between different ethnic groups. Efforts to promote Malay, however, have yet to make it an international language like English. Malay has been quite successful within the country, but internationally, it is not considered one of the major languages of the world. It is not the case that Malay is in competition with the other languages; rather all other languages are in competition with English or have to find a way to coexist with English.

It is therefore important to ensure that, in the rush towards economic development, national unity and ethnic sensitivities are safe-guarded as well. Bilingualism and multilingualism must be promoted for national identity, for instrumental use, for ethnic and personal identity, and the importance of culture and values. While English is clearly the language of international trade and business and global interactions, the other languages must be recognized as languages of cultural identity and ethnic cohesion.

To summarize, language and education policies in the country have undergone a number of phases. Firstly, before independence, a bilingual and multilingual education system existed. This was followed by the switch to Malay as the medium of instruction in national schools and Mandarin and Tamil for the national-type schools. Still later, we have seen a switch back to English for science and maths heralding once again a bilingual and trilingual education system. Globalization has led to an emphasis on the importance of English and a policy change to enable English to be made a medium of instruction. The debate regarding this matter is still ongoing, with some voices claiming that students in rural areas are being victimized due to the lack of support given to them. Studies have been carried out to determine the effectiveness of this policy change and findings are still un-confirmed. Alis (2006), for example, provides arguments against this policy by stating that research has found that the majority of rural students are weak in English and their standard not satisfactory, that teachers in primary schools who are supposed to teach science and maths in English are themselves weak in the language. Furthermore, the Ministry report in 2003 showed that the results of Form One students in science and maths were not good. On the other hand, there are frequent comments in the media that this move is to be welcomed in view of the deteriorating standard of English throughout the country and the need for measures to be taken for the country to compete with the rest of the world.

Malaysian English and English as a Lingua Franca

The greater importance accorded to English in recent years "has led to the old politics of identity being increasingly abandoned in favour of a new pragmatic position where language and culture are valued as commodifiable resources" (Wee 2003: 211). This section will look at the consequences of this new situation in Malaysia, the effects on the other languages, the variety of English that is used, and implications for the teaching of English.

To some, the emphasis on English is to the detriment of the education system, the national language, national unity, and the Malays. Alis (2006) provides a quotation by Noss (1994: 11) who states that:

> Many countries around the world have tried to give the national language and some international languages equal status. It is by now fairly clear that this solution does not work. From the education system on up to all the other sectors of the economy and the society, one of the two languages becomes dominant in the popular mind and becomes associated with success, the other with failure. At worst, class distinctions are widened, racial feelings are stirred up, and polarization of society is encouraged.

To a certain extent this is true; however, English has not been given equal status, but merely assigned separate domains from Malay and other languages. While English is considered the language for access to information and for progress, Malay and other languages are linked to cultures and values. Nevertheless in many ways, Malay is still regarded as an important language, firmly entrenched in the civil service and education, and a requirement to pass it at the school leaving exam is still a prerequisite to getting a good grade and needed for employment in the civil service and to study in local universities. There has also been considerable evidence to show that despite the medium of instruction being Malay for the years 1982 to 2002, Malaysians have been successful in many fields in the country and abroad. The transformation of Malay from being an indigenous language to one that is able to cope with research and scholarship shows that there has been some degree of success in the implementation. Unlike Singapore where Malay is one of the national languages but not spoken outside the Malay community (McKay and Bokhorst-Heng 2008: 92), Malay in Malaysia is very much alive and used by all ethnic groups.

How then do we resolve the paradox between protecting national identity and giving English an important place in the linguistic ecology? An important consideration is what English we are talking about, and in the context of Asia, at least two varieties of English need to be considered. First, the spread of English in Malaysia has resulted in the development of a variety of English peculiar to Malaysia that is used by all English-knowing Malaysians, and which is now accepted as a neutral language between different ethnic groups and has an integrative function. Moreover, many non-native speakers use English as a language for communication especially in trade, education and online communication; Graddol (2006) states that there are currently more non-native speakers of

English than there are native speakers, and in Asia, most speakers of English can be considered to be "English-knowing" multilinguals (Pakir 2000, cited in Kirkpatrick 2007). English in this context is not a first language and the speakers are more likely to use English with other English-knowing bilinguals or multilinguals from within the region than with people who speak native-speaker varieties (Kirkpatrick 2007). It is clear therefore that it is increasingly and widely used as a lingua franca within the Asian region. According to Bolton, the extraordinary recent growth of the use of English in Asia has resulted in 812 million English users (2008:7). In the ASEAN grouping itself, speakers comprise some 450 million English-knowing multilinguals.

With the tremendous pressure to learn English, more attention needs to be given to how and which model English is to be taught and used. As English gets to be accepted as a language that belongs to Malaysians, as can be seen in the increasing use of English in creative work and advertising, for example, the local variety gets highlighted and is often used to promote the shared identity of the different ethnic groups. It is not only a language for international communication but also for intranational communication. Although it is a colonial legacy, the nativized variety has generally been accepted and is believed to have the advantage of being ethnically neutral. It is, however, not class neutral and is the language of the middle and upper classes of the society. Therefore, the debate about the medium of English in education must be seen in this context.

The challenge, however, is that in debates on English as a medium of instruction and on language policy (as discussed in the sections earlier), there is hardly any mention of the local variety; what is often emphasized is the international use of English. This has been noted by Tan (2005:59–60) in his study of newspaper data on the medium-of-instruction debate, who states that "avoiding reference to English as a Malaysian language could point to a difficulty in accepting that English could be an ingredient in the Malaysian national identity". Although Malaysian English is used in the media, in creative writing and in plays locally, there appears to be an assumption that "only a single language can serve the function of national identity and national integration" (Tan 2005:60). Schneider (2003:152–153), observing that English has been relegated to certain domains of use, though very much used in urban areas, also notes, like Tan (2005), that Malaysian English is not yet accepted in formal contexts and that "the linguistic orientation is still exonormative". In scholarship, although endonormative standards and a codification of Malaysian English has been talked about, as yet no dictionary of Malaysian English is in the making, though a distinct lexicographic coverage of Malaysian English, together with Singapore English, has begun with the publication of the second edition of the *Times-Chambers Essential English Dictionary* (1997) and with the inclusion of Malaysian words in the *Macquarie Junior Dictionary* (1999) and the *Grolier International Dictionary* (2000) (Schneider 2007:152–153).

To sum up, the interaction between English and other languages and the learners' linguistic repertoires require a pedagogy that recognizes the complex ways in which languages are used in the country and region. In particular a recognition is needed of the fact that contact involves many partners in multi-dialectal and multilingual contexts and changes statuses and functions of languages (Leitner 2004), as well as the reality that a nativized variety of English has a dual structure, one being the local and the other the global.

Recent change: English to Malay

As I write this article (July 2009), the Malaysian Ministry of Education has announced that there will be a switch back to Malay as medium of instruction for maths and science . The reasons given are the poor success rate of the implementation of English for the teaching of maths and science , and the pressure by parents and teachers from both national and Chinese and Tamil schools for a move back to Malay and the vernacular languages for these two subjects; studies have indeed shown that the teaching of maths and science in English has been problematic and has not improved proficiency (e.g. Hazita 2004; Nor Hashimah et al. 2008). The switch will take effect in 2012 to give teachers enough time to prepare for the change; and the Dewan Bahasa dan Pustaka and the National Institute of Translation will be tasked with translating science, technology and maths terminology into Malay. In addition, in lieu of using English for the teaching of maths and science , the time allotted to English lessons will be increased by 14% for the time being, up to an increase of 70% starting in 2012, and more skilled teachers, a review of textbook use, and the setting up of English laboratories will also be introduced (*The Malaysian Insider* 2009).

This change again raises questions that have been raised in the past: Should we not wait until Malay has achieved the goal of being a fully developed language for maths and science? Does it have the linguistic resources like English to deal with these two subjects? Will learning maths and science in Malay disadvantage students as they would not be able to access the wealth of knowledge and information that takes place in English? Materials, textbooks and reference books in Malay must be made available and teachers linguistically equipped in the language of instruction for this shift to be a success.

Conclusions

This paper has discussed the contestation and negotiation among the different ethnic groups that surround the choice of language in Malaysia. Shifts in policies and media of instruction have taken place, efforts in setting up integrated schools using a common curriculum and language projects or programmes have been implemented, achieving only part of the desired target or failing to achieve satisfactory integration. In the mid-1980s, integrated programmes to bring together Malays, Chinese and Indians under one building did not fare well. From 1995 to 2000, Vision schools were set up to bring together schools with the three languages of instruction — these were also not very successful. Until today, the question of how we can develop a national system of education that is not intrinsically linked to race has not been answered.

The main challenge for any policy chosen is that it should, apart from maintaining the national language, Malay, also ensure the maintenance and preservation of the other languages. Ideally, there should be a common national school system which accommodates the varying preferences of all the different ethnic groups, and all schools within this system should be funded by the government. All Malaysians should be given access and opportunities regardless of their ethnic backgrounds. A common framework needs to be established, and this framework should integrate the different needs and priorities of all ethnic groups. Enforcing a national language as the sole medium of instruction makes sense as long as it is practicable and as long as the goal is a common identity and social integration. Otherwise, enforcing such a language will quickly appear to be a chauvinistic attempt at ignoring other languages which will then result in social disintegration instead.

A comparison of figures taken from the Household Survey of 1967–68 with the Strategic Plan for Education 2007 shows that divisiveness among the ethnic groups in the education system has worsened. While in the past, 87% of the Malay children went to Malay schools, 85% of the Chinese to Chinese schools, and 67% of the Indians to Tamil schools, 40 years on, about 93% of the Chinese are in Chinese schools while the same percentage of the Malays are in national schools with Malay as the medium of instruction (Syed Husin 2008: 163).

The education policies implemented were meant to create a common Malaysian identity using a common curriculum and language. However, it can be concluded that national schools have fallen short of their objective to bring about the desired integration of the main ethnic groups. While they have enabled many to obtain the basic education from Primary One to secondary school, they have not solved the problem of a divisive school system. Chinese and Tamil schools remain presently divided according to ethnic groups. Many Chinese and Indian parents still feel the need to send their children to Chinese and Tamil schools mainly to ensure their cultural and linguistic heritage. They, especially the Chinese, also tend to believe that the vernacular schools are academically superior. The education system should be reviewed as at present it has led more to diversity than unity. Every ethnic group feels that they are discriminated against by the present policies. Certain ethnic groups are found in certain schools and even universities. Schools using the Malay medium continue to be dominated by Malays while national- type schools in urban areas continue to be dominated by non-Malays. In secondary schools in urban areas the majority of the students are non-Malays while the MARA science schools until recently have admitted only Malay students.

At the tertiary level, Universiti Teknologi Mara is mainly for Malays, and the Tunku Abdul Rahman University mainly for Chinese. In general, the majority of students in public universities are Malays, although an increasing number of non-Malays have been admitted, and the majority in private universities are non-Malays. There seems little likelihood of acculturation in education with many factors tending to preserve ethnic differences. The Chinese feel they deserve a right to autonomous education, and this is seen by some Malays to be disloyal. The Chinese, on the other hand, feel that they lack the benefits given to the Malays.

The latest news (July 2009) is the shift back from English to Malay as the medium of instruction for maths and science to start as of 2012. While this has appeased some people from all ethnic groups, it has also raised fears that the standard of English will drop even further. Some would prefer maths and science to be taught in Malay or Chinese or Tamil at the primary level when many children lack the ability to understand instructions, but feel that the two subjects should be taught in English at the secondary level. With the switch back into Malay, teachers who have undergone training programmes to teach in English will have their knowledge and skills go to waste.

Unlike large and fully industrialized countries, Malaysia may not have the resources, and neither would it make a great deal of sense to establish an exclusively Malay-speaking community, as is the case for the English-speaking, Spanish-speaking or even German-speaking world regions. That makes it necessary especially in economic terms to consider the importance of the different languages which are vital to economic advancement, namely English and Chinese, which everyone should be free to choose from. However, it should not be forgotten that language planning and education policy should not rest entirely on economic considerations but on the recognition of and respect for linguistically expressed cultural identities. For Malaysia, this is important when coming up with a solution to the educational questions without creating racial and ethnic tensions or conflict.

Every effort must ensure that the implementation of any medium of instruction is a success. The implementation of a policy is contingent on factors that determine if language resources are available and adequate, and not simply on government action. More English classes must be given in schools and more teachers trained to teach in the medium of instruction. The national schools must be made more attractive to the Chinese and Indians. A dual medium of instruction and teaching of Chinese and Tamil as electives will lead to students being at least bilingual. Fluency in at least three languages can be achieved or at least attempted.

Ethnic configuration in Malaysia is complex, with diversity within each ethnic group, and the outcomes of the policies have also been unclear. A reversal of the policies is not likely to happen in the very near future. If at the time of independence it was necessary to have a communal approach to politics and education, more effort is necessary to solve the problems that have arisen, efforts that are based more on needs than on race.

While Malay remains the national language, Malaysia's other languages can be preserved while we strive to increase English proficiency in schools. It must be borne in mind that firstly, preserving a language and still keeping the option open for the individual choice of a preferred language is not necessarily a contradiction, and secondly, that promoting or supporting a language or culture that its bearers feel have been neglected in the past by no means represents a threat to other languages and cultures.

Considering the fact that Malay is defined as the national language, there are several ways of going about the changes that need to take place. One possibility could be to have primary education in Malay plus an optional language (English, Mandarin, Tamil or other) in a bilingual mode, and then in secondary education to have a certain percentage of classes in Malay and to make it optional for students whether they wish to go to Mandarin- or English-medium maths and science classes. All schools that adhere to such a national framework would receive government funding, while independent private schools may offer any other language or curriculum and be self funded. The education system can place emphasis on the mastery of at least three languages: Malay, English, and Chinese or Tamil. All these languages are useful and necessary in trade and economic dealings with China, Indonesia and India. The economic advantage could outdo the racial factor. With national schools the main choice of all races, this would also be a productive way of encouraging the mix of the different ethnic groups and facilitate racial integration. With a more liberal and conducive educational environment in which all learners feel that they are valued, a single national school system may be possible, which would augur well for racial stability and harmony in Malaysia.

Note
* The research conducted here was supported in part by a grant from the Humboldt Foundation for work in Germany, 2009. I would like to thank Jan-Peter Herrmann for his assistance in the preparation of this paper.

References
Alis Putih (2006) *Language and Nation Building: A Study of the Language Medium Policy in Malaysia*. Petaling Jaya: SIRD.
Asmah Haji Omar (1979) *Language Planning for Unity and Efficiency – A Study on the Language Status and Corpus Planning of Malaysia*. Kuala Lumpur: University of Malaya Press.
Asmah Haji Omar (1982) *Language and Society in Malaysia*. Kuala Lumpur: Dewan Bahasa dan Pustaka.
Asmah Haji Omar (1987) *Malay and its Sociocultural Context*. Kuala Lumpur: Dewan Bahasa dan Pustaka.
Asmah Haji Omar (1992) *The Linguistic Scenery in Malaysia*. Kuala Lumpur: Dewan Bahasa dan Pustaka.
Asmah Haji Omar (2007) Malaysia and Brunei. In A. Simpson (ed.) *Language and National Identity in Asia*, pp. 337–359. Oxford: Oxford University Press.
Azirah Hashim (fc 2010) Englishes in advertising. In A. Kirkpatrick (ed.) *The Handbook of World Englishes*. Oxford: Routledge.
Barnes Report (1951) Ministry of Education Malaysia. Kuala Lumpur: Government Press.
Bolton, K. (2008) English in Asia, Asian Englishes and the issue of proficiency. *English Today* 24(2): 3–12.
David, M.K. (2000) The language of Malaysian youth: An exploratory study. In H. Mohd. Said and Ng K.S. (eds) *English is an Asian Language*, pp. 64–72. Persatuan Bahasa Moden and Macquarie Library.
David, M.K. and S. Govindasamy (2003) Language education and 'nation building' in multilingual Malaysia. In J. Bourne and E. Reid (eds), *Language Education*, pp. 215–225. Great Britain: Kogan Page.
Department of Statistics Malaysia (2002) www.statistics.gov.my
Gill, S.K. (2004) Medium-of-Instruction policy in higher education in Malaysia: Nationalism versus internationalization. In J.W. Tollefson and A.B.M. Tsui (eds) *Medium of Instruction Policies: Which Agenda? Whose Agenda?*, pp. 135–152. USA: Lawrence Erlbaum.
Gill, S.K. (2005) Language policy in Malaysia: Reversing direction. *Language Policy* 4: 241–260.
Graddol, D. (2006) *English Next*. London: The British Council.
Hazita Azman (2004) Global English and English literacy education in Malaysia. In P. Lee and Hazita Azman (eds) *Global English and Primary Schools: Challenges for Elementary Education*. Melbourne: CAE Press.

Kirkpatrick. A. (2007) *World Englishes: Implications for International Communication and English Language Teaching*. Cambridge: Cambridge University Press.

Lee, H.K. (2007) Ethnic politics, national development and language policy in Malaysia. In Lee, H.G. and L. Suryadinata (eds) *Language, Nation and Development in Southeast Asia*, pp. 118–149. Singapore: Institute of Southeast Asian Studies.

Leitner. G. (2004) *Australia's Many Voices*. Berlin, New York: Mouton de Gruyter.

Malaysian Insider, The (2009) 11 July. http://www.themalaysianinsider.com

McKay, S.L. and W.D. Bokhorst-Heng (2008) *International English in Its Sociolinguistic Contexts: Towards a Socially Sensitive EIL Pedagogy*. New York, London: Routledge.

Morais, E. (2000) Talking in English but thinking like a Malaysian: Insights from a car assembly plant. In H. Mohd. Said and Ng K.S. (eds) *English is an Asian Language*, pp. 90–106. Persatuan Bahasa Moden and Macquarie Library.

Nor Hashimah Jalaluddin, Norsimah Mat Awal and Kesumawati Abu Bakar (2008) The mastery of English language among Lower Secondary school students in Malaysia: A linguistic analysis. *European Journal of Social Sciences* 7(2): 106–117.

Ooi, V. (ed.) (2001) *Evolving Identities: The English Language in Singapore and Malaysia*. Times Academic Press: Singapore.

Ozog, A.C.K. (1993) Bilingualism and national development in Malaysia. *Journal of Multilingual and Multicultural Development* 14: 59–71.

Powell, R. (2008) *Motivations for Language Choice in Malaysian Courtrooms: Implications for Language Planning*. Kuala Lumpur: University of Malaya Press.

Schiffman, H.F. (2002) Malaysian Tamils and Tamil linguistic culture. *Language and Communication* 22: 159–169.

Schneider, E.W. (2007) *Postcolonial English: Varieties of English around the World*. Cambridge: Cambridge University Press.

Syed Husin Ali (2008) *The Malays: Their Problems and Future*. Kuala Lumpur: The Other Press.

Tan, P.K.W. (2005) The medium-of-instruction debate in Malaysia: English as a Malaysian language? *Language Problems and Language Planning* 29(1): 47–66.

Tate, M.D. (2008) *The Malaysian Indians: History, Problems and Future*. Petaling Jaya: SIRD.

Wee, L. (2003) Linguistic instrumentalism in Singapore. *Journal of Multilingual and Multicultural Development* 24(3): 211–224.

Beyond fear and loathing in SG

The real mother tongues and language policies in multilingual Singapore

Lisa Lim
University of Hong Kong

This paper considers the real mother tongues of Singapore, namely the Chinese 'dialects' and Singlish, the linguistic varieties which, respectively, arrived with the original immigrants to the rapidly developing British colony, and evolved in the dynamic multilingual ecology over the decades. Curiously these mother tongues have been regarded with fear and treated with loathing in the official language policies and accompanying prestige planning that have been developed and executed in Singapore since independence, being actively denigrated and discouraged in official discourse, viewed as not having a place in the globalization goals of the nation. Looking beyond the official line and census figures, actual linguistic practices of the community of speakers testify to the vitality of these varieties, in spite of the official sanctions; moreover, in spite of itself, the government does in fact allow itself the use of these mother tongues when certain contexts call for it. This paper suggests that an enlightened consideration of native 'dialects' and nativized Singlish and the plurilingual practices in which they are used, as well as of the question of intelligibility, must point policy makers in directions where fears are assuaged and spaces made for the natural existence and evolution of such varieties in multilingual ecologies.

Fear and loathing in SG

In an age where vernaculars, whether endangered languages spoken by a last community or languages with minority status in larger nation states, are receiving greater (positive) recognition, support and funding, from linguistic organizations and bodies such as UNESCO, it is always intriguing to examine a context where the mother tongue of a people is regarded with fear and loathing. This paper has as its focus the real mother tongues of Singapore's multilingual population — not the officially designated 'Mother Tongues' (MTs) of English, Mandarin, Malay and Tamil, which are the linguistic varieties which are officially associated with the official races of the state, namely Chinese, Malay and Indian, and learnt as second languages in school, but the actual linguistic varieties that arrived with the original immigrants to Singapore or that have evolved in the Singapore context.

While this paper has as its main focus the English language, the situation with the Chinese languages is also examined, first because it parallels that of English, as will be seen in the sections following, and second because the possibility of (a) Chinese language(s) as competitor to English needs to be considered. In examining English, a significant aspect involves the contact dynamics of Singapore's multilingual context and the emergent variety of English which has been nativized and

AILA Review 22 (2009), 52–71. DOI 10.1075/aila.22.05lim
ISSN 1461–0213 / E-ISSN 1570–5595 © John Benjamins Publishing Company

appropriated by Singaporeans. In examining the various other Chinese languages, a crucial consideration is what functions they represent for the Chinese community in Singapore.

In both cases, two things are to be borne in mind: one is the fact that an ecology is by definition dynamic and thus outcomes of earlier policies or shifts due to new population movements in different eras also impact on the situation at hand; the other involves the tensions between the government's official policies and the people's actual practices in negotiating the languages and their meanings for Singaporeans — and while fear and loathing may be seen to underlie the official discourse on the real mother tongues, the actual communities of speakers appear to be embracing them with confidence and affection.

The Singapore 'success story'?

Singapore is often held up as the success story of "ascendant English-knowing bilingual communities for a globalized world" (Pakir 2001), in no small part due to the language policies instituted post-independence.[1] It has been hailed, by some scholars, as "a unique case study of a successful program of bilingualism and language management … an impressive case of a well-planned and effectively implemented language-policy program", having "negotiated carefully its language policy and the attendant-sensitive choice of a language for the medium of instruction in its state educational system" (Pakir 2004: 117). Indeed, Singapore appears to have demonstrated how it is apparently easy to find place for the English language — the former colonial language — positioning it as the main H language, as neutral language and foil to the local languages who themselves fulfil other functions. The fundamentals of the Singapore story and its language policies are well known and analyzed, and are summarized in this section. Where the endogenous languages are concerned, while the multilingual situation in Singapore involves numerous Chinese languages, Indian languages, and Malay (see e.g. Lim 2007, fc a for a fuller account of these), this paper focusses on the Chinese languages.

First, in contrast to other Asian countries who at independence elected to redress the imbalance in opportunity that different ethnolinguistic groups of the population afforded during colonial rule by making the vernacular of a single group (that was perceived or presented as the original and/or rightful inhabitants of the country) the national language and language of education, such as Malay in Malaysia and Sinhala in Sri Lanka, Singapore, leading up to and at independence in 1965, opted for "pragmatic multilingualism" (Kuo and Jernudd 1994: 72), with a nod to ideologies of both vernacularization and internationalization. Three of the four official languages, chosen to represent the three official races 'Chinese', 'Malay' and 'Indian', are Mandarin, Malay and Tamil respectively, referred to in official discourse as 'Mother Tongues' (MTs); and English, the former colonial language was retained as the fourth official language. As has been widely discussed in scholarship as well as in government discourse, the MTs and English are positioned such that there is functional allocation. English, as the language of science and technology and of international trade and commerce, was a basic need; further being a neutral non-native language and not associated with any of the Asian cultures, and not the mother tongue of any of the ethnic groups, it gave none of the ethnic groups an advantage (Kuo 1980: 59ff). The MTs on the other hand were there to act as cultural ballast and provide Asian values. With regard to the MTs, of note is that the Chinese language chosen, Mandarin, was in fact not any of the actual mother tongues of the original Chinese immgrants, the vast majority of them hailing from Southern China, mainly Chaoshan in northeastern Guangdong (the Teochews), Xiamen in southern Fujian (the Hokkiens), and Guangdong (the Cantonese), as well as sizeable representations of Hakka and Hainanese (Lim fc a); the choice was primarily motivated by the status of Mandarin in China once the Chinese republic was founded (Bloom 1986: 359ff; Kwok 2000) (more of this later).

Second, English was very rapidly institutionalized as medium of instruction (MoI) in all schools (with the exception of a few government-sanctioned Malay-medium *madrasahs*). The first

English-medium school was, as with all former British colonies, established during British colonial rule in 1834, and, as has been the norm, such schools were for the purpose of educating and cultivating a minority of English-speaking elites in the local population, with the majority of children going to schools run by the individual ethnolinguistic communities whose MoI were the vernaculars. By the end of the 19th century though, with the increasing recognition of the advantages that the English language afforded, enrolment in such schools increased rapidly, such that by the 1950s, in a system where education was effectively universal, English-medium education became increasingly the norm, with 43% of school enrolment being in English-medium schools. Leading up to independence in 1965, English was made a compulsory language in schools; this was either as a first language, or, in the vernacular (Chinese-, Malay- or Tamil-medium) schools, as a second language, in the bilingual education system advocated in the 1956 Singapore White Paper on Education, and in 1987 English was implemented as MoI in all schools. This has resulted in a population of people who have been described as English-knowing bilinguals (for an overview of the sociohistorical and political details of English in Singapore, see e.g. Bloom 1986; Gupta 1994; Lim and Foley 2004; Lim 2007, fc a).

Third, aggressive prestige planning was also a large part of the picture, with the aforementioned language policies being supported and promoted actively in what have been viewed as 'invisible language planning policies' (Pakir 1994, 1997). Particular attention was paid to the Chinese group and their languages — they comprising the largest proportion of the population at 78% — and when after a few years the bilingual education programme was assessed as having failed (Goh et al. 1979), with students evaluated as not performing well in Mandarin because the various other Chinese languages, referred to in national discourse as "Chinese dialects"[2] were still being used at home, the annual Speak Mandarin Campaign (SMC) was launched in 1979 (for more indepth discussion of the SMC, see e.g. Bokhorst-Heng 1998). Discouragement of the use of the Chinese 'dialects' has been the official line ever since the SMC was launched in 1979 as one of the modes of supporting the bilingual policy with Mandarin as official language. This was on the basis of the following belief, propounded at the inaugural launch in 1979 of the SMC by the then Prime Minister Lee Kuan Yew:

(1)   It is most difficult for the average, and impossible for the slow, to keep in mind, for
      immediate recall and use, enough words in English, Mandarin and dialects.[3]

Other reasons for SMC was that the disparate Chinese community needed a single language to foster unity, as argued in 1991 by the then Prime Minister Goh Chok Tong:

(2)   Singaporean Chinese should be a single people, speaking the same primary language.

While over the years, the themes of SMC have had various foci (including specific domains, such as at work, or specific population groups such as the youth and the English-educated), the primary thrust, especially in the early years, was to pit Mandarin against the other Chinese 'dialects'. This discourse was explicit in the SMC's slogans, manifesting in the following forms over various years: "Speak more Mandarin and less dialect" (1979, inaugural year), "Mandarin's in, dialect's out" (1983), "Start with Mandarin, not dialect" (1986), "Better with more Mandarin, less dialect" (1988).

Political rhetoric in the early years of the campaign, playing on the layman's misconceptions of 'language' versus 'dialect', also served to denigrate the 'dialects' and discourage their use. For instance, the then Senior Minister of State (Foreign Affairs) Rabim Ishak suggested (The Straits Times 11 July 1980) how vulgarity was associated with 'dialects' when he noted that he:

(3)   learnt swear words in Cantonese, Hokkien, Teochew and Hainanese whereas in
      Mandarin, the swear words were less common and was a language for the refined people.

That the Chinese 'dialects' could not develop to fulfil the communicative needs of its speakers, and that they were inconsistent, was implied by the then Prime Minister Lee Kwan Yew (4), and Goh Chok Tong, then Second Defence and Health Minister (5), the latter at the opening ceremony of the SMC in his constituency (*ST* 10 January 1980; 9 June 1981):

(4)   Mandarin is a developing language; on the other hand, dialect is a stagnant language.

(5)   The spoken and written form in Mandarin are in unison and do not create problems, unlike dialects where one word can have several meanings depending on the dialect it is spoken in.

Perhaps most crucially in this powerful show of prestige planning, the economic capital of Mandarin versus the Chinese 'dialects' was underlined, drawing on the fear that most would have of falling behind. The then Prime Minister Lee Kwan Yew stressed (*ST* 17 October 1980) that, unlike Mandarin which:

(6)   has cultural value and will also have economic value twenty years later, [dialects] have no economic value in Singapore. Their cultural value is also very low.

The ominous advice to parents that followed (*ST* 17 November 1980) was that:

(7)   ... dialect will hinder the learning of the child if he uses dialect ... to speak dialect with your child is to ruin his future.

It would appear that the goals of the government in the first instance in its language planning for Singapore were met, and with resounding success, in particular if census data are consulted. Linguistic practices show drastic shifts (the following account, analyzed from census data from Ng 1995 and Leow 2001, derives from Lim and Foley 2004; Lim 2007a, fc a; also see Li, Saravanan and Ng 1997 for a specific study of language shift in the Teochew community). As a result of compulsory education in English, the proportion of the population having English as a dominant home language doubled in twenty years, from 12% in 1980 to 23% in 2000, with 70% of Primary 1 children (aged 6 years) reporting as having English as a dominant home language. English literacy increased from less than half the population (47%) in 1970 to some three-quarters of the population (71%) thirty years on, in 2000. In general, around the late 1970s to early 1980s, English started displacing Hokkien and Bazaar Malay as lingua franca, especially among the younger and more educated. Similarly, the bilingual policy, coupled with the SMC, can certainly be evaluated as having fulfilled its goal: census data over the decades show clearly how Mandarin has displaced the other Chinese languages as the main home language, from 10% in 1980 to 30% in 1990 to 45% in 2000, with the Chinese languages decreasing in use from 81% in 1980 to 50% in 1990 to 31% in 2000 — a 50% decrease in twenty years. Some 87% of the Chinese population claimed to be able to understand Mandarin by 1988, and it has become the language of choice for many younger Chinese Singaporeans' intraethnic communication in all domains. To restate the obvious, part of the 'success' of the execution of Singapore's language policy where the Chinese languages was concerned was the fanning of fear at all levels — cultural, social, economic — leading to a population that was loath to speak its own dialects.

Even its harshest critics would concede that the decisions of the government in early independence — viz. having English as one of the official languages and MoI, and selecting Mandarin as the official Chinese language — were pragmatically made. It should be noted of course that, at the time of independence in 1965, Singapore had to deal with a context that included the imminent withdrawal of the British military and the income this provided, threats of invasion from Indonesia, communist guerilla movements in Malaysia and elsewhere, and the Vietnam war, and their immediate goal was survival; it is only after internal as well as regional stabilization was achieved that its language policies — of course amongst other political decisions taken — may be seen to have afforded Singapore a chance in fulfilling its goal of participating in a globalizing world.[4] That said, proficiency in English — the global language of business, politics, international relations, culture and entertainment — has certainly given Singapore leverage, and its "high standard of English language education" (S.P. Jain n.d.) is certainly a factor for drawing professionals and investors to the country. Singapore was recently ranked the most attractive Asian city for expatriates to live, work and play in (Mercer 2006), in terms of a solid educational system, alongside efficient government, first-world infrastructure, and clean crime-free streets. And if a correlation between a competence in Mandarin for communicating with China is to be believed, then the proof is in the excellent bilateral ties that Singapore and China have developed in the last decades: China is currently Singapore's 3rd largest trading partner, and Singapore China's 8th largest trading partner, with Singapore's trade with China at a record high of S\$ 91.6 billion in 2007; China is also Singapore's top investment destination, and Singapore is China's 7th largest investor, with Singapore's cumulative actual investments amounting to more than US\$ 33 billion as of end 2007 (Ministry of Trade and Industry 2008).

The dollars, perhaps, have been taken care of as a consequence of these initial language policies; but what about the sense? Understanding and managing Singapore's true multilingual situation has in fact been the greater challenge, and a closer look beyond the official language policies and their purported results reveals a much more complex situation. The next section examines the consequences that followed from these initial language policies.

The problem with a multilingual ecology

Multilingual matters

Multilingualism is undoubtedly challenging to any governing body in numerous ways. At face value, Singapore would appear to have been more sensitive to its multilingual population than most, being one of only three states of the 233 in the world recognizing more than three official languages (Switzerland also with four, and South Africa with 11). But acknowledging multilingualism is more than recognizing a number of languages in official discourse and pigeonholing them both for specific ethnic groups and for specific functions. Singapore's language policies in fact seem to stem from a particular understanding and application of what it means to be part of a multilingual community, and what seem not to be taken into consideration are the following issues: (i) That in a multilingual ecology, languages in contact quite naturally exert influences on each other; and the English language, in all the diverse contexts it has been transplanted to, has always evolved, often as a result of new identity construction, to manifest features from other languages in the ecology (see e.g. Schneider 2007; Ansaldo 2009; Lim and Gisborne 2009), and that these should not be viewed as "negative interferences". (ii) That language policies can be — and indeed usually are — a very significant force in the external ecology (Lim 2007, fc a), in raising or lowering the profile of different languages, and consequently affecting language choice and language shift; but that other forces in the ecology also have a role to play, demography, strongly impacted upon by migration patterns, being another force to reckon with (Lim 2007, fc a). (iii) That, in language acquisition, the learning of one language is not at the expense of the mastering of others. (iv) That while the instrumental value of a language is indeed one of the most powerful motivations for its adoption, the identific and integrative function is not necessarily so easily overridden.

Non-neutral, native-speaker English

As outlined in the previous section, post-independence, the English language was retained to fulfil the role of primary working language and neutral language as foil to the three ethnic Mother Tongues. One of the problems arising with regard to the role of English has been discussed in previous scholarship, and will only be summarized here, as follows. Falling outside the three official races mentioned earlier is the fourth official race, that of the 'Others' — a category which groups together a mix of people including the Eurasians, descendants of primarily Portuguese and local alliances. Crucially, for many of this latter group of Singaporeans, English has been a de facto mother tongue for many generations; this situation thus challenges the discourse of English as 'neutral' language, yet this cannot be recognized in the statal narrative — the requirement that they be assigned and therefore have to study one of the three official Mother Tongues in school is upheld — since it would run counter to the English vs. Mother Tongues divide (Wee 2002). (A similar linguistic situation holds for the Peranakans, a group who are classified as Chinese and thus are assigned Mandarin as their official Mother Tongue, but in fact once had Baba Malay, a variety of Malay with Hokkien influences, as their vernacular, and now for all intents and purposes also have English as a mother tongue (Lim 2009a).)

The other problem, which this paper focusses on, is this: as a consequence of ensuring competence in English in the state, the prominence of English in Singapore has led to an increasingly large critical mass of younger generations becoming native speakers of English. This is of course an English that has evolved in a multilingual ecology, and thus has seen much linguistic restructuring due to contact with the endogenous languages. Singapore has been analyzed as having attained endonormative stabilization, phase 4 of Schneider's (2007) Dynamic Model for the evolution of postcolonial Englishes.[5] The emergent variety of English, Singlish (or colloquial or basilectal Singapore English),[6] which exhibits particular phonological patterning, syntax and vocabulary derived from the various local languages, in particular Malay, Hokkien, and Cantonese (see e.g. Ansaldo 2004, 2009; Bao 2001, 2005; Bao and Lye 2005; Bao and Wee 1999; Lim 2004a, 2009b,c, fc b; Wee 2004; Wee and Ansaldo 2004), can in fact be said to be much more Asian than English (Ansaldo 2009). Crucially it is this variety of English which fulfils identification and integrative functions for Singaporeans.

In this globalized world, however, a major concern of the government is that Singaporeans retain their global competitive edge, and one vital way, which sets Singaporeans apart from all its Asian neighbours, is the possession of ('good' i.e. 'standard') English skills as a commodity. The emergence and prominence of Singlish has given the government significant pause in this respect, and their fear, masked as loathing, is illustrated in statements by the nation's leaders. The then Prime Minister Goh Chok Tong, in his 1999 National Day Rally speech to the nation, declared it a corruption of the English language:

(8)   Singlish is not English. It is English corrupted by Singaporeans and has become a Singapore dialect.

The reason for their concern — the need to remain a global player — is also made explicit by both the then Senior Minister Lee Kuan Yew (9) in 1999, and PM Goh (10, 11) in 1999 and 2000:

(9)   We are learning English so that we can understand the world and the world can understand us.

(10)   Speaking good English is crucial if the country is to achieve its goal of becoming a first-world economy and a world-class home … We cannot be a first-world economy or go global with Singlish … Poor English reflects badly on us and makes us seem less intelligent.

(11)   Investors will not come if their supervisors and managers can only guess what our workers are saying. It will be hard for Singapore to be a financial centre. TV programmes

and films will be difficult to succeed [sic] because foreigners do not understand Singlish — this will affect the first-world economy we hope to achieve.

This culminates in a clear directive against Singlish by SM Lee (1999):

(12)   Do not popularize Singlish. Do not use Singlish in our television sitcoms, except for humorous bits, and in a way that makes people want to speak standard English … The people who will benefit most are those who can only master one kind of English. Singlish is a handicap we must not wish on Singaporeans.

Putting their words into action, the annual Speak Good English Movement (SGEM) was initiated in 2000, whose aim is "to encourage Singaporeans to speak grammatically correct English that is universally understood" (SGEM 2009). At the inaugural launch, PM Goh reminded Singaporeans of the responsibility they had:

(13)   If they speak Singlish when they can speak good English, they are doing a disservice to Singapore.

A critical mistake with SGEM (and for detailed critical evaluations of SGEM, see e.g. Rubdy 2001; Chng 2003; Bruthiaux fc; Gupta fc) has been the inability to recognize that different varieties of English can co-exist, each serving different functions in different domains. Instead SGEM pitched 'good English' against 'Singlish', and had as an aim, in particular in the first five years (2000 to 2004), amongst other things, "to help Singaporeans move away from the use of Singlish" (SGEM 2009). Almost a decade on, SGEM, which has seen a number of prominent language specialists at the helm, plus an advisory board which includes local linguists, still adopts a prescriptive stance, and has also, as noted by Gupta (fc) fostered a maven culture for English in Singapore, breeding insecurity in ordinary users of English without any serious effort at improving their English. Significantly, an identification function of language was brushed aside, with Singaporeans told — by PM Goh in 2000 — that they:

(14)   should not take the attitude that Singlish is cool or feel that speaking Singlish makes them more 'Singaporean'.

Crucially, subaltern practices demonstrate how distant government discourse is from reality. Academic scholarship analyzing the features of Singlish is vast (see e.g. the research bibliography in Lim, Pakir and Wee fc), and data of naturally occurring speech document how widespread and entrenched the use of Singlish is in the repertoire of Singaporeans (see e.g. chapters in Lim 2004b, based on the Grammar of Spoken Singapore English Corpus (GSSEC; Lim 2001; Lim and Foley 2004), comprising data of naturally occurring spontaneous speech of young Singaporeans). In (15) and (16), both from GSSEC, numerous Singlish features are observable, including zero copula (Ansaldo 2009b), *kena* passive (Fong 2004), absence of inflection on 3rd-person singular and past tense verbs (Fong 2004), *is it* question tag, use of *one* (Wee and Ansaldo 2004), reduplication (Ansaldo 2004; Wee 2004), *lah, ah, what* and *lor* particles (Lim 2004, 2007; Wee 2004), and borrowing from and code switching with local languages.

(15)   B: So just go down … ya just go down go straight down
       C: Go straight down and turn into Zion Road *ah*.
       A: Careful! The *ah pek*!   (Hokkien 'old man')
       B, C: (laughter)
       C: You remember that guy that was running across the other day?
             {Just run across like that. (laughter)

B: {****

A: Hey, you know that Razid in Pizza Hut, right?

B: Which one?

C: Razid *ah*, Razid…the other { *mat.*   (Malay (slang) 'a Malay male')

A: { Razali…Razali's friend…you know what he was doing
    or not?

B: The one who always like to *kow peh* { is it?   (Hokkien 'complain')

A, C: { Ya ya…

C: The one who always making { noise…

B: { I don't like him, you know … he *ah* … like *macam*
                                                              (Malay 'like')

C: The *botak botak* { fella   (Malay 'very bald')

B: { Ah… the like ****

A: The fella centre *botak* three side hair {*one*   (Malay 'bald')
    'The fellow is (has the quality of being) bald in the centre with hair on three sides'

C: {Eh, that guy got problem *ah*, that fella…

(16) A: Lee was calling me his buddy yesterday.

B: He quite poor thing also *lor*, come to think of it.

C: Why?

B: At first, I dunno *lah*, I didn't really like him because he's just too … his PR is quite
    bad *ah*.

C: Oh, PR

B: That's why. That's the point *ah*. Come to think of it, okay *lah* … he also *kena* play out
    lor.   (Malay 'get')

C: By who?

B: He *kena* sabotage *what*, the airport … last minute, they send him to Brunei, you
    know, instead of Taiwan.   (Malay 'suffer')

C: But is that a true story, or is he making a fast one?

B: I dunno *lah*.

C: It's a bit difficult to believe that they do that to him at the last minute … right?
    But I mean … I mean, by virtue of the fact that he accepted the overseas posting so
    willingly *ah*, it does say something about the family situation. Most people won't be
    too willing to run away like that.

B: Money is good *ah*.

C: True *ah*.

B: Good, you know, and the fella still dare to {complain about ****

C: {**** signal, you can still turn on this lane.
    Ah chek ah, ka kin tam po ah, ah chek!
    'Youngest uncle, go a little faster, youngest uncle!'   (Hokkien)
    Horn the fella, horn him! Horn him!

C: In the States, this fella with the Volkswagen Beetle put a Porsche engine under the
    hood. All the { coppers couldn't catch him you know

A: { all the *mata* couldn't catch him.   (Malay 'police')

Interestingly — and perhaps this is what worries the government more — Singlish is not just found
in colloquial speech in informal domains, as in (15) and (16), but is also used in the domain of
education. Teachers have been documented as moving between more standard English and Singlish

features in classroom talk, as a means of negotiating identities and achieving goals (Alsagoff fc). The extract in (17) from Alsagoff (fc) illustrates how, when a teacher moves into a focus on content, more non-standard features appear in her speech, including the increased use of discourse markers (e.g. *a*, *eh*), clauses without overt subjects or objects (e.g. *we mark [ ]*), absence of auxiliary (e.g. *how [ ] you start [ ]*), absence of conditional (e.g. *[ ] You go and buy a story book, …*), use of *don't have*, etc:

(17)   Scaffold (…) always *ah*, in any writing. You it, *eh*, Band B, you need to know all this, you know, because when we *mark [ ] ah*, we'll check *ah*. Intro, that one, you all know *ah*, introduction, how you start. Very important, when I pick up a story, the first thing that does is the intro. *[ ] You go and buy a story book, the intro doesn't always start, 'long time ago, once upon a time, far, far away in a long lost land ter ra ra ra. Don't have.* Theme? What theme? Although it's a suspense story, but what you doing, which theme are you going about?

Local filmmakers have also not only used authentic Singlish in their scripts (e.g. award-winning *Singapore Dreaming*, Woo, Goh and Wu 2006) but also reflected a monolectal-type code switching (see Meeuwis and Blommaert 1998) between English, Mandarin and Hokkien (Lim 2008b); in (18) and (19) below, the code used by younger-generation characters Mei and Seng are particularly representative of this. Such a view goes beyond considering the act of CS as unmarked (e.g. Li Wei's 1994 Chinese-English CS in second-generation British-born Chinese bilinguals in northeast England, and Myers-Scotton's 1993 Swahili-English CS in the younger generation in Nairobi, Kenya), but views the code as a single code in its own right (e.g. Meeuwis and Blommaert's 1998 Lingala-French code used by Zaireans, and Canagarajah's 1995 Englishized Tamil as the unmarked everyday code in Jaffna, Sri Lanka). In (18) and (19), only the English idiomatic gloss is provided, and languages are indicated using different formatting, as follows: **Hokkien**, <u>Mandarin</u>, *Malay*, English, *Sinitic particles*.

(18)   Ma: *Here, Ah Seng*
         Seng: *Thanks Ma.*
         Pa: *Come, Seng.*
         Seng: *Drink, Pa.*
         Ma: *Don't drink too much.*
         Pa: *Eat la, eat la!*
         Mei: Seng *a21*, time to get a job *ho24*? Pa and Irene spend all their savings on you already *le21*. Are you waiting for Pa <u>to buy Toto [the lottery] and get it all back</u> *me55*?
         Pa: You say other people for what? You are just a secretary.
         Irene: *Aiya*, never mind, never mind. Anyway Seng already has a job interview on Monday.
         Pa: *Wah*, real or not?
         Seng: I arranged the meeting through email. Now American degrees <u>all in demand</u>.
         CB: *Wah*, congratulations, man.
         Seng: Thanks.
         Ma: **What did they just say?**
         Mei: <u>Seng said that on Monday…</u>
         Pa: Now you've come back, you can't play the fool anymore, okay? <u>*What if*</u> you end up selling insurance like this guy? **Don't make me lose face!**

(19)   Mei: So Irene *a21*, when are you and Seng going to get married *a24*?
         Irene: Maybe after he gets a job.

Mei:	Hh you're not tired of waiting *a21*? [to mother] <u>Ma, I was just saying, since</u> <u>Irene lent Seng so much money, it's only right that they get married.</u>
Irene:	<u>Aiya, Seng really needed it…</u>
Mei :	<u>I know! I'm just saying I couldn't do such a thing. Before you're even married,</u> <u>you're lending so much money to a man… And even living in his home…</u>
Ma:	*It's right to support your husband!*
Mei:	*Ma, Seng is not her husband yet!* <u>Women shouldn't be so stupid!</u> <u>Do you know why Seng is like that? It's because every time he screws up, the</u> <u>two of you are there behind him</u> *to help him wipe his backside.*

Websites such as *TalkingCock.com* (founded in 2000) and *The Dictionary of Singlish and Singapore English* (launched 2004) have emerged in the last decade, not only comprising laypersons' documentation of the Singlish lexicon, but also using Singlish in texts — and these have garnered tremendous support and nurtured immense popularity. A perusal of these and/or any website or blog addressing English in Singapore will attest to how Singlish has long been recognized (and documented) as part of the Singaporean identity. Example (20) is an excerpt from one of the regular satirical columns, *Lim Peh Ka Li Kong* (Hokkien 'let your father tell you…') of *Talkingcock.com* (Talkingcock.com 2004), stereotyping conversations on topical issues amongst Singaporeans, in this case about mother tongues. While the cynical may suggest that these are stereotyped, exaggerated examples of Singlish, other pages of the website involve the creators directly addressing their readership, as in (21), where Standard English features and Singlish features (here, involving Hokkien terms, as well as the Singlish existential *got* structure) mix naturally to construct a Singaporean identity.

(20)   Ter Koh chimed in: "It's *si beh* condemn that as Chinese peepur, our standard of Chinese am not as powderful as our Engrand."
"If you all so worrage about your Chinese," I ask them, "how come you send all your chewren to English school and not Chinese school?"
"*Wah piang!*" sneered Ah Pek. "What, you want my *gin nah* to come out and be like all those *cheenagherk cheenapiangs, ah*? They all gone case one!"

(21)   Just a note to let you know we're still on hiatus working on our new top-secret projects. *Pai say*. Looks like Singapore is damn exciting at the moment — got terrorist captured, got feminists fighting… we feel damn too *lan* that we're not at the frontlines making *wu liao* jokes. But *boh pian*. These new projects demand our attention. But we really hope to be back in action soon. Stay tuned!

But perhaps what is more significant is this: in certain government activities, Singlish has in fact been permitted. A music video was produced by the Ministry of Health during the outbreak of SARS (Severe Acute Respiratory Syndrome) in 2003, in order to publicize healthy practices to Singaporeans. The performer was a local actor/comedian in his (lead) character from the well-known local sitcom *Phua Chu Kang* — which, after the first two series, had been instructed by the government to use 'proper' (i.e. standard) English rather than Singlish in its shows, for fear that the series' popularity would encourage the use of Singlish in Singaporeans; this was worked into the storyline with PCK enrolling himself for English night class. However this *SAR-vivor Rap* incorporated many Singlish features, using, for example, as in the extract in (22), discourse particles *leh, lah* and *ah*, the *kena* passive and Malay lexical items *kaya* ('coconut jam') and *tahan* ('to endure'):

(22)   Some say "*leh*", some say "*lah*"
Spread *kaya*, but don't spread SARS!

> Everybody, we have a part to play
> To help fight SARS at the end of the day!
> …
>
> Hey if you *kena* home quarantine,
> Don't go out, except in your dreams.
> *Tahan* a while, and co-operate
> Don't give everybody a big headache *ah*!

The point here is this: that when push comes to shove, and a governing body needs to communicate with its people on matters of utmost urgency, with enough confidence that the message is conveyed and taken to heart, it is the real mother tongue of the people that it must call on — which in the case of (English-speaking) Singaporeans would appear to be Singlish.

The Chinese languages

Turning our attention now to the Chinese varieties in the Singapore context, it is clear that Mandarin has been the variety afforded most importance, having been selected as the Mother Tongue for those of the Chinese ethnic group, elevated through this, as well as via the SMC, as outlined in the first section. In relation to the other official MTs, too, we see that some are 'more equal than others', with Mandarin holding a higher position compared to the other two MTs. In addition to the fact of the numerical dominance of the Chinese in the population (78%) (Lim 2007, fc a), this has been, in particular in recent years, due to Mandarin's economic value, motivated by the anticipated economic development of China. The SMC's thrusts have clearly changed over the years, with more recent aims framed as follows: "Apart from promoting Mandarin as an avenue to understanding one's roots and Chinese culture, the campaign also highlights the importance of Mandarin for economic and business competitiveness" (SMC 2006). The instrumental value of Mandarin is clearly perceived to the point that non-Chinese Singaporeans also wish to study it as a MT, rather than the MT (Malay or Tamil) designated for their own ethnic group (Wee 2003; Wee and Bokhorst-Heng 2005). We see then how the discourse of the MTs serving as cultural ballast — against English, the language of progress but also potentially of negative Western values — is reconstructed on instrumentalist grounds as a consequence of perceptions of what it means to be globally competitive (Wee 2003). The problem, as argued in Wee (2003), is that this undermines strict complementarity between English and MTs. Wee (2003) notes that this situation presents an interesting challenge since intralinguistic considerations (reconciling a language's function as bearer of authenticity with its economic value) need to be dealt with alongside interlinguistic ones (the desire to maintain parity or equal status amongst the official MTs).

There are two twists to this story, the first to do with the purported instrumental function that Mandarin serves, and the second to do with the implication that the other Chinese varieties cannot fulfil such a function.

As is the case with any ecology, the situation is always dynamic, and this is nowhere more so than in Singapore, in no small part due to the two factors of immigration patterns and languages policies in different periods (for a detailed account of these see Lim fc a). In what is identified as the third sociohistorical era of late modernity (Lim fc a), where foreign manpower is relied on to overcome the limits of local resources, the sources of 'foreign talent' have shifted from the traditional bases of the United States, Britain, France, Australia, Japan and South Korea to China and India, due to policies instituted in the 1990s targetting non-traditional source countries (Yeoh 2007). The fourth sociohistorical era, based on the government's 'Singapore 21' (Singapore in the 21st century) vision (Goh 1999) involves, amongst other things, policies which have targeted mainland Chinese individuals as desired immigrants to Singapore, either for education or for business, as analyzed in

Lim (fc a). Together these have brought about a change in the composition of Singapore's Chinese population: there is now a significant mainland Chinese population in Singapore, with the number of 'new' migrants from China estimated to be close to 100,000 (Chan 2006: 9). Of these, there are now approximately 36,000 students from mainland China studying in Singapore's local schools, making up half of the foreign students in Singapore. Often accompanying the students are their mothers — an estimated 5,000 *peidu* (Mandarin 'accompany study') *mamas* 'study mamas' — who often work as salespersons, tutors, workers in local coffeeshops, cleaners, as well as KTV lounge hostesses and in the sex trade (Toh 2008), and along with other female mainland Chinese business-women, have "made their presence felt" (Ee 2008) over the last couple of decades; crucially, as Lim (fc a) notes, they have in many cases significant contact with the local population. The impact of their presence is attested in the numerous strong — usually negative — reactions of many Singapor-eans, usually non-Chinese, to the fact that these Chinese nationals who are working in major retail outlets such as English bookstores and department stores speak only Mandarin and no English (Teo 2008); there is even a Facebook site — surely a sign of the times — called 'I am Singaporean and tired of service staff who can only speak Mandarin' (Teo 2008).[7] In spite of this, the indisputable ascendance of Mandarin in this current sociohistorical era and prediction of continued dominance in the future (see Lim fc a) does raise the question of whether Mandarin now presents competition for English, as not just an economic resource but also a social one.

Then there are the other Chinese languages. At the level of the government, the discourse has not changed since the launch of SMC three decades ago. Most recently the principal private secre-tary to Lee Kuan Yew, now Minister Mentor,[8] reiterated their reasons for having "discouraged the use of dialects", since it "interferes with the learning of Mandarin and English", going to the extent of saying (Chee 2009) that

(23)   it would be stupid for any Singapore agency or NTU [Nanyang Technological University] to advocate the learning of dialects, which must be at the expense of English and Mandarin.

He also reiterated that the emphasis on transforming Mandarin into:

(24)   the mother tongue for all Chinese Singaporean, regardless of their dialect groups [is because it] is the common language of the 1.3 billion people in China. To engage China, overseas Chinese and foreigners are learning Mandarin and not the dialects of the different Chinese provinces.

However we see again linguistic practices which run counter to the official discourse. Perhaps the starkest show of strength comes from what has been transpiring in the Chinese clan associations (the collectives that developed amongst the immigrants to Singapore in the 1800s that were run along the lines of 'dialect' groups, that is, the provinces from which they hailed). In the last 30 years, since the government's emphasis on Mandarin through the bilingual education policy and the SMC, the clan associations too have been offering Mandarin lessons. The most recent decade has, how-ever, seen a shift in practice and attitudes, a consequence of the evolution of Singapore's ecology, which has seen ascendance in the official Chinese language, Mandarin, to the detriment of the other Chinese languages. These associations are now conducting dialect classes — for Hokkien, Teochew, Cantonese, Shanghainese — with people "clamouring for the sessions" (*ST* 9 Sep 2002), and enrol-ments of some 300 students in Teochew classes since they were started six years ago, and up to 600 students in Cantonese and Shanghainese classes since they were started six to nine years ago (Oon 2009). It is telling to identify the reasons for such a surge in interest.

On the one hand, it can be seen that the other Chinese languages do in fact fulfil instrumental functions, contrary to the strong official statements that it is (only) Mandarin that is needed to engage in business with China. Many of the younger generation Singaporeans who were brought up with Mandarin as their Mother Tongue are in recent years specifically seeking out Chinese 'dialect' classes for the purpose of doing business in China, in fact comprising the focus group of this initiative (Oon 2009), and the functionality of these languages for economic purposes in the region for Singaporeans is exemplified in the following account (Ang 2009):

(25)   When I go to Kuala Lumpur and Hong Kong on business, I conduct business discussions with my clients in Cantonese. In Penang and Taipei, it helps when I talk to my business partners in Hokkien. And when I do business in Bangkok, I often speak to clients in Teochew.

This echoes what has been documented in other multilingual contexts, where multilingualism is an asset in companies with multilingual workforce, and vernaculars as the languages with economic capital in informal (local) markets (Stroud 2001, 2004). Put another way, globalization does not mean homogenization.

Even within Singapore itself, the Chinese 'dialects' figure quite significantly, for example, in interethnic interactions, with Hokkien being an important vernacular for all males, regardless of ethnicity, in the National Service (army), where young men of extremely varied socioeconomic backgrounds are forced to work and interact together, serving especially well for neutralizing class differences so as to get along with fellow soldiers and simply get things done (Stroud and Wee fc). Additionally Singaporeans use 'dialects' not of their own 'dialect' group: a Hakka medical social worker reports valueing Cantonese as it helps her to communicate with many of the elderly patients she encounters in her work (Hing 2004: 56, cited in Stroud and Wee fc).

On the other hand, more obvious and predictable, the Chinese 'dialects' are still felt to be the language which connects people not only to their culture but also to their community (though Stroud and Wee fc, in an analysis of Singapore's mother tongues from the point of view of sociolinguistic consumption, describe situations where the Chinese 'dialects' are seen as neither crucial to speakers' ethnic identity nor to the preservation of tradition). The major reason for enrolment in the 'dialect' classes is to speak with grandparents and better connect with their roots (Oon 2009). Singaporeans also report (Ang 2009) how, upon visiting their ancestral village (in the following quote, in Fujian), it was:

(26)   so meaningful to talk to distant relatives in Hokkien, the only language spoken and understood in the village my great-grandfather came from … And when my father died recently, the Hokkien Huay Kuan clan members impressed me with their show of support during our bereavement.

As succinctly put by Oon (2009), while motivation for the learning of 'dialects' for business may be affected by the economic crisis, "the urge to *xun gen* or explore one's roots appears to be recession-proof".

The various Chinese languages have recently also been widely used in local films, such as those of Colin Goh and Woo Yen Yen (*Singapore Dreaming*, with Hokkien alongside Singlish and Mandarin) Eric Khoo (*Be With Me, My Magic*), Jack Neo (*I Not Stupid, Money Not Enough*), Djinn Ong (*Perth*, with Hokkien alongside English and Mandarin), Tan Pin Pin (*Singapore Gaga*, with Hokkien), Royston Tan (*Sons*, narration entirely in Hokkien; *881*, with Hokkien in dialogue and songs), Kelvin Tong (*Love Story*, in various Chinese languages), these filmmakers believing that dialects are "an important part of Singapore", which "work for their expressiveness", giving a "realness that locals enjoy" (cited in Foo 2008), and "an authentic flavour" (Tan, cited in Biston 2007). Indeed these films have seen great success and popularity, both locally and on the international scene: the film *881* on *getai* (Mandarin 'song stage') has revitalized Hokkien amongst the younger generation in Singapore by making it cool; and numerous awards and accolades have been won by these filmmakers in international film festivals. Although it may seem that restrictions on the use of dialects (in television programmes) have been relaxed in recent years, as recommended in 2003 by the Advisory Committee for Chinese programmes (ACCESS) — the Censorship Review Committee's 2003 report recommended allowing films with limited use of dialects, full dialect use on cable TV, the Arts Central TV channel, some radio news programmes, and limited screening of full Chinese dialect films at cinemas on a single film print per title basis television programme — as a sign of the continuing official line on the Chinese 'dialects' in Singapore, one of the trailers of *Singapore Dreaming* was banned from being aired on Singapore television for having too much Hokkien in it.

This makes it even more significant, perhaps, when we note the instances when these other Chinese languages **are** used in government contexts, and there have been two main arenas. First, the Chinese 'dialects' are commonly used by electoral candidates, from both the ruling and opposition parties, during the general elections, not only when campaigning door-to-door, but also in public election rallies. In the lead-up to the general elections in 2001 and 2006, for example, ministers, including the then Prime Minister, gave election rally speeches in not only the official languages (English, Mandarin, etc) but also in Hokkien, Teochew and Cantonese, in order to to reach out to older Chinese Singaporeans and better connect with their voters. The second instance where reaching out to Singaporeans was crucial was during the SARS outbreak in 2003, as already noted with Singlish. Then, the government permitted the use of dialect on television and radio, in order to broadcast the message "in a language that [every Singaporean] understands", with the Media Development Authority (MDA 2003) explaining such an adjustment of programming guidelines was necessary "in these exceptional circumstances… so that everyone will be aware of the SARS problem".

Beyond fear and loathing in SG

To conclude, this final section first reflects on practices related to multilingualism — documenting, defining and directing it — in the context of how it seems to have been managed in the Singapore context, and then goes on to specifically reconsider the position of English in Singapore, in particular with regard to the important role it has in Singapore's globalization visions, and the implications for policy and education.

Multilingualism and the real mother tongues

The first reflection is on **documenting** multilingualism — this is a fundamental and widely recognized problem, that multilingual practices are not so very well captured, especially in standard census data. While official statistics have shown increases and decreases in the use of various languages in Singapore, this perhaps hides more than it reveals. In the first place, one needs to scratch the surface beyond 'Chinese' to determine the use of the individual Chinese languages. More detailed analyses pertaining to specific Chinese dialect groups can be found in the newsletter of the Singapore Department of Statistics (Lee 2001). There, for example, one discovers that Cantonese is in fact still rather vital, being spoken by the Cantonese at home more frequently than Mandarin (36% vs. 32% in 2000).[9] The same simplification applies to 'English', which could just as well (and probably indeed does) include Singapore English varieties ranging from more acrolectal through basilectal Singlish, but such distinctions are not attempted in these standard national surveys.

Second, and perhaps more critical and fundamental, is our reflection on **defining** multilingualism. As is recognized by linguists, but less so by governments, the fact that, for a multilingual community, selecting a single language to report as the main home language may not be straightforward, given that there may well be two or three or more languages being spoken at home, in various manifestations of bilinguals' competence, such as using different varieties for different interlocutors, and/or code switching between the different varieties, as described earlier, not unlike the plurilingual practices noted for South Asia (Canagarajah this volume).

As a means of addressing both these limitations, more fine-tuned, linguistically informed surveys need to be designed and administered for a more accurate account of linguistic practices in such a multilingual context as Singapore.

Finally, one needs to critically assess the practice of **directing** multilingualism. The attempt by the government to assign a multilingual repertoire of their choosing to the population, via language policies and language campaigns, can lead to what may be considered by some as success, but success that is skin deep. The power of a multilingual ecology is too great to be constrained by directives, and certainly too diverse and dynamic to be contained in two official standard languages of 'English' and 'Mandarin'. As described earlier, one natural — perhaps inevitable — development beyond official language policy is the evolution of a nativized, restructured variety of English, which, with all the linguistic influences of the actual mother tongues of the people, serves much better as a marker of identity than a more standard — albeit 'good' — English. The other overflowing beyond official language policy are the Chinese 'dialects'. The original mother tongues of the original immigrants of the first, colonial era (Lim fc a) where natural immigration created the nation's population, the Chinese 'dialects' have not been subdued by the language policies and campaigns, even if they have been dealt a hard blow. In spite of official policy, Chinese Singaporeans still find that the 'dialects' resonate much more strongly when it comes to cultural values and roots, in contrast with Mandarin, which was the mother tongue of no Chinese community in the original immigrants to Singapore. In other words, in the Singapore situation, in spite of the government's linguistic engineering, it would appear that Singaporeans still make choices for the languages which serve to express their identities etc., namely Singlish and the Chinese 'dialects' — the real mother tongues. Language planners need to recognize this, for future policies that would actually make sense in multilingual Singapore.

At the same time, there are two curiosities which give one pause. First, the government does appear to recognize that mother tongue education in an additive (and preferably late exit) bilingual education system is the most effective means of learning of both first and second language (if one can identify those) as well as of other skills. However, instead of using the population's actual home languages in education, their solution was to change the language at home instead. Second, in spite of all the official discourse, the government does still recognize what Singaporeans' real mother tongues are — Singlish and the Chinese 'dialects' — and does not hesitate to use them in situations of states of emergency (elections, pandemics). One may only surmise that the government has decided that, as perhaps with most other vices in the country, these unsanctioned linguistic varieties are only permissible in small doses and under their careful control.[10]

A prognosis for English in multilingual, globalizing Singapore

Given the vitality not just of English but also of the Chinese languages, it remains for this final section to attempt a prognosis for the English language in Singapore. As a result of the language planning and policy making in the early years, English is very much entrenched in Singapore — two decades ago Singapore was already described as "well on its way towards becoming a largely English-speaking country" (Newbrook 1987: 12) and a decade after as "English-dominant" (Schneider 1999: 193) — and in this respect, Singapore must be recognized as being successful in managing the myriad languages in its ecology — or at least some of them — with an eye on maintaining English in order to keep Singapore a highly competitive global player. But: What does one mean by 'English' in Singapore in such discussions? What 'English' is a player in Singapore's story? What 'English' outcome is desired — and by whom? The government? The people? Linguists? And how can current and future decisions, beyond the original language policy making, address this or take it into consideration?

The government's concern over how the presence and use of Singlish will affect Singapore's (economic) future does need to be given serious intellectual attention — but not just in how they have (mis-)managed SGEM. The various manifestations of a nativized variety of English, used in plurilingual practices, as illustrated earlier, need to be examined for their potential threat. To recapitulate, there are — alongside Standard Singapore English, the variety which does exhibit a certain amount of nativization (e.g. in phonology and to some extent in lexis), but for all intents and purposes does not differ from internationally recognized and accepted standard varieties of English, which is used in more formal and public contexts — perhaps at least three manifestations of nativized 'English' that exist in Singapore:

i.   There is Singlish, the restructured variety that is officially disinherited, but is certainly a linguistic variety that is (a) a dominant language for many, (b) a variety that is widely used, (c) a variety that is an important identity marker for Singaporeans.

ii. There are plurilingual practices, which in one incarnation are viewed as a glocalized linguistic practice in which Standard English and Singlish features are used in a fluid mix, and which has been noted to be used effectively in the domain of education; and which in another incarnation have been treated as a monolectal code switching practice of English (Singlish), Mandarin and Hokkien (or other Chinese 'dialects'), a code which is used as an intracommunal medium.

Speakers engaging in some or all of these linguistic practices appear to know when to use them: (i) is used in colloquial contexts, amongst Singaporeans (or non-Singaporeans who have been in Singapore sufficiently to warrant being part of the speech community); the former incarnation of (ii) has been noted to be used systematically, not randomly, to serve various goals of Singaporean classroom discourse (organization vs. content), while the latter is a code used within the community which share such a code. None of these manifestations of English thus need be viewed as threats to the globalization dreams of the government. And in fact, as mentioned previously, the government would appear to realize this anyway, using, as they have, Singlish when needing to connect with and communicate effectively with their people — in this sense, no different from the linguistic practice of (ii).

Second, fears of unintelligibility and/or lack of prestige are not objective facts. The more exposure the rest of the world has to a variety like Singlish — through scholarly work, film and media, etc. — the more the variety will become increasingly intelligible and possibly increase in positive attitudes. Gupta's (fc) example of how the Singlish term *kiasu* (Hokkien '(the quality of being) afraid to lose out') moved into mainstream usage — from army slang in the late 1970s and general colloquial use in Singapore to usage in formal domains, and, only a decade after having appeared in 1990 in the Singapore press, to appearances in the British press from 2001 and, soon after, inclusion in the *Oxford English Dictionary* — is a case in point. The current reality of the internet, with easy access to audio and video and participation in blogs and chats, which allows not just passive exposure to any variety of English but also active interaction with speakers of those varieties, will only aid such processes.

This paper has examined the natural evolution of language and linguistic practices in Singapore's multilingual ecology, focussing in particular on Singlish, as well as on the Chinese 'dialects', in terms of their status in official language policy and their use in actual practice, and two general points may perhaps be underlined in conclusion. First, the early language policies of the government have in fact set Singaporeans up to be English-knowing bilinguals, and as a result, even with the significance of the Chinese 'dialects' as rekindled mother tongues, and even with the continued ascendance of Mandarin as a regional lingua franca in Greater China, a region vital to Singapore's economy, and its continued dominance in Singapore (Lim fc a), it is highly doubtful that the pre-eminence of English will be threatened any time in the future. Second, the (Standard) English-medium education system developed over the decades, even with its shortcomings (see Rubdy fc), has also set Singaporeans up to be proficient (Standard) English users (see Bruthiaux fc; Gupta fc), and as a result, even with the emergence of nativized Singlish, it is also highly doubtful that Singaporeans will cease to be able to be intelligible, and therefore successful, globally. Rather than react with fear and loathing to natural linguistic processes in multilingual ecologies, language policy would instead do well to recognize and create a space for these linguistic varieties — only in reaching out and grasping them with courage will they not sting.

Notes

1. This is of course coupled with the fact that policies and practice are far more easily implemented in a small, rich city-state, compared with geographically vaster, politically more fragmented, and/or economically poorer nations, such as some of her Asian neighbours.

2. The term 'dialect', in single quote marks to distinguish it from linguistic definitions, will be used in this paper.

3. It should — and will — be noted that most of the statements, such as (1), by the political figures are not supported by research on the relationship between multilingualism, IQ, and acquisition; nor is there reflected in statements, such as (3) to (7), any linguistic understanding of the fact that all linguistic varieties, whether 'languages' or 'dialects' (or 'creoles', etc), are capable of expressing any concepts and of developing to fulfil any communicative needs. I thank one of the reviewers for pointing out that the fact that the statements are untutored and unsupported needed to be underlined.

4. I am grateful to one of my reviewers for pointing out the immediate concerns that Singapore would have had at independence (as mentioned here), with its goal of participating in a globalizing world only coming later, after internal and regional stability.

5. In the widely used Three Circles model of Englishes world wide (Kachru 1985), Singapore is classified as belonging to the Outer Circle; in addition to the limitations of the model itself, Singapore's linguistic situation has changed over the decades and its reality is not captured in such a model.

6. While in previous writing (e.g. Fong, Lim and Wee 2002; Lim 2004b, 2007, 2009b, c) I have shown a preference for a term such as *colloquial Singapore English* (also more widely used in most SgE scholarship) rather than *Singlish*, as the latter tends to evoke numerous negative connotations, I have chosen to use *Singlish* here, partly to be in line with the term used in the various discourses discussed in this paper, and partly to underline its proximity more to Asian varieties than English (also see Lim fc b).

7. The dissatisfaction voiced over the fact that Mandarin seems to be gaining prominence over English in Singapore echoes the situation of the late 1980s when culturally marginalized English-speaking minority communities, mostly middle-class, including Indians and Eurasians, perceiving a favouring of the Chinese community in the bilingual policy and the particular emphasis on Mandarin, emigrated in large numbers (see Lim fc a).

8. When Goh Chok Tong became Prime Minister (PM), the post of Senior Minister (SM) was created for outgoing PM Lee Kuan Yew; later, when Lee Hsien Loong became PM, and Goh then moved to the SM role, the title of Minister Mentor was created for Lee senior.

9. This is argued to be partly attributable to the arrival of a significant number of Hong Kong 'foreign talent' immigrants in the late 1980s and 1990s (Lim 2007, fc a).

10. Though the extent to which this can be 'controlled' is doubtful, as evidenced by the dogged survival and/or re-emergence of such varieties. I thank one of my reviewers for pointing this out.

References

Alsagoff, L. (fc 2010) Hybridity in ways of speaking: The glocalization of English in Singapore. In Lim et al. (eds).

Ang, K.C. (2009) Dialects make business sense. *The Straits Times*. Forum. 9 March.

Ansaldo, U. (2004) The evolution of Singapore English: Finding the matrix. In Lim (ed.), pp. 129–151.

Ansaldo, U. (2009a) *Contact Languages: Ecology and Evolution in Asia*. Cambridge: Cambridge University Press.

Ansaldo, U. (2009b) The Asian typology of English: Theoretical and methodological considerations. In Lim and Gisborne (eds), pp. 133–148.

Bao Z. (2001) The origins of empty categories in Singapore English. *Journal of Pidgin and Creole Languages* 16(2): 275–319.

Bao Z. (2005) The aspectual system of Singapore English and the systemic substratist explanation. *Journal of Linguistics* 41: 237–267.

Bao Z. and Lye H.M. (2005) Systemic transfer, topic prominence, and the bare conditional in Singapore English. *Journal of Pidgin and Creole Languages* 20: 269–291.

Bao, Z. and L. Wee (1999) The passive in Singapore English. *World Englishes* 18(1): 1–11.

Biston, J. (2007) Singapore film on music for dead brings Hokkien to life. *Reuters*. Retrieved 8 June 2009 from http://www.reuters.com/article/inDepthNews/idUSSP27516220070901

Bloom, D. (1986) The English language and Singapore: A critical survey. In B.K. Kapur (ed.), *Singapore Studies: Critical Surveys of the Humanities and Social Sciences*, pp. 337–452. Singapore: Singapore University Press.

Bokhorst-Heng, W.D. (1998) Language planning and management in Singapore. In J.A. Foley, T. Kandiah, Bao Z., A.F. Gupta, L. Alsagoff, Ho C.L., L. Wee, I. Talib and W. Bokhorst-Heng. *English in New Cultural Contexts: Reflections from Singapore*, pp. 287–309. Singapore: Oxford University Press.

Bruthiaux, P. (fc 2010) The Speak Good English Movement: A web-user's perspective. In Lim et al. (eds).

Canagarajah, S.A. (1995) The political economy of code choice in a 'revolutionary society': Tamil-English bilingualism in Jaffna, Sri Lanka. *Language in Society* 24: 187–212.

Chan, B. (2006) Virtual communities and Chinese national identity. *Journal of Chinese Overseas* 2(1): 1–32.

Chee, H.T. (2009) Foolish to advocate the learning of dialects. *The Straits Times*, Forum, 7 March.

Chew, P.G.-L. (2007) Remaking Singapore: Language, culture and identity in a globalized world. In A.B.M. Tsui and J.W. Tollefson (eds), *Language Policy, Culture, and Identity in Asian Contexts*, pp. 73–93.

Chng, H.H. (2003) "You see me no up": Is Singlish a problem? *Language Problems and Language Planning* 27(1): 45–62.

Dictionary of Singlish and Singapore English. http://www.singlishdictionary.com/

Ee, W.W.J. (2008) Men from China at your service. *The Straits Times*, 20 April.

Fong, V. (2004) The verbal cluster. In Lim (ed.), pp. 75–104.

Fong, V., L. Lim and L. Wee (2002) 'Singlish': Used and abused. *Asian Englishes* 5(1): 18–39.

Foo, L. (2008) Local filmmakers include more Chinese dialects in recent works. *Channel NewsAsia*, 6 July. Retrieved 8 June 2009 from http://www.channelnewsasia.com/stories/singaporelocalnews/view/358575/1/.html

Goh, K.S. and the Education Study Team (1979) *Report on the Ministry of Education 1979*. Singapore: Ministry of Education.

Gupta, A.F. (1994) *The Step-Tongue: Children's English in Singapore*. Clevedon, Philadelphia, Adelaides: Multilingual Matters.

Gupta, A.F. (fc 2010) Singapore Standard English revisited. In Lim et al. (eds).

Hing, K. (2004) Chinese dialects in Singapore: Reversing language shift. BA Honours thesis, National University of Singapore.

Kachru, B.B. 1985. Standards, codification and sociolinguistic realism: The English language in the outer circle. In R. Quirk and H. Widdowson (eds), *English in the World: Teaching and Learning the Language and Literatures*, pp. 11–36. Cambridge: Cambridge University Press.

Kuo, E.C.Y. (1980) The sociolinguistic situation in Singapore: Unity in diversity. In E.A. Afendras and E.C.Y. Kuo (eds), *Language and Society in Singapore*, pp. 39–62. Singapore: Singapore University Press.

Kuo, E.C.Y. and B.H. Jernudd (1994) Balancing macro- and micro-sociolinguistic perspectives in language management: The case of Singapore. In S. Gopinathan, A. Pakir, Ho W.K. and V. Saravanan (eds), *Language, Society and Education in Singapore: Issues and Trends*, 1st ed., pp. 25–46. Singapore: Times Academic Press.

Lee, E.F.E. (2001) Profile of the Singapore Chinese dialect groups. *Statistics Singapore Newsletter*, pp. 2–6. Singapore: Singapore Department of Statistics.

Leow, B.G. (2001) *Census Population 2000 Statistical Release 2: Education, Language and Religion*. Singapore: Department of Statistics, Ministry of Trade and Industry.

Li, W. (1994) *Three Generations, Two Languages, One Family: Language Choice and Language Shift in a Chinese Community in Britain*. Clevedon: Multilingual Matters.

Li, W., V. Saravanan and L.H.J. Ng (1997) Language shift in the Teochew community in Singapore: A family domain analysis. *Journal of Multilingual and Multicultural Development* 18(5): 364–384.

Lim, L. (2001) The Grammar of Spoken Singapore English (GSSEC): Final report. National University of Singapore.

Lim, L. (2004a) Sounding Singaporean. In Lim (ed.), pp. 19–56.

Lim, L. (ed.) (2004b) *Singapore English: A Grammatical Description*. Amsterdam, Philadelphia: John Benjamins.

Lim, L. (2007) Mergers and acquisitions: On the ages and origins of Singapore English particles. *World Englishes* 26(4): 446–473.

Lim, L. (2008a) Dynamic linguistic ecologies of Asian Englishes. *Asian Englishes* 11(1): 52–55.

Lim, L. (2008b) *Singapore Dreaming*, Singapore English and Singapore's languages: How linguistics can be enriched by popular culture. 14th International Conference of the International Association for World Englishes (IAWE). World Englishes and World Languages: Convergence, Enrichment, or Death? Hong Kong, 1–5 Dec 2008.

Lim, L. (2009a in press) Peranakan English. In D. Schreier, P. Trudgill, E. Schneider and J.P. Williams (eds), *Lesser Known Varieties of English*. Cambridge: Cambridge University Press.

Lim, L. (2009b) Revisiting English prosody: (Some) New Englishes as tone languages? In Lim and Gisborne (eds), pp. 218–239.

Lim, L. (2009c) "Not just an 'Outer Circle', 'Asian' English: Singapore English and the significance of ecology". In T. Hoffmann and L. Siebers (eds), *World Englishes: Problems, Properties, Prospects*. Amsterdam, Philadelphia: John Benjamins.

Lim, L. (fc 2010a) Migrants and 'mother tongues': Extralinguistic forces in the ecology of English in Singapore. In Lim et al. (eds).

Lim, L. (fc 2010b) Tone in Singlish: Substrate features from Sinistic and Malay. In C. Lefebvre (ed.), *Substrate Features in Creole Languages*. Amsterdam, Philadelphia: John Benjamins.

Lim, L. and J.A. Foley (2004) English in Singapore and Singapore English: Background and methodology. In Lim (ed.), pp. 1–18.

Lim, L. and N. Gisborne (eds) (2009) *The Typology of Asian Englishes*. Special Issue, *English World-Wide* 30(2).

Lim, L., A. Pakir and L. Wee (eds) (fc 2010) *English in Singapore: World Language and Lingua Franca*. Hong Kong: Hong Kong University Press.

Media Development Authority (MDA), Singapore (2003) Allowing the use of dialect on television and radio. The New Desk, 30 April. Retrieved 8 June 2009 from http://www.mda.gov.sg/wms.www/thenewdesk.aspx?sid=491

Meeuwis, M. and J. Blommaert (1998) A monolectal view of code-switching: Layered code-switching among Zairians in Belgium. In P. Auer (ed.), *Code-Switching in Conversation: Language, Interaction and Identity*, pp. 76–98. London, NY: Routledge.

Mercer (2006) Mercer Singapore Watch — Q3 2006. *Mercer*. Retrieved 27 September 2008 from http://www.mercer.com/referencecontent.htm?idContent=1246080

Ministry of Trade and Industry, Singapore (2008) Singapore China FTA Agreement Concluded. Press Release, 4 September. Retrieved 8 June 2009 from http://practicesource.com/australian-asian-legal-eye/singapore-china-fta-agreement-concluded.html

Myers-Scotton, C. (1993) *Social Motivations for Code Switching: Evidence from Africa*. Oxford: Clarenden.

Ng, P.S., (ed.) (1995) *Singapore Facts and Pictures 1995*. Singapore: Ministry of Information and the Arts.

Oon, C. (2009) Dialects draw more new learners: Younger people taking classes to connect with old folk or for business. *The Straits Times*, 7 April.

Pakir, A. (1994) Education and invisible language planning: The case of English in Singapore. In T. Kandiah and J. Kwan-Terry (eds), *English and Language Planning: A Southeast Asian Contribution*, pp. 158–181. Singapore: Times Academic Press for Centre for Advanced Studies, National University of Singapore.

Pakir, A. (1997) Education and invisible language planning: The case of the English Language in Singapore, In J. Tan, J., S. Gopinathan and Ho W.K. (eds), *Education in Singapore: A Book of Readings*, pp. 57–74. Singapore: Prentice Hall.

Pakir, A. (2001) Which English? The nativization of English and the negotiations of language choice in Southeast Asia. International conference on Anglophone Cultures in Southeast Asia: Appropriations, Continuities, Contexts. Chinese University of Hong Kong, Hong Kong. 8–11 Oct 2001.

Pakir, A. (2004) Medium-of-instruction policy in Singapore. In J.W. Tollefson and A. Tsui (eds), *Medium of Instruction Policies: Which Agenda? Whose Agenda?*, pp. 117–133. Lawrence Erlbaum Associates.

Rubdy, R. (2001) Creative destruction: Singapore's Speak Good English movement. *World Englishes* 20(3): 341–355.

Rubdy, R. (fc 2010) Problematizing the implementation of innovation in English language education in Singapore. In Lim et al. (eds).

Schneider, E.W. (2007) *Postcolonial English: Varieties of English World Wide*. Cambridge: Cambridge University Press.

S.P. Jain Center of Management Dubai, Singapore (n.d.) Why Singapore? Retrieved 8 June 2009 from http://www.spjain.org/why_singapore.asp

Speak Good English Movement (SGEM) (2009) Retrieved 8 June 2009 from http://www.goodenglish.org.sg/2009/

Speak Mandarin Campaign (SMC) (2009) Retrieved 8 June 2009 from http://www.mandarin.org.sg/2009/index-en.html

Stroud, C. (2001) African mother tongue programs and the politics of language: Linguistic citizenship versus linguistic human rights. *Journal of Multilingual and Multicultural Development* 22(4): 339–355.

Stroud, C. (2004) The performativity of codeswitching: Women street vendors in Mozambique. *International Journal of Bilingualism* 8(2): 145–166.

Stroud, C. and L. Wee (fc 2010) Language policy and planning in Singaporean late modernity. In Lim et al. (eds).

TalkingCock.com (2004) Lim Peh Ka Li Kong: Father's troubles with mother tongue. *TalkingCock.com*, 28 November. Retrieved 7 August 2009 from http://www.talkingcock.com/html/article.php?sid=1577

TalkingCock.com (2009) Still on hiatus. *TalkingCock.com*, 26 May. Retrieved 10 August 2009 from http://www.talkingcock.com/html/index.php

Teo, E. (2008) Speaking up for minorities. *The Straits Times*, My Thoughts, 24 November.

Toh, M. (2008) Tough life for 'study mamas'. *The Straits Times*, 28 September.

Wee, L. (2002) When English is not a mother tongue: Linguistic ownership and the Eurasian community in Singapore. *Journal of Multilingual and Multicultural Development* 23(4): 282–295.

Wee, L. (2003) Linguistic instrumentalism in Singapore. *Journal of Multilingual and Multicultural Development* 24(3), 211–224.

Wee, L. (2004) Reduplication and discourse particles. In Lim (ed.), pp. 105–126.

Wee, L. and U. Ansaldo (2004) Nouns and noun phrases. In Lim (ed.), pp. 57–76.

Wee, L. and W.D. Bokhorst-Heng (2005) Language policy and nationalist ideology: Statal narrative in Singapore. *Multilingua* 24: 159–183.

Woo, Y.Y., C. Goh (Producers/Directors) and W. Wu (Producer) (2006) *Singapore Dreaming*. [Motion Picture.] Singapore: 5C Films Pte Ltd.

Yeoh, B.S.A. (2007) Hungry for foreign workers at all skill levels. *Migration Information Source. Country Profiles*. Washington, DC: Migration Policy Institute. January. Retrieved 22 September 2007 from http://www.migrationinformation.org/Profiles/display.cfm?ID=570

Towards 'biliteracy and trilingualism' in Hong Kong (SAR)

Problems, dilemmas and stakeholders' views*

David C.S. Li
Hong Kong Institute of Education

Despite the Hong Kong SAR (Special Administrative Region) government's determination to implement the 'mother tongue education' policy amid strong social resistance one year after the handover, English remains a prestigious language in society. The need for Putonghua (Mandarin/Standard Chinese) is also increasing following ever-expanding trade and other activities with mainland China. The societal demand for both English and Putonghua in postcolonial Hong Kong is important for understanding the SAR government's language-in-education policy called 'biliteracy and trilingualism'. The learning of English is fraught with two main problems: (a) the absence of a conducive language-learning environment outside the classroom, which makes English in Hong Kong more like a foreign than a second language, and (b) tremendous typological difference between Chinese and English on one hand, and considerable linguistic differences between Cantonese and Putonghua on the other. Given the significant phonological differences and, to a lesser extent, lexico-grammatical divergence between the majority's vernacular and modern written Chinese, the learning of Putonghua is no straightforward task either. The dilemmas of the medium-of-instruction (MoI) debate will be discussed by elucidating the main concerns as seen from the respective vantage points of the government and five key stakeholder groups: employers, parents, school principals, teachers and educationalists, and students.

Introduction

A good decade has elapsed after the sovereignty of Hong Kong was returned to China on 1 July 1997. Within the space of barely 1,100 square kilometers, Hong Kong SAR is home to over seven million inhabitants (as of 2009), making it one of the most densely populated cities in the world. Over 95% of Hongkongers are ethnic Chinese, with an overwhelming majority being native speakers of Cantonese (Census and Statistics Hong Kong 2007: 39). This demographic detail helps explain why Cantonese is widely perceived as the unmarked language choice among Chinese Hongkongers, and that initiating or maintaining an English-only conversation is so highly marked except in the presence of non-Cantonese speakers. Natural resources being negligible, trade and commerce have always been the lifeline of this former colony. Since the 1980s, the principal economic activities gradually shifted from manufacturing to those which are characteristic of a knowledge-based economy. In terms of manpower development and educational needs, therefore, English is regarded by policy makers as

AILA Review 22 (2009), 72–84. DOI 10.1075/aila.22.06li
ISSN 1461–0213 / E-ISSN 1570–5595 © John Benjamins Publishing Company

important linguistic capital for the continued well-being of 'Asia's World City', and by Hongkongers as an indispensable language for upward and outward mobility.

This paper will first briefly discuss how the Hong Kong SAR government's language policy of 'biliteracy and trilingualism' is shaped by the socioeconomic realities outlined above. It will then address two main issues: (a) problems pertaining to the effective acquisition of English and Putonghua (Mandarin/Standard Chinese) by Chinese Hongkongers; and (b) the social tension between Cantonese, English and Putonghua in the education domain, as epitomized in various concerns of different stakeholder groups regarding the controversial medium-of-instruction (MoI) debate: the Hong Kong government, employers, parents, school principals, teachers and educationists, and students. The primary purpose of this review paper is to help readers who are unfamiliar with the Hong Kong language situation to better understand the predicament faced for over two decades by Hong Kong language policy makers and the key stakeholders affected.

HKSAR's language-in-education policy: Biliteracy and trilingualism

Like many other parts of the world, Hong Kong's manpower needs have been largely conditioned by its principal economic realities. From the period between the two World Wars to about the end of the 1950s, Hong Kong prospered essentially through bustling entrepôt trade. In the next three decades until around the mid-1980s, manufacturing became the mainstay of economic activities, with 'Made in Hong Kong' being the hallmark of this former British colony which came to be known as 'The Pearl of the Orient'. Throughout this period, the needs for English in society were by and large limited to the upper echelons of government officials and business people, as well as senior administrators in the domains of education and law. This was reflected in the relatively restricted numbers of and societal needs for university graduates with a high level of English proficiency. Up until the early 1980s, the competition for a place in one of the two local universities — especially the English-medium University of Hong Kong — was very keen, with a success rate of barely 2% of all secondary school leavers (Form 7 or Grade 13, aged around 18) per year.

From the mid-1980s onwards, the manufacturing sector gradually gave way to several other sectors which are more characteristic of a knowledge-based economy. Of these, the most vibrant are banking, investment and finance, import/export, tele-communications, transport and logistics, tourism, hotels, restaurants, insurance, retail trade, and real estate services. The 1980s also witnessed the gradual transformation of mainland China from a self-secluded communist state to an increasingly export-oriented economy after the open-door policy was enthusiastically embraced and actively implemented by the Beijing government under the leadership of its helmsman Deng Xiaoping. China's gradual integration into the global economy, which culminated in her successful accession to the WTO in 2001, has tremendous implications for Hong Kong's manpower needs. To the extent that business opportunities and transactions with non-Cantonese-speaking mainlanders take place increasingly in Putonghua, pragmatically minded Hongkongers have little choice but to expand their linguistic repertoire to include at least some Putonghua. In April 2009, the government-initiated Task Force on Economic Challenges (TFEC) identified six potential industries for future development: testing and certification, medical services, innovation and technology, cultural and creative industries, environmental industries, and (international) educational services (GovHK 2009). It can be seen that these niche industries, which are viewed by the government as crucial for Hong Kong's sustained vitality and further development, all require a high level of proficiency in English and Chinese (i.e. Cantonese, Putonghua, and modern written Chinese).[1]

Above is thus the background to the SAR government's needs-driven language-in-education policy called 'biliteracy and trilingualism'. Accordingly, one important policy goal of higher education is to graduate students with a reasonably high level of ability to speak Cantonese, English and

Putonghua, and to read and write Chinese and English. The increasing need for a biliterate and trilingual workforce is also reflected in the percentage of students gaining access to postsecondary education: from a mere 2% in the early 1980s to 18% in the mid-1990s (Lin and Man 2009).

Learning English and Putonghua: Two unfavourable acquisitional factors

English in Hong Kong (SAR): Second language or foreign language?
As the absolute majority of Chinese Hongkongers (over 90%) is Cantonese-speaking, Cantonese has always been the dominant vernacular cum lingua franca among Hongkongers. This fact has important implications for the ease — or rather a lack of it — with which English and Putonghua are acquired. Since the non-Chinese population has rarely exceeded 5%, the English-speaking people, including the British during colonial times, have always been minority groups. This demographic detail helps explain why, despite the conspicuous presence of English in society — from shop names and street signs to textbooks and menus; from newspapers and magazines to public announcements and broadcast media — English is rarely used by (Chinese) Hongkongers for intraethnic communication among themselves. Indeed, in the absence of non-Cantonese speakers, the choice of English as the medium of communication is widely perceived as highly marked, probably out of concern for the co-speakers' ethnolinguistic identity. One consequence of such a concern is that whoever initiates or persists in maintaining an English-only conversation with no non-Cantonese-speakers around is expected to come up with some justification for that unusual language choice. This is what sets Chinese Hongkongers and, say, Chinese Singaporeans apart. In terms of opportunities for language practice or authentic use, what this means is that for the majority of Hongkongers, English has very little reality outside school premises or in their lifeworld. In this regard, sociolinguists would say that Hong Kong lacks a conducive environment relative to the important goal of learning English effectively. No wonder many 'errors' or accuracy problems at the lexico-grammatical level are found at various stages of the learning process, thereby fueling criticisms in an ongoing public discourse mediated by both the print and broadcast media (e.g. Li and Chan 2001; Chan et al. 2002). In his extended treatise on 'Chinese Englishes', including 'Hong Kong English', Bolton (2003) points out that for a long time, there has been a widely shared perception in Hong Kong society that the standards of English have been declining. In this connection, he speaks of a 'complaint tradition' (cf. Milroy and Milroy 1985). However, those who complain fail to realize that following the gradual shift from elite education to mass education, the percentage of young people receiving higher education, especially at the university level, has increased considerably, leading to a general decline in average academic performance, including a lower level of language-learning attainment. Above all, what is often ignored in such complaints and criticisms is the absence of a conducive environment for Hongkongers to practise and use English beyond the language classroom. Owing to Chinese Hongkongers' inhibition against speaking only English among themselves, it is not at all obvious how the learners' classroom inputs may get consolidated through active meaning-making in natural communication with others.

This brings us to one interesting issue related to the functions and status of English in Hong Kong: is it more like a second language or a foreign language (cf. Li 1999)? As mentioned, English is seldom used by Chinese Hongkongers for intraethnic communication among themselves (except in Cantonese-English code-switching, which takes place more often at the intra- than inter-sentential level, Li and Tse 2002). This makes English more like a foreign than a second language (Li 1999). At the same time, to the extent that English is one of the official languages (alongside Chinese) which is commonly and actively used, more in print than in speech, in the key domains of government, education, law and business, it functions more like a second language. Such characteristics make

English in Hong Kong an untypical second or foreign language. This is probably why in the literature on 'Hong Kong English', different analyses and conclusions are arrived at depending on the World Englishes scholar. Kachru (2005: 90) categorizes English in Hong Kong, along with that in China, as a foreign language, albeit a "fast-expanding" one. McArthur (2001: 8–9), on the other hand, places Hong Kong along with Bangladesh, Brunei, Ghana, India, Malaysia, Nigeria, and Singapore as one of "the ESL territories". Likewise, in his extended treatise of 'Hong Kong English', Bolton (2003) places it in the Outer Circle. The placement of Hong Kong in the Outer Circle or the Expanding Circle has theoretical implications in Kachru's Three-Circle model (1985), namely 'norm-developing' (Outer Circle) vs. 'norm-dependent' (Expanding Circle). The above analysis suggests that a model featuring three concentric circles based essentially on nation-states in abstraction of tremendous variation within them is not as useful for characterizing the status and functions of English in a place like Hong Kong, where percentage-wise only a minority speaks English as a quasi-L1, while the majority of Chinese-English bilinguals fall within a cline of proficiency levels with 'proficient' at one end and 'barely intelligible' at the other. In any case, what is clear is that English in Hong Kong is an untypical second or foreign language which defies any attempt to have it placed in one Kachruvian circle or the other in a cut-and-dry manner.[2]

Typological distance between Chinese and English, and linguistic differences between Cantonese and Putonghua
In addition to the absence of a conducive social environment for using and practising English, another major problem is linguistic, which is rooted in the fact that English and Chinese are typologically very dissimilar languages. English is an Indo-European language whereas Chinese belongs to the Sino-Tibetan language family (Gordon 2005). Phonologically, many of the pronunciation features are alien to Chinese ears, including the dental fricatives, stress-timed rhythm (as opposed to syllable-timed rhythm in Chinese), and consonant clusters, the latter being uncommon or not found in Chinese varieties (Hung 2000, 2002). Still other pronunciation difficulties are due to the Chinese learner's ignorance of phonotactic constraints regarding which English consonants may occur in the syllable- or word-final position. This is a major source of difficulty for Chinese learners of English in general, which often combines with the problems created by consonant clusters.[3]

Grammatically, most of the subsystems in English such as tenses and articles are non-existent in Chinese. In terms of lexis, apart from a small subset of loanwords borrowed from English (e.g. Cantonese words for *taxi* and *bus*, *foreman* (of a company/enterprise) and *counter* (of a bank/hospital)), the number of cognates in English is negligible. As for the way the two languages are written, English is alphabetic while Chinese is logographic (Gordon 2005). As a result of salient typological differences, therefore, very little of Chinese learners' knowledge of their mother tongue is of any use in the process of learning English — unlike learners from other cognate language pairs such as English and German, or French and Italian. This linguistic factor helps explain why, for the majority of Chinese learners, English is so difficult to learn, let alone to master.

What about Mandarin or Putonghua? Do Cantonese-speaking Hongkongers find it easy to acquire this national lingua franca of Greater China? The answer is a qualified "yes". Since written Chinese is based essentially on Putonghua, learning to read Chinese means that one naturally becomes familiar with a large number of vocabulary words in the national language, even though in Hong Kong SAR, students continue to pronounce Chinese texts in their vernacular, Cantonese. This is the background against which Cantonese and Putonghua have evolved many cognates (Luke 2005). In other words, many Putonghua expressions are pronounceable in Cantonese because learners in Hong Kong are taught to pronounce them in Cantonese rather than in Putonghua, as is the rule in mainland schools. As far as writing is concerned, one additional complication is that, in accordance with the Hong Kong (SAR) Basic Law, Chinese characters in Hong Kong SAR continue to be written in traditional forms, as opposed to simplified forms in mainland China (Snow 2004; for more details about Chinese as a lingua franca in Greater China, see Li 2006).

Despite the commonalities outlined above, for the majority of Hongkongers, the learning of Putonghua somehow exhibits certain characteristics of the learning of a second language. Most of the learning difficulties are related to the rather different phonological systems between the two Chinese varieties, notably with regard to their systems of tones. There are four tonemes in Putonghua but six in Cantonese, with marked differences in their respective tone contours (Matthews and Yip 1994). Other phonological problems that Cantonese learners have to grapple with include morpho-syllables pronounced with neutral tones or tone sandhi, the latter being triggered by systematic allophonic changes necessitated when morpho-syllables of the third tone co-occur (e.g. the expression 很好, 'well' or 'very well', consists of two morpho-syllables which are pronounced in isolation as *hěn* and *hǎo*, but together they should be articulated as *hén hǎo*). In addition, perhaps more importantly, learners' exposure to Putonghua tends to be restricted to the language classroom, for like in English, there are hardly any opportunities for meaningful practice beyond school premises.

Toward biliteracy and trilingualism: Challenges and dilemmas in the MoI debate

The language-in-education policy in Hong Kong has been a source of tremendous social tension in the last two decades (Lin and Man 2009). Few would dispute the usefulness of English in the white-collar workplace. Given that English is seldom used for intraethnic communication, however, for the majority of Hongkongers schooling is almost the only domain in which they get exposure in English, which is taught and learnt from kindergarten onwards. Until the end of Primary education (Primary 6 or Grade 6, aged around 12), with few exceptions the teaching medium is mainly Cantonese. At the onset of Secondary education (roughly Grade 7), however, since September 1998 the 'mother tongue education' policy stipulates that schools must teach in Chinese (Cantonese and Standard Chinese written in traditional, as opposed to simplified, Chinese characters), unless they can demonstrate that students and teachers have the ability to learn and teach through the medium of English effectively. There are about 30% of over 400 secondary schools which meet this EMI (English as a medium of instruction) requirement.

The language situation became more complicated after the sovereignty of Hong Kong was returned to China in July 1997. Being the national language taught and learned by practically all Chinese nationals across mainland China, Putonghua is an important symbol of national unity, and so there seems no reason why Hong Kong Chinese should be exempted from learning to understand and speak Putonghua — a state of affairs which is currently 'tolerated', as stipulated in the Hong Kong (SAR) Basic Law.

English has evolved into an international or global lingua franca (Jenkins 2003; Seidhlhofer 2004; Kirkpatrick 2007). While Putonghua/Mandarin is as yet nowhere near being a contender for that position, it is fast becoming a regional lingua franca in Greater China among ethnic Chinese. The number of Confucius Institutes — comparable in mission and objectives to other more established national counterparts like British Council, Alliance Française, Goethe-Institut and Instituto Cervantes — keeps expanding in different parts of the world. The increasing demand for the Chinese language worldwide is indicative of China's expanding sociopolitical influence internationally, suggesting that in the not-too-distant future a knowledge of Putonghua and Chinese literacy has great potential for making the speaker more competitive in the global job market. In short, being able to speak English **and** Putonghua/Mandarin fluently will be an important asset for anyone preparing for a professional career in the multilingual workplace. This is why English and Putonghua figure so prominently in the SAR's language-in-education policy of 'biliteracy and trilingualism'.

The rationale behind the needs-driven 'biliteracy and trilingualism' policy is hardly disputable. What remains controversial is the right and reasonable target level of attainment (e.g. is it '**balanced** biliteracy and trilingualism' or '**functional** biliteracy and trilingualism'?),[4] and, once the goal post is agreed, how to get from where we are to where we want to be. At the moment, no attempts have been made to define exactly what level of 'biliteracy and trilingualism' is intended, although this is often understood implicitly as native-speaker-based standards in terms of the four skills (hence 'balanced' rather than 'functional'), as evidenced in the 'complaint tradition' and public discourse on 'errors'. Since explicit instruction through classroom teaching tends to be the only means by which the majority of Hongkongers can gain access to English and Putonghua, for over two decades there has been an ongoing debate regarding the most productive way(s) of teaching these two important languages (see e.g. Lin 1996, 1997, 1999; Johnson 1997; Johnson and Swain 1997). Lin and Man (2009) offer a timely, detailed account of the key issues involved in this debate. Various bilingual education models and experiences which have been implemented in other countries like Canada, Singapore and Malaysia are discussed and their relevance to Hong Kong carefully analyzed. The 'mother tongue education' policy, introduced in September 1998, consists of streaming Primary-school leavers to English-medium (EMI) and Chinese-medium (CMI) Secondary schools depending on their relative academic performance in Chinese and English (for the streaming mechanism, see below). This 'late immersion' policy, effective for three years till the end of Junior High School (Secondary 3, Grade 9, aged around 15), is premised on the theoretical assumption that teachers and learners ought to stick to the same language of classroom interaction, be it English or Cantonese. Any form of 'code-mixing' is seen as undesirable and detrimental to the development of the target language.[5] After having been implemented for over a decade, the late immersion policy did not seem to be as effective as hoped, as shown in the English language attainment of students' public examination results (Hong Kong Certificate of Examinations, HKCEE; Hong Kong Advanced Level Examinations, HKALE). This has sparked criticisms and triggered suggestions for alternative modes of bilingual education (e.g. mixed-mode teaching, whereby less language-dependent subjects such as Music, Art and Mathematics are taught in English, while more language-dependent subjects such as History and Geography are taught in the students' mother tongue; see Lin and Man (2009) for more details). As of the time of writing (June 2009), the Education Bureau (EDB) has just announced the timeline for implementing the 'fine-tuning policy' (effective from September 2010), with Secondary schools being given more flexibility — subject to specific EDB guidelines — when deciding which language to select as the medium of teaching and learning for a particular class/subject. Still, the MoI debate mediated by mass media shows no signs of abating.

The debate is further compounded by the need to introduce Putonghua into the Primary school curricula. To date, Putonghua is taught and learnt as a school subject at the Primary (in some schools, Secondary) level. The learning outcomes are clearly unsatisfactory, a fact which adds ammunition to those who are advocating for teaching Chinese subjects (mainly Chinese Language and Chinese History) in Putonghua. The PMI (Putonghua-medium instruction) project has been piloted at the Primary level under the aegis of the government; many educationalists believe that it will eventually be implemented Hong Kong-wide. Opponents (see e.g. Bauer 2000) are concerned about the continued vitality of the community's (now) dominant vernacular, once school children are no longer taught to pronounce Chinese characters in Cantonese. And, in terms of facilitating learning and teaching, there is no doubt that using the students' (and teachers') most familiar vernacular — Cantonese for the majority — as the medium of instruction will remove unwanted language barriers in the give-and-take between teachers and students. One way out of the quagmire, according to some advocates of a radical position, is to implement real 'mother-tongue education' by officially declaring Cantonese to be the primary (i.e. unmarked) language of instruction in secondary education across the board (e.g. Bauer 2000). It remains unclear, however, how such a position would be received by stakeholders — notably the government, parents and educationalists — and whether the outcome of English learning would be compromised.

Below, I will briefly outline the main concerns of the SAR government and various stakeholder groups vis-à-vis the vicissitudes of the MoI policy with regard to English as the medium of instruction: employers, parents, school principals, teachers and educationalists, and students. The purpose is to help disentangle the complexity of the picture viewed from the respective vantage points of these groups.

The MoI debate: Key stakeholders' concerns

Hong Kong (SAR) government. It is almost a cliché today to say that Hong Kong is the meeting place between East and West. Her success story, one that features a remarkable transformation from a sleepy fishing village set against a barren rock in the 1840s to an international metropolis cum global financial centre rivalling New York, London and Tokyo in the 21st century, is arguably sui generis. For all this to happen, it can hardly be denied that English has played an instrumental role, albeit with the key players being members of the English-educated elite. Like the central government in Beijing, the SAR government is acutely aware of the significance of English to the continued well-being of Hong Kong, and so English figures prominently in the curricula of the local education system. Every year, a significant percentage of the SAR's GDP amounting to multi-million (HK) dollars is budgetted for education-related expenses, with a view to improving the quality of English language teaching and learning (Miller and Li 2008), but the overall returns are disproportionate and disappointing by any standards. The two main factors discussed above — a lack of a conducive English-learning and English-using environment on one hand, and tremendous typological differences between the two languages Chinese and English on the other — represent two main obstacles which militate against the government's efforts to upgrade Hongkongers' general proficiency and standards of English. The promotion of Putonghua through classroom teaching is no easy task either. Apart from considerable phonological differences between Cantonese and Putonghua, a lack of opportunities for meaningful practice outside the classroom is another real obstacle. A further thorny issue is the limited number of qualified teachers of Putonghua, who are needed in the thousands given the size of the schooling population at Primary level (around 100,000 at Primary One) each year. These obstacles notwithstanding, there are two recent trends which seem to provide some room for optimism: (a) in the 'fine-tuning policy' the government seems to have adopted a more tolerant stance toward the 'mixing' of languages in the school curriculum which, as Lin and Man (2009) have observed, could be an effective bilingual education strategy if done properly (cf. Lin 1996, 1999); and (b) independently of the government's efforts to raise the quality of the teaching of English and Putonghua in school, more and more Hongkongers (especially working adults) are willing to learn English and Putonghua in an attempt to enhance their competitiveness when job-hunting (Miller and Li 2008).

Employers. Opening the job advertisement pages of any local newspapers on any day, including e-dailies, one will notice that virtually all of the job adverts — from managers to messengers — require applicants to have at least some knowledge of English, in addition to Cantonese. Where interaction with non-Cantonese-speaking business representatives in mainland China is an important part of the job specification, an additional working knowledge of Putonghua is a must. Today, the business environment in Hong Kong, like elsewhere in Greater China, clearly favours multilingual workers. Those who are conversant in more than one Chinese 'dialect' (e.g. Shanghainese or Chiu Chow, the latter being the home dialect of Mr. Li Ka-Shing, a well-known philanthropist and the richest person in Hong Kong) will have an advantage — if their wider linguistic repertoire could be put to meaningful use on the job. Indeed, multilingualism is increasingly valued by multinational consortiums as an important asset and a key to business success (Li 2007). No wonder employers from the business sector are among the most vocal critics, whose voices deploring Hong Kong students' 'declining English proficiency' are often amplified in mass (both print and electronic) media (cf. the 'complaint tradition' discussed above). While similar criticisms have not yet been extended to Hong-kongers' non-standard Putonghua, such criticisms are conceivable the more widespread Putonghua becomes in the local business sector. It is therefore understandable why some business enterprises are among the staunchest supporters of various language enhancement schemes (e.g. HSBC's support for workplace English), typically in addition to boosting their staff's language skills through in-house, on-the-job corporate training, which tends to include some elements of ESP (English for Specific Purposes) (and increasingly Putonghua as well).

Parents. Hong Kong parents have an unmistakable preference for their children to be educated through the medium of English, to the point of moving into neighbourhoods with a marked concentration of English-medium schools, so as to maximize the chance of their children being allocated to an English-medium Secondary school (Li 1999). Such a preference has been variously analyzed as a form of passive, uncritical submission to the global hegemony of English ('English linguistic imperialism' being a form of 'linguicism', Phillipson 1992), as opposed to an active, conscious wish to embrace and partake of the linguistic capital of the de facto global language (Li 2002). In any case, it cannot be denied that many Hong Kong parents tend to be unaware of the kinds of support or preconditions needed — if the placement of their child in an EMI school is to be an educationally sound decision. Crucial to this decision are two key factors: the amount of home support for English (e.g. one or more English-speaking parent, access to a private tutor, availability of learning resources such as language games, etc.), and their child's aptitude to learn through the medium of English. Research in SLA has shown that some children/learners are more gifted at foreign language learning than others (see e.g. Skehan 1989; Dörnyei 2005). In the absence of either condition — or worse, both conditions — then requiring one's child to learn content subjects through English is not at all a wise decision. Indeed, in whichever direction the MoI policy may be further developing, there is clearly a need for the government to step up the efforts to 'educate' parents in order to bring home this important message. This could be done, for example, by making available or pointing the way to useful resources, including those on the internet, so that parents could find out more about various factors which are conducive to effective language learning. This type of information may be useful for helping at least some parents to arrive at their own informed decisions.

School principals. School principals have the responsibility of ensuring the survival of their school, which hinges on how successful it is in attracting academically high-performing students. Given Hong Kong parents' preference for English-medium education, being able to claim 'EMI status' would naturally work to the advantage of the school. The government is clearly aware of this, and so a lot of effort has been made to monitor the qualifications and actual EMI-teaching capabilities of the teaching staff in self-proclaimed EMI schools. One critical issue arising from the mother tongue education policy is stigmatization: other things being equal, a CMI school/student is generally perceived as lower in standard compared with an EMI school/student. This has been a major point of contention between supporters and opponents of this policy; it is also ostensibly the main reason for the most recent 'fine-tuning' initiative, which according to government officials is intended to deliberately blur the distinction between CMI and EMI schools as part of an attempt to counteract social stigmas engendered by the labelling effect of 'dual-medium-of-instruction' streaming.

Teachers and educationalists. Stigmatization as a direct consequence of the 'dual-medium-of-instruction' streaming policy is one of the most serious concerns among conscientious teachers and educationalists. Another main concern of frontline teachers is the government's stance toward (Cantonese-English) 'code-mixing', which is commonplace in those EMI lessons (including English lessons in CMI schools) where keeping to English often makes it difficult for students to follow. As mentioned earlier, until recently the government was rather intolerant of 'code-mixing', largely out of a concern that 'mixing' the languages would deprive students of precious exposure to good English. This concern is well taken; yet one lingering problem remains nevertheless: by sticking to a language which is less familiar to some students and unfamiliar to others, the immediate and arguably higher-order objective of learning is being sacrificed. In this regard, if the conjecture that the government has adopted a more tolerant stance toward language alternation (i.e. the use of bilingual teaching strategies) in class is accurate, that would be pedagogically a most welcome development.

Students. Hong Kong students are clearly aware of the linguistic capital associated with the successful acquisition of English and, to a lesser extent, Putonghua. Owing to the abovementioned obstacles, however, the majority find it a very difficult if not an impossible task to master both effectively. For Primary students, the dual-medium-of-instruction streaming or selection process is a source of anxiety. Once the results of the streaming are announced, both EMI and CMI students have their respective worries. EMI students would worry about, among other things, having to learn — typically by rote — a seemingly endless list of English vocabulary words in the textbook of practically every school subject (except Chinese Language and Chinese History). The teachers' input is often difficult to follow if not downright incomprehensible. Whether the EMI student is able to cope depends to a large extent on the availability of home support and/or access to additional private tuition. CMI students, on the other hand, may have the 'luxury' of learning through their mother tongue, but they will have to put up with a lingering concern that, in the long run, they may be worse off as they do not have a body of English lexicon for academic purposes, which is an important prerequisite for securing a place in a local university. In the past decade, there is ample evidence, including longitudinal research and news reports, showing how CMI Secondary school leavers are disadvantaged by a lack of EAP (English for Academic Purposes) knowledge in high-stake public exams such as HKCEE and HKALE (e.g. research conducted by Tsang Wing Kwong and associates, CUHK 2008; see also Clem 2008) and/or after they have successfully entered an EMI university. The research question — when the most opportune time for effecting a transition from CMI to EMI education (i.e. Secondary Four, Five, Six or Seven) is — remains a tricky one. Finally, it should be remembered that CMI students, who make up the majority (ca. 70%) of all Secondary-school leavers, are the most vulnerable of various stakeholder groups, for they are the ones who bear the brunt of stigmatization. Many have to cope really hard to overcome the psychological barrier of being socially labelled 'second best'.

Conclusion
At the dawn of a new millennium, there is no doubt that Hong Kong SAR, the most cosmopolitan and internationalized of all Chinese metropoles, has evolved into and depends for its survival on how well it fares as a knowledge-based economy. Most of the economic activities require a workforce with a reasonably high level of proficiency in English and Putonghua. Given the significance of these two languages to Hong Kong's socioeconomic vitality, continued prosperity and sustainable development, it comes as no surprise that English and Putonghua should figure so prominently in the Hong Kong SAR government's language-in-education policy, which came to be known as 'biliteracy and trilingualism'. There are however two rather serious problems as the government and citizens of 'Asia's World City' alike grapple with the task of becoming biliterate in Chinese and English, and

trilingual in Cantonese, English and Putonghua. The first problem is concerned with a lack of a conducive language environment for using and practising English and Putonghua in authentic situations. Another way of putting it would be to say that, being foreign languages, English and Putonghua are hardly used for authentic meaning-making purposes among Cantonese-speaking Hongkongers. The use of only English or Putonghua when conversing with fellow (Cantonese-speaking) Chinese Hongkongers is so highly marked that one is burdened with some sort of justification if one initiates, and seeks to maintain, an English-only or Putonghua-only conversation. Conversely, one could say that the widely perceived unmarked language choice for intraethnic communication is Cantonese, a fact that may be explained by the demographic or ethnolinguistic pattern of Hong Kong, which has always been a Cantonese-speaking Chinese society. Indeed, as Bolton (2003) has observed, in earlier sociolinguistic research on Hongkongers' language use patterns, it was not uncommon to find commentaries that Hong Kong was ethnically a (relatively) homogenous society.

Another major problem concerns the high degree of linguistic dissimilarity between Chinese and English (Li in press). Typologically, they belong to different language families with very different linguistic characteristics from phonology to lexico-grammar, from orthography to information sequencing. In terms of the relative (un)ease of acquisition, one consequence for Hong Kong Chinese learners of English — as a foreign rather than a second language — is that linguistically very little of what they know about their mother tongue (Cantonese) has any reference value in the strenuous process of learning English. While the same cannot be said of the learning of Putonghua, which shares many cognates with Cantonese lexico-grammatically and which adopts the same orthography, it is no easy task for Cantonese-speaking Hongkongers to master the pronunciation system in Putonghua. The considerable discrepancy between the vernacular and standard written Chinese suggests that the term 'mother tongue education' is in one sense a misnomer, for Hong Kong Chinese school children do not write the way they speak (Li 2000, 2006).[6]

In short, for Chinese Hongkongers the road toward biliteracy and trilingualism is a bumpy one and those on board are riddled with plenty of dilemmas. Everyone knows that the continued well-being of Hong Kong SAR depends crucially on a biliterate and trilingual workforce. However, the collective ethnolinguistic identity of Chinese Hongkongers is so strong that initiating or maintaining a conversation in a language other than Cantonese is generally perceived as highly marked and in need of some sort of justification (sometimes implicitly, e.g. to avoid excluding a non-Cantonese-speaker in the conversation). This results in an odd situation commonly found in foreign language learning settings: many eager learners of English and Putonghua are ready to pay an exorbitant fee to some tutorial centre, typically charged by the hour, just to be given the opportunity to practise using the target language with other like-minded learners, often under the guidance of a native-speaker tutor. This consumer demand is probably what the writer of the following advertising slogan for a learning centre has in mind (english town, May 2009): "It is wrong to study English!" ("學英語是錯的!", subtext in Chinese: you can't master English by studying it; practice is the key, which is our teaching philosophy). The same may be said of the learning of Putonghua: many are aware that a high level of proficiency in the national language is a key that helps open many doors in the workplace, and yet outside the classroom it is very difficult to find natural opportunities for meaningful practice.

What this means is that the learning of English and Putonghua is very much confined to classroom teaching as a school subject. The limitations of this teaching and learning approach are well known, and so for over a decade, the Hong Kong (SAR) government has sought to enhance teaching and learning effectiveness by providing EMI education to those students who have demonstrated a certain level of ability to learn through English (students are selected through a scoring mechanism known as MIGA, or Medium of Instruction Grouping Assessment, see Lin and Man (2009) for more details).[7] Some 11 years after the 'mother tongue education' policy has been implemented, the results leave much to be desired. In addition, as briefly discussed above, the policy has also antagonized various stakeholder groups, who are displeased with it in one way or another. Some of their more salient concerns are summarized as follows:

- Employers find it difficult to recruit employees with a high-enough level of English and Putonghua skills needed for the workplace;
- Parents resent dwindling opportunities for their children to be educated through English;
- Principals of CMI schools are weary of adverse consequences brought about by the public's perception that their teachers and students "lack the competence" to teach and learn in English; should this lead to dwindling student numbers, it would pose a threat to the school's survival (according to the policy, schools can only 'survive' if they have attained a certain student number);
- Teachers — of CMI and EMI schools alike — find it difficult to abide by an EDB guideline against any form of code-alternation (Lin 1996, 1999); and
- Students of CMI students have to put up with being stigmatized and socially labelled as 'second best', while many EMI students have to cope with varying degrees of cognitive problems in the process of learning through a language that they are less familiar/unfamiliar with.

The rationale behind the 'biliteracy and trilingualism' policy is beyond dispute, which to a large extent may be regarded as a linguistic reality thrust upon Hongkongers as the former British colony gradually evolved into a knowledge-based economy toward the end of the last century. In the absence of a conducive language-learning environment, and given the considerable linguistic differences between Cantonese/Chinese and English on one hand, and Cantonese and Putonghua on the other, it does not seem obvious how the many dilemmas of various stakeholder groups outlined above may be resolved. The 'fine-tuning policy', due to be implemented in September 2010, is expected to give schools more flexibility in terms of language choice for a particular class or subject (subject to specific EDB guidelines). Insofar as it aims to minimize social divisiveness by blurring the CMI/EMI divide, it is worthy of support. In the long run, late immersion may be a way out. No doubt it will be an uphill battle; to inform ongoing policy adjustments, what is needed is sound empirical research in locally based bilingual teaching strategies, as well as methodologically well-conceived experimentation with different modes of immersion and models of bilingual education (Lin and Man 2009).

Notes

* This article has benefited from constructive comments and insightful feedback from two anonymous reviewers as well as Angel Lin and Evelyn Man. I alone am responsible for any inadequacies that remain.

1. For a discussion of the nuanced conceptual distinction between such related terms as 'Modern Chinese' (*xiandai Hanyu*, literally 'modern language of the Han people'), 'Modern Standard Chinese', 'Putonghua' and 'Modern Written Chinese', see Li (2006: 152–153).

2. For a discussion of the extent to which English in Hong Kong may be characterized as a 'new variety' (cf. five criteria, Butler 1997: 106), see Li (2008a) and Li (in press).

3. I am indebted to Reviewer B for pointing this out to me.

4. Being functionally trilingual does not mean that the learners/users are 'balanced trilinguals' in terms of being equally highly proficient in all three languages. Instead, functional trilingualism is a more realistic goal, in that it is broadly understood as the learners'/users' ability to use the three languages to varying degrees of proficiency and for different purposes.

5. There is some empirical evidence showing that code-mixing is due in no small measure to a 'medium-of-learning effect', i.e. English-L2 learners' cognitive dependence on English terminology as a direct result of studying through the medium of English (Li 2008b).

6. Of course the same learning difficulties can be expected when English-speaking or Putonghua-speaking learners learn Cantonese, but research has shown that the former can get by with little or no knowledge of Cantonese (Tinker Sachs and Li 2007), while the latter can often assume that Hongkongers will make an effort to speak to them in the national language (e.g. mainland tourists shopping in Hong Kong).

7. From September 2010 onwards, a new version of the Secondary School Places Allocation (SSPA) mechanism will be used for streaming all primary-school leavers to CMI/EMI schools; see EMB (2005).

References

Bauer, R.S. (2000) Hong Kong Cantonese and the road ahead. In D.C.S. Li, A.M.Y. Lin and W.K. Tsang (eds), *Language and Education in Postcolonial Hong Kong*, pp. 35–58. Hong Kong: Linguistic Society of Hong Kong.

Bolton, K. (2003) *Chinese Englishes: A Sociolinguistic Survey*. Cambridge: Cambridge University Press.

Butler, S. (1997) Corpus of English in Southeast Asia: Implications for a regional dictionary. In M.L.S. Bautista (ed.), *English is an Asian Language: The Philippine Context*, pp. 103–124. Manila: Macquarie Library.

Census and Statistics Department, Hong Kong Government (2007) *Hong Kong 2006 Population By-Census Main Report Volume I*. Retrieved 28 Sept 2008 from http://www.censtatd.gov.hk/freedownload. jsp?file=publication/stat_report/population/B11200472006XXXXB0400.pdf&title=Hong+Kong+2006 +Population+By-census+Main+Report+%3a+Volume+I&issue=-&lang=1&c=1

Chan, A.Y.W., B.S.C. Kwan and D.C.S. Li (2002) An algorithmic approach to error correction: Correcting three common errors at different levels. *JALT Journal* 24(2): 201–216.

Chinese University of Hong Kong (CUHK) (2008) CUHK Faculty of Education releases findings of the study: "The Effect of Medium-of-Instruction Policy on Education Advancement". Press Release, 14 March. Retrieved 12 July 2009 from http://www.cuhk.edu.hk/cpr/pressrelease/080314e.htm

Clem, W. (2008) Research casts doubts on mother-tongue education. *South China Morning Post*, 15 March.

Dörnyei, Z. (2005) *The Psychology of the Language Learner: Individual Differences in Second Language Acquisition*. Mahwah, NJ: Lawrence Erlbaum Associates.

Education and Manpower Bureau (EMB), Government of HKSAR (2005) Medium of instruction for secondary schools and secondary school places allocation. Education and Manpower Bureau, The Government of the Hong Kong Special Administrative Region. Retrieved 12 July 2009 from http://www.edb.gov.hk/ FileManager/En/Content_1914/moisspa%20booklet%20dec%202005_eng.pdf

Gordon, R.G., Jr. (ed.) (2005) *Ethnologue: Languages of the World*, 15th ed. Dallas, TX: SIL International. http://www.ethnologue.com/web.asp

GovHK (2009) Task force identifies 6 industries to be developed. *news.gov.hk*. 3 April. Retrieved April 2009 from http://news.gov.hk/en/category/businessandfinance/090403/html/090403en03004.htm

Hung, T.T.N. (2000) Towards a phonology of Hong Kong English. *World Englishes* 19(3): 337–356.

Hung, T.T.N. (2002) English as a global language: Implications for teaching. *The ACELT Journal* 6(2): 3–10.

Jenkins, J. (2003) *World Englishes: A Resource Book for Students*. London, New York: Routledge.

Johnson, R.K. (1997) The Hong Kong education system: Late immersion under stress. In Johnson and Swain (eds), pp. 171–189.

Johnson, R.K. and M. Swain (eds) (1997) *Immersion Education: International Perspectives*. Cambridge: Cambridge University Press.

Kachru, B.B. (1985) Standards, codification, and sociolinguistic realism: The English language in the outer circle. In R. Quirk and H.G. Widdowson (eds), *English in the World: Teaching and Learning the Language and Literature*, pp. 11–30. Cambridge: Cambridge University Press.

Kachru, B.B. (2005) *Asian Englishes: Beyond the Canon*. Hong Kong: Hong Kong University Press.

Kirkpatrick, A. (2007) *World Englishes: Implications for International Communication and English Language Teaching*. Cambridge: Cambridge University Press.

Li, D.C.S. (1999) The functions and status of English in Hong Kong: A post-1997 update. *English World-Wide* 20(1): 67–110. Reprinted in K. Bolton and Y. Han (eds) (2008) *Language and Society in Hong Kong*, pp. 194–240. Open University of Hong Kong Press.

Li, D.C.S. (2000). Phonetic borrowing: Key to the vitality of written Cantonese in Hong Kong. *Written Language and Literacy* 3(2): 199–233.

Li, D.C.S. (2002) Hong Kong parents' preference for English-medium education: Passive victims of imperialism or active agents of pragmatism? In A. Kirkpatrick (ed.), *Englishes in Asia: Communication, Identity, Power and Education*, pp. 29–62. Melbourne: Language Australia.

Li, D.C.S. (2006) Chinese as a lingua franca in Greater China. *Annual Review of Applied Linguistics* 26: 149–176.

Li, D.C.S. (2007) Multilingualism and commerce. In P. Auer and Li Wei (eds), *The Handbook of Multilingualism*, pp. 423–443. Berlin: Mouton de Gruyter.

Li, D.C.S. (2008a) Review of K. Bolton (2003) *Chinese Englishes: A Sociolinguistic Survey*. Cambridge: Cambridge University Press. *Hong Kong Journal of Applied Linguistics* 11(1): 99–102.

Li, D.C.S. (2008b) Understanding mixed code and classroom code-switching: Myths and realities. *New Horizons in Education* 56(3): 17–29.

Li, D.C.S. (in press) Improving the standards and promoting the use of English in Hong Kong: Issues, problems and prospects. In A.W. Feng (ed.), *English Language Use and Education across Greater China*. Clevedon: Multilingual Matters.

Li, D.C.S. and A. Chan (2001) Form-focused negative feedback: Correcting three common errors. *TESL Reporter* 34(1): 22–34.

Li, D.C.S. and E.C.Y. Tse (2002) One day in the life of a 'purist'. *International Journal of Bilingualism* 6(2): 147–202.

Lin, A.M.Y. (1996) Bilingualism or linguistic segregation? Symbolic domination, resistance, and code-switching in Hong Kong schools. *Linguistics and Education* 8(1): 49–84.

Lin, A.M.Y. (1997) Bilingual education in Hong Kong. In J. Cummins and D. Corson (eds), *The Encyclopedia of Language and Education: Bilingual Education*, Vol. 5, pp. 279–289. Dordrecht: Kluwer Academic Publishers.

Lin, A.M.Y. (1999) Doing-English-lessons in the reproduction or transformation of social worlds? *TESOL Quarterly* 33(3): 393–412.

Lin, A.M.Y. and E.Y.F. Man (2009) *Bilingual Education: Southeast Asia Perspectives*. Hong Kong: Hong Kong University Press.

Luke, K.K. (2005) Cong shuangyu shuangyan kan Xianggang shehui yuyan bianqian [Bilingualism and diglossia: Sociolinguistic changes in Hong Kong]. *Zhongguo Shehui Yuyanxue [The Journal of Chinese Sociolinguistics]* 1: 82–88. [In Chinese.]

Matthews, S. and V. Yip (1994) *Cantonese: A Comprehensive Grammar*. London: Routledge.

McArthur, T. (2001) World English and world Englishes: Trends, tensions, varieties and standards. *Language Teaching* 34: 1–20.

Miller, L. and D.C.S. Li (2008) Innovations in ELT curricula and strategies of implementation in Hong Kong SAR. In Y.H. Choi and B. Spolsky (eds), *ELT Curriculum Innovation and Implementation in Asia*, pp. 71–100. Seoul: Asia-TEFL.

Milroy, J. and L. Milroy (1985) *Authority in Language: Investigating Language Prescription and Standardization*. 2nd ed. London, New York: Routledge.

Phillipson, R. (1992) *Linguistic Imperialism*. Oxford: Oxford University Press.

Seidlhofer, B. 2004. Research perspectives on teaching English as a lingua franca. *Annual Review of Applied Linguistics* 24: 209–239.

Skehan, P. (1989) *Individual Differences in Second-Language Learning*. London: Edward Arnold.

Snow, D. (2004) *Cantonese as a Written Language: The Growth of a Written Chinese Vernacular*. Hong Kong: Hong Kong University Press.

Tinker Sachs, G. and D.C.S. Li (2007) Cantonese as an additional language: Problems and prospects. *Multilingua* 26: 95–130.

English in China

Convergence and divergence in policy and practice

Anwei Feng
Bangor University, UK

This paper starts with an overview of the sociolinguistic context and a series of policy documents concerning English language education promulgated recently in China. It moves on to an analysis of disparities in English language education policies practised in different regions, differences between urban and rural areas, between social classes and between linguistic minority and majority groups. The juxtaposition aims to reveal what different regions and social and ethnic groups in China have in common and how divergent they can be in terms of local policies and practices in English language provision. Also discussed in the paper are issues such as tensions between the spread of English and Chinese language education, and between mother tongue, Chinese and English language education in the case of minority groups, inequality in education and other linguistic, political and cultural dimensions.

Introduction

Recent scholarship on English in China has shown a consensus that the role and status of English in the society and in education have reached unprecedented heights (Hu 2008; A.W. Feng in press; Gil and Adamson in press). The exponential spread of English has been particularly evident since the turn of the century when the central education authorities promulgated a series of documents promoting the language in schools and tertiary institutions. The whole country seems to be mobilized for their implementation. Official statistics cited in Wen and Hu (2007) claim that the overwhelming majority of over 226,000,000 students in primary and secondary schools and in universities study English taught by a strong force of English teachers numbering 850,000 in the country. There is common agreement that the last couple of decades have witnessed the fastest growth in English language education.

Despite the rapid increase of English use in Chinese society in general and the popularity of English language education, tensions remain high between the spread of English and the national language, Mandarin Chinese,[1] for the majority group of the country, and between the minority home language,[2] Mandarin Chinese as a second language and English as a third language in the case of a typical minority group. The provision of the English language in schools in economic and socio-political powerhouses and in coastal regions differs enormously from that in inland and remote regions. Even within the same geographical location, whether it is an economic and sociopolitical centre or a small town in a remote region, access to resources for English language learning can vary greatly from one social group to another. Arising out of this context are vexing issues such as social and ethnic divisiveness and inequality in education. This paper provides a general description of the

AILA Review 22 (2009), 85–102. DOI 10.1075/aila.22.07fen
ISSN 1461–0213 / E-ISSN 1570–5595 © John Benjamins Publishing Company

policies and practices pertinent to English language education at various governmental levels, state and regional, and a critical analysis of the thorny issues in this most populous country in the world.

State policies from a historical perspective

To discuss how state policies regarding foreign language education are formulated and implemented in China, scholars usually start with detailed reviews of the history of sociopolitical changes and examine how these changes were reflected in foreign language policies and practices (Fu 1986; Li et al. 1988; Ross 1993; Adamson 2004; Wen and Hu 2007). Many trace the policies and practices to the 19th century when China established its first formal foreign language schools in Beijing, Shanghai and Guangzhou in the early 1860s after the country had lost in the Opium War and realized its backwardness and the importance of learning Western technology to strengthen the country. This led to the Self-Strengthening Movement in the late 19th century (see Fu 1986; Li et al. 1988; Ross 1993). The underlining rationale for these reviews is clear: there is always a strong link between education, including foreign language education, and politics (UNESCO 1996: 92–94; Byram 1997: 43–47, 2008).

Numerous descriptions of foreign language education policies made in the P.R.C. period clearly show the interrelationship between foreign language education and the country's political agenda. Since 1949 when the Chinese Communist Party (CCP) took power, there have been several major policy shifts in foreign language education (Fu 1986; Ross 1993; Adamson 2004). In the early P.R.C. period when the CCP turned to the Soviet Union for mentorship, they condemned English officially as the language of the enemy and made Russian a prestigious foreign language in China. In the late 1950s, however, when the Sino-Soviet relation turned sour, Russian lost its popularity and English gradually became the favoured foreign language. During the first half of the Cultural Revolution (from 1966 to 1976), foreign languages were broadly associated with bourgeois ideology and foreign language teaching was literally banned. Many teachers of foreign languages, particularly Western language teachers, were victimized (Cortazzi and Jin 1996; Adamson 2004). Some foreign language education programmes resumed after China regained membership in the United Nations at the end of 1971 and when the then US president, Richard Nixon, visited the country in the following year (Wen and Hu 2007). Nevertheless, these programmes were run on a limited scale at the university level and there was hardly any formal foreign language provision for the whole education system until 1976 when the Cultural Revolution ended due to the death of the then paramount leader, Mao Zedong, and in the following year when the country resumed its entrance examination for university education.

Since 1977, English language education has been part of China's 'reform and open-door' strategy, and English has been increasingly taken as essential for its 'Four Modernizations' ambition, aiming to modernize agriculture, industry, national defence and science and technology (Ross 1993; Adamson 2004). Numerous national policies have been promulgated to promote English language teaching all over the country. To Wen and Hu (2007: 8–9), before the turn of the century, the most impactive policies included: the 'Proposals for Enhancing Foreign Language Education' disseminated by the Ministry of Education in 1979; the 'Plan for University English Teacher Training' issued by the State Council in 1980; and the 'College English Syllabus for Science and Technology Students' and the 'College English Syllabus for Arts and Social Sciences Students' promulgated in 1985 and 1986, respectively. These documents pushed the popularity of English language learning to an exceptional height in the country. Among them, the most prominent were the two College English syllabuses issued in 1985 and 1986. The impact of the policies on English language education was largely attributed to the fact that the tests for both syllabuses, called CET 4 (College English Test — Band 4) and at a higher level CET 6 (College English Test — Band 6), have been nationally perceived as the key to personal and institutional success since it was first administered nation-wide in 1987.

As test designers and educators long believed in giving priority to reading skills for Chinese students (Dong 2003; Yang 2003), the TOEFL-like tests traditionally placed great emphasis on reading skills and vocabulary (65% of marks were given to reading and vocabulary and the remaining 35% to listening and writing). The two tests are administered twice annually nation-wide.

For a long time, the pass certificates of the tests, particularly CET 4, have put huge pressure on students and other stakeholders in tertiary institutions. First of all, the CET 4 certificate is linked in many tertiary institutions with the university degree; this was especially so in the 1990s (Wang 1991; M. Feng 1995; Q.D. Wu 2005). On the job market, many employers in China, not only private or foreign-owned companies but also public sectors such as government departments, regard the certificate(s) as an important recruitment criterion. For a university, the pass rate of its students is often associated with its academic reputation; for College English teachers, the pass rate may have direct effect on promotion. It can be argued that it is the nation-wide CET 4 (and the CET 6), which has been at the centre of debate in recent years (see Yang 2003; Liu and Dai 2004), rather than the Syllabuses, that has brought about a national campaign for English since its appearance in 1987. This campaign has affected all stakeholders in tertiary institutions and impacted strongly on the society as a whole. Primary and secondary schools have been particularly impinged upon due to the common belief that the nurturing of real communicative competence in English should start from an early age and thus English language education should be systematized for all stages of education.

A 'typical pupil' today

Since the turn of the century, China has continued to develop rapidly, particularly on the economic front, and the English language has become even more popular in society as well as in education. In 2001, against the backdrop of the country's successful bid for the 2008 Summer Olympics and its successful application for the WTO (World Trade Organization) membership, three policy documents were disseminated by the Ministry of Education to promote English language education throughout the country. The first two specify new English Curriculum Standards (ECSs) for primary and secondary schools (see Figure 1 for a graphic representation of different levels) (Cheng in press). The first was issued to primary schools, stipulating that English provision was to start from Year 3 in all primary schools by the autumn of 2002 (Ministry of Education 2001a). On the premise that primary school leavers achieve Level 2 in the language, the second set up specific English standards for secondary schools, with Level 5 being for junior secondary school leavers and Level 8 for senior secondary school leavers (Ministry of Education 2001b). Attached to the second document as its appendices are specific requirements for pronunciation, vocabulary, phrases, grammar, functional and notional inventories, and even a long list of English expressions to be used in classrooms. Both documents are claimed to have been formulated with extensive consultations with experts and educators and are intended to be applied nation-wide. Suggestive in the documents is the intention to robustly promote English teaching and learning and to standardize teaching philosophy, approaches, as well as levels of English proficiency for school children at different stages, even though mention is made of the diversity of pupils' background, resources, and other contextual factors.

While the ECS documents for primary and secondary schools appear conventional with very specific inventories of lexical and grammatical items for acquisition (similar to the College English syllabuses issued in 1985 and 1986, but for different levels), the third document makes a short but significant 'suggestion' for a new approach to English language education at the tertiary level. Although it is not a document specifically written for foreign language education, under its general title, *Guidelines for Improving the Quality of Undergraduate Teaching* (Ministry of Education 2001c), it stipulates that 5 to 10% of the tertiary courses for undergraduate students be conducted in English or another foreign language within three years after the issuing of the documents, a tall order few

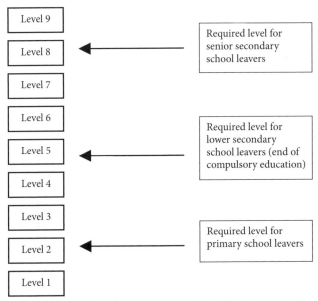

Figure 1. English proficiency levels from primary up to secondary school graduation (Source: Ministry of Education 2001a, b).

in China could miss. The paragraph containing this stipulation is short but significant for it was the first official endorsement of this strong form of bilingual education, i.e. using 'two majority languages' as the media of instruction (Baker 2001: 194), in this case, English, the international language, alongside Chinese, the national language of the country. The endorsement was partly due to the wide dissatisfaction of the outcomes of traditional EFL teaching (A.W. Feng 2005) and partly due to the increasing awareness of research published internationally that provides evidence of the effectiveness of the Content-Language Integrated Learning (CLIL) approach (Baetens Beardsmore 1993; Khoo et al. 1994; Met 1998) and to the fact that many schools and universities in coastal cities had already been practising it (A.W. Feng 2005). It is, however, important to point out here that the fact that the paragraph in the document legitimizes the use of a foreign language as a medium of instruction contradicts the language law of the country (this issue will be taken up later).

At the same time, at the tertiary level, College English education has continued as usual, though its syllabus has undergone several revisions in the new century because of the impact of the three 2001 documents. The most notable revision was made in 2004 when the Ministry of Education issued the *College English Curriculum Requirements* as a trial version and formally promulgated it to the whole country three years later (Ministry of Education 2007). The document suggests changes to teaching approaches, learning objectives and assessment, and a better link with the ECSs for schools. On entrance, tertiary students are to be allocated into three tiers according to their 'levels' as defined in Figure 1 above. Those who achieved Level 7 are to be allocated to the 'Normal Requirement' tier; those at Level 8 are classed into the 'High Requirement' tier; and those who managed to get Level 9 are streamed into the 'Advanced Requirement' tier. As far as objectives of learning are concerned, there is clear emphasis on the overall competence of English rather than on only certain language skills such as reading. Specific requirements are set for all language skills, namely speaking, listening, reading, writing and translation. Even the teaching approach is specified. Computer-Aided Language Learning is strongly promoted. Formative assessment is encouraged with criteria specified in the document. The summative tests, CET 4 and CET 6, are played down (in fact, they are not mentioned in the document). More freedom is given to individual institutions to set up their own assessment systems. Noticeably, the time for English teaching and learning which used to be given in terms of hours/week in its predecessors is missing, but the document stipulates that in principle English takes 10% of the total credits required for undergraduates.

In the meantime, the tests, CET 4 and CET 6, were under reform, not to make them more popular in the society, but quite the contrary, to reduce the social impact of the tests (Q.D. Wu 2005). To this end, it is stated in policy documents that only registered university students can take the tests. There will be no certificate to differentiate test takers by grades such as 'fail, pass or good pass' in percentages but only a report to show individual scores up to 710. Apparently, the test report resembles that of TOEFL. What is more, the link between the test certificate and the university degree established in many universities is officially claimed to be inappropriate and thus should be severed (Wen and Hu 2007). Despite the reforms and official speeches aiming to reduce the social impact such as that by Q.D. Wu (2005), the tests have remained as popular as ever (Zhang 2008), and a commonplace statement made in mass media is that the CET 4 and CET 6 certificates, now called reports, are as important as the graduation certificate for university students.

The current policy documents depict a seemingly elastic but linear model envisaged by policy makers, which is much more complex than those developed in the past. To enable readers to see an overall picture of the model as elaborated in the recent policy documents, particularly in terms of exposure to English, Figure 2 gives a graphical representation of the class time a 'typical pupil' is expected to spend on English from primary schooling up to graduation from a tertiary institution.

It is important to note in Figure 2 that for the nine-year compulsory education, standards of English proficient are clearly defined. A pupil has to meet the required level to proceed to the next stage. Flexibility appears only when a pupil enters senior secondary school. However, the document for tertiary education explicitly requires a minimum Level 7 for tertiary English education. The same is true for College English tests. Although formative assessment is encouraged, CET 4 and CET 6 are as popular as ever. The bottom line for a 'typical pupil' is that, if he/she wishes to move upwards to a good senior secondary school upon finishing compulsory education, he/she has to reach Level 5. If he/she wishes to attend university, Level 7 is the minimum. At the university, he/she has to get a certificate, now called a 'report', of CET 4 and ideally CET 6 as well in order to gain access to a decent job in a big company or a government department. The flexibility as suggested in policy documents, thus, may seem politically right but the system is as rigid as ever.

To sum up, the development in English language education has been unprecedented due to China's 'reform and open door' strategies aimed at modernizing the country's economy and at geopolitical influence. Policies on English language education have been ambitious. There has been a dramatic increase in English-knowing graduates since the end of the Cultural Revolution. In today's China, rapid development of its economy and its growing political influence seem to justify all the means (i.e. policies). So far, the balance between various ideologies, sociopolitical forces, and the spread of English seems to be maintained well in general. How long can this balance be upheld? How are state policies implemented locally? To what degree are they altered in different geographical conditions and social and ethnic contexts? What factors may affect the maintenance of this balance? The following sections shall examine these questions.

Cultural and linguistic tensions

Despite the popularity of English language education, there are fervent debates on the sociopolitical and cultural consequences. First of all, many policy makers show concerns about the wide spread of English language education and make frequent calls to emphasize Chinese in school curriculums,

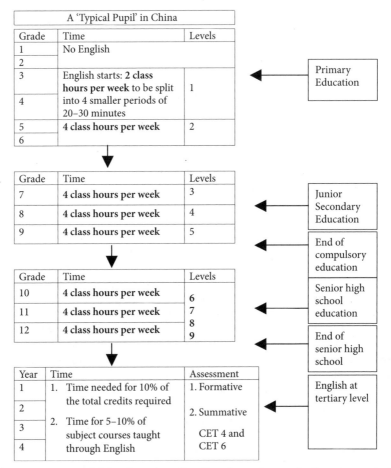

Figure 2. Time spent on English by a 'typical pupil' in China from primary schooling up to graduation from a tertiary institution

or to keep Chinese at the centre of language education (*Zhongguo Jiaoyubao* 2003; Yuan 2005). In the same vein, some educators assert that learning English as a lingua franca is a double-edged sword (K.Q. Xu 2003). It eases communication with people all over the world, but at the same time it threatens mother tongue language and culture. Therefore, Xu (2003) argues that patriotism, traditional values, and 'mother tongue'[3] language and culture must remain at the core of school curriculums. Some other educators, however, adopt a utilitarianist view which A.W. Feng (2007:272–273) defines as instrumental value given to a language such as English for accessing the knowledge of sciences and technology in that language in order to facilitate economic development and nation building in general. Feng gives two examples. The first is B.H. Wang's (2003:16) assertion that "we must enhance our study of English so as to enable us to rapidly grasp the advanced scientific knowledge and technology of the developed countries". The other is G.Y. Huang's (1997:2) strong statement made in the preface of his monograph on English language education:

> In the open-door era, we emphatically promote English language education because we wish to acquire stones from other mountains to build our own garden into a genuine place of civilisation

for new generations. We hope that our new generations will no longer need to spend so much time on foreign languages. They should have more time engaging in creative activities. (author's translation)

The strongest challenge is posed to the use of English as a medium of instruction in classrooms. As a strong form of bilingual education (Baker 2001), it is widely reported as effective and as a solution to the long-felt ineffectiveness of traditional EFL teaching. It has become extremely popular in recent years, mostly in metropolitan areas and other prosperous regions (B.H. Wang 2003; A.W. Feng 2005). In his critical analysis of the phenomenon, Hu (2007, 2008) characterizes the spread of this form of bilingual education as a 'craze' for English and draws parallels between the 'craze' and the 'Great Leap Forward', a campaign for economic modernization launched in 1958 by the then paramount leader, Mao Zedong, which led to disastrous consequences. On legal, political and cultural bases, opponents of Chinese-English bilingual education such as Ma (cited in *Nanfang Dushibao* 2004) make stern calls to prevent using English as a medium of instruction in the classroom. Ma, first of all, sturdily rejects such practice from the patriotic perspective of protecting national sovereignty and national security. He further robustly argues that the strong form of bilingual education violates the national language law promulgated in 2000 by the Standing Committee of the People's Congress. Indeed, Article 10 of the Law of the People's Republic of China on the Use of Language and Script which came into effect in January 2001 ordains that all educational institutions in China, excluding those of minority groups, must use Mandarin as the primary teaching language and adopt standard Chinese written characters as the written form. Ironically, this legal accusation against using a foreign language as a medium of instruction has not resulted in any official response to clarify the situation. According to Chen (2002), linguists, lawyers, and policy makers are aware of the 'unlawful' situation bilingual education is in, but they argue that bilingual education is a recent phenomenon and regulations or laws governing it will follow soon. Up till now, however, there has been no new law known to the author to rectify the situation. This ambiguous situation markedly demonstrates tensions between various ideological and social-cultural forces, hidden or overt, and between globalization and patriotism or nationalism. These tensions impact strongly on academic discussions and bilingual education practice.

While most discussions are focussed on the issues and challenges faced by the majority Han group in relatively developed regions, relatively fewer voices are heard from educators and researchers who teach and study minority nationalities about the impact of English language education on them. Both the policy documents and the unprecedentedly high status of English in prosperous societies have clearly impacted powerfully on minority groups in China (A.W. Feng 2005; J. Yang 2005). Linguistically, it is widely accepted that minority home languages are further threatened by foreign languages in addition to the strong influence of the majority language, Chinese. B.L. Huang (2007, in press) has observed that in Guangxi Zhuang Autonomous Region, the home language, Zhuang, is being increasingly ignored in societies and schools, while the importance of English for the region and for individuals has radically increased due to highly profitable international mega-events such as the China-ASEAN Exposition that is held annually, and because of the regional government policies to promote English language education. Feng and Sunnudula (2009) report that many Zhuang student interviewees in their research referred to Zhuang, unconsciously perhaps, not as a language for the indigenous group but as a 'dialect' of Chinese. In a remote village school in Yunnan attended by Naxi children, according to Blackford and Jones's research (in press), an English teacher, though poorly trained, has been available to the school to offer English in recent years, but the Dongbawen (the Naxi written language) teacher who used to be there disappeared. In the Naxi-dominated area, they were told that less than 2% of the indigenous Naxi people could read and write in their own language. These findings help explain why, in discussing the impact of English on minority groups, many authors (e.g. Bastid-Bruguiere 2001; Beckett and MacPherson 2005) argue that the national drive for English language education is further empowering the already powerful majority Han group, leaving minority and indigenous peoples further behind.

Divergence of policy and practice

Even though China is a country that has been traditionally characterized by a centralized, top-down system, regional variations do exist in terms of state policy implementation. The process of policy formulation at the local level in response to state policies can be rather complex (Feng and Sunnudula 2009), and the real-world practices can differ tremendously (Cortazzi and Jin 1996). These variations can be broadly grouped into three categories: coastal-inland and urban-rural disparities; variations in terms of access to English due to socioeconomic factors; and differences between ethnic groups. In the following sections, these differences will be elaborated on sequentially, but a focus is placed on the last category, i.e., disparities in English provision between ethnic groups. The rationale behind this focus will be provided in the discussion section.

Regional and urban-rural differences

In this most populous country, it can be argued that it is impossible for any policy to be implemented in a uniform, homogeneous fashion, and thus regional differences should be the norm. In Hu's (2003) report of his survey among 439 students from different parts of China but studying in Singapore, he notes significant differences in English language education between what he calls coastal regions such as Shanghai, Beijing and Guangdong and inland regions such as Gansu, Hubei, Hunan, Anhui and Sichuan. He states that these regions differ not only with regard to infrastructural resources and thus pupils' language proficiency, but also in terms of teaching pedagogy and pupils' learning behaviour. Indeed, differences in terms of policy implementation, exposure to English and language learning resources can hardly be overestimated. A local government may carry out a state policy exceedingly far or water it down in its implementation (Feng and Sunnudula 2009). Learners of English in major economic and political powerhouses such as Shanghai and Guangzhou may have access not only to teaching by qualified teachers at any age from kindergarten to an advanced level, but also to all modern facilities such as multimedia laboratories and computers, to private tuition by native speakers of English and even to tours abroad to gain direct exposure to English used in naturalistic settings (A.W. Feng 2005; Zou and Zhang in press), whereas in underdeveloped regions, it is an issue to provide even the basic foreign language education specified in policy documents.

An empirical research study is reported by Y. Wu (2008) in which great disparities were found between urban and rural schools. This was a comparative study of two urban schools and two rural schools, one primary and one secondary for each, in Shiyan, a major city in the northwest of Hubei. With regard to the qualifications of teachers of English, Table 1 gives a clear comparison of the teachers in the four schools. The most notable finding in Wu's study is that the rural primary school did not start English teaching from Year 3 until 2003. This school enrolled 624 students at the time of the study, but the only teacher of English left the school after one year of teaching there. Although the pupils are still said to have two lessons of English per week, they do so through distance learning — VCDs and satellite TV — and there is hardly any face-to-face support by a professional teacher. On the other hand, both the urban schools have offered English teaching far beyond the hours required by the policy document. The urban primary school, for example, starts English from Year 1 — three class hours per week — and the city secondary has employed two foreign teachers of English.

Table 1. Comparison of the qualifications of teachers of English in four schools in Shiyan (slightly adapted and translated from Y. Wu 2008)

Highest degree earned	City secondary	City primary	Rural secondary	Rural primary	Total
Master	3	1	0	0	4
Bachelor (4 years)	4	2	3	0	9
Certificate (3 years)	3	2	3	0	8
High school	0	1	5	1	7
Total	10	6	11	1	28

Differences in English accessibility by socioeconomic status
It is a commonplace headline in mass media that English courses are widely available in the market, but they can be exceedingly costly. The fee for a kindergarten place in a bilingual preschool in 2005 in Harbin in northern China was as high as RMB 16,000 (roughly USD 2,300) which was well above the average family income of RMB 10,000 (USD 1,430) in the same year (*Harbin Ribao* 2005). In Guangdong, there are even stories of rich parents who hire temporary helpers to queue for bilingual school places for their children (A.W. Feng 2005). The Wall Street Institute with its headquarters in Baltimore, Maryland, USA, established in 2000 its sub-colleges in Shanghai and Beijing and charged a high fee of RMB 29,200 (USD 4,200) per student for a flexible 6- to 12-month course. However, it managed to enrol more than 7,000 students in 2002, most of whom were reportedly white-collar office workers (J. Wang 2002). The high costs of bilingual preschools and schools and other kinds of private English providers themselves show how popular English courses are in metropolitan areas and prosperous regions. Individuals and parents are apparently willing to invest in English at all cost because of the perceived high social status of English.

As far as English education at schools is concerned, many agree that the national drive for English language acquisition exerts more pressure on parents than on pupils. Zou and Zhang (in press) provide empirical evidence to show how parents in Shanghai attach high value to English and what measures they take to ensure that their children do not lose out in the 'national movement'. They report that the most popular schools are Min Ban Schools (MBSs), literally 'People-Managed Schools', which are known as the best schools, but fee-paying, and which are required to follow national curricula. Entering such a school is on a competitive basis and attending it is financially challenging for most families (RMB 7,000–10,000, roughly USD 1,000–1,470). Nonetheless, MBSs are extremely popular, especially if an MBS is claimed to feature strong English education. One of Zou and Zhang's findings is a comparison of English learning effectiveness in the three types of schools: MBSs claimed to feature strong English education, ordinary MBSs, and ordinary state schools. They administered a proficiency test among 2,034 students in Grade 9 in these schools and obtained the results as shown in Table 2.

The correlation between the expenditure and the test results is obvious, although Zou and Zhang (in press) caution that the MBS students should score higher as they entered the schools with higher marks in all subjects including English. Interestingly, they also surveyed among the same group of students what types of commercial extracurricular activities and schools available in the Shanghai market the students choose to attend, or which their parents select for them (they listed eight types of extracurricular classes and activities in their questionnaire for the students to choose from), and what effect these have on their English language learning. Table 3 gives the results of their survey.

Table 2. Comparison of the results of English Proficiency Test by types of schools (extracted from Zou and Zhang in press)

	MBSs featuring strong English education	Ordinary MBSs	Ordinary urban schools
Expenditure per student (Chinese RMB)	19,028	10,974	6,531
Mean scores	75.19	69.64	53.67

Table 3. English Proficiency Test scores by types of English learning activities students attend, their family income, and expenditure on the activities (adapted from Zou and Zhang in press)

Family income	None	One type	Two types	Three or more types	Total	
High	5 (3.2%)	52 (32.9%)	55 (34.8%)	46 (29.1%)	158	$X^2 = 114.95$
Mid-high	8 (1.8%)	149 (34.4%)	151 (34.9%)	125 (28.9%)	433	$df = 9$ $p = .000$
Mid-low	41 (6.4%)	273 (42.8%)	203 (31.8%)	121(19.0%)	638	
Low	42 (18.2%)	121 (52.4%)	54 (23.4%)	14 (6%)	231	
Cost/student (RMB)	1,830	4,387	7,006	8,978	$F = 96.735$	$p = .000$
Mean scores	56.55	57.59	59.52	61.02	$F = 2.848$	$p = .036$

Though the correlation between the quantity of English learning opportunities and the test scores is discernable, it is not as plain as that between the MBSs and state schools as shown in Table 2. The most relevant point of the data, as far as this paper is concerned, is that the parents of all economic conditions have invested heavily in their children's English. In a highly commercialized society such as Shanghai, however determined parents are, access to English as a commodity is no doubt in the hands of the rich.

The findings suggest that even in the same geographical location, socioeconomic factors contribute to a worsening situation with regard to inequality in education which may lead to further social divisiveness. Research and discussions on English language provision in China from a socioeconomic perspective are still rare. However, the importance of a thorough understanding of the socioeconomic dimension in education can hardly be overestimated because consequences of further social stratification and uneven socioeconomic development can be dire.

Disparities in English provision by ethnicity
Divergence in terms of local policies and practice in English provision is most outstanding when it comes to China's minority groups, numbering more than 100,000,000 in population, most of whom are spread in remote and mountainous regions in the country. Because of geographical, historical and political reasons, there have always been attempts by policy makers in the central government to set up separate policies for minority groups, although many state policies such as the ECSs are claimed to apply to all schools in the country. One year after the promulgation of the ECSs, in 2002, the State Council issued a directive on minority language education with a statement that implicitly excluded minority groups from the promotion of English language education. The directive (The State Council 2002) states that, in bilingual education, which usually refers to minority language and Mandarin Chinese education, "the relationship between minority home language and the Mandarin Chinese

should be correctly managed. ... English should be provided in regions where favourable conditions exist". The directive offers no explanation of how 'correct management' is defined and what the 'favourable conditions' are. It therefore leaves much room for interpretation, and for justifying local policies which deviate from the state system.

Despite the incompatibility in the policy documents, in minority education, the past few years have witnessed a growing literature on the notions of *Sanyu Jiantong* ('trilingualism' or 'mastery of three languages': the minority home language, Mandarin Chinese and English) and *Sanyu Jiaoyu* ('trilingual education'). The literature gives some evidence on how the ECSs are implemented locally: they may be watered down or even ignored in some minority regions and prefectures. Regional responses are usually determined by various contextual factors, political, geographical and/or sociocultural. While some authors (e.g. W.Z. Wang 2000; Jing 2007) show optimism for trilingualism and trilingual education for minority pupils, most commentators and practitioners list the difficulties minority students face in learning English, from lack of resources to cognitive, affective and sociocultural problems minority pupils show to experience in learning a foreign language (Ju 2000; Tian 2001; Y.M. Wu 2002; Y.L. Li 2003; Xiang et al. 2004; J. Yang 2005). Many policy makers and educators hold the view that minority pupils do not cope with foreign language learning as well as their majority counterparts, and the required standards for them should thus be lower than those specified in the state policy documents.

In terms of local policy making and implementation, most local governments in minority dominated or minority and majority mixed regions and communities have responded to the 2001 policies, with some more so than others. Quangxi, the Zhuang Autonomous Region, is such an example. The Regional education authority responded with strategic plans; even in poor areas such as Baise, efforts are made by local authorities to train English teachers for schools. Most Zhuang students are kept in the system, although it is acknowledged that it takes more time to provide pupils in remote areas with English from primary school onwards than in geographically advantaged regions such as major towns and cities (Feng and Sunnudula 2009). English language education may be further enhanced with the rapid economic development in the region (B.L. Huang in press). In Yunnan Province where 25 minority groups are distributed in different regions, mostly mountainous areas, efforts have been made by the provincial government to provide English for minority pupils according to the state policies, even though resources are very limited at the present stage (Blachford and Jones in press). In these regions, minority children appear to follow the same system as the majority children, although, as mentioned before, the issue of maintaining their linguistic identity has become more acute (B.L. Huang 2007, in press; Feng and Sunnudula 2009; Blachford and Jones in press).

In some regions, however, minority children are apparently kept out of the national system. Unlike their majority counterparts in the same region, according to Olan's (2007) research, most minority students in Xinjiang were not offered English during their nine-year compulsory education. Most of her research subjects — tertiary students — did not start English learning until they entered university. Sunnudula and Feng (in press) found that a 'draft plan' issued by the education bureau of the Uyghur Autonomous Region in 1977 is apparently still in effect today. The plan states explicitly that while majority Han children start foreign language learning from Year 3 onwards, "no foreign language courses are to be provided for minority schools". Today, even in minority-majority mixed schools in Xinjiang, according to Tsung and Cruickshank's (2009) study, the draft plan is still followed: the majority Han children start English from Year 3 and the Uyghur children begin Mandarin Chinese as a second language from the same year onwards. A disheartening situation has thus arisen:

> Before the 1980s, Chinese schools offered Uyghur lessons to Han students from Year 3, so Han students could speak Uyghur language; so Han and Uyghur children would play together. It was good for them to have this language exchange and mutual understanding. It is different now. After the open and reform policy, Han parents are only interested in their children learning English and schools have replaced Uyghur language lessons by English lessons. Han students don't learn Uyghur language any more. After school many Han parents send their children to English tutoring classes or mathematics tutoring. Han and Uyghur children no longer play together. (A quote by a teacher, Tsung and Cruickshank 2009: 8)

In this case, the local policies to provide English to the majority group but not the minority groups have apparently widened the gap and created more segregation, rather than integration, between children of different ethnic groups.

The second disparity that exists between the minority and majority groups is, strictly speaking, not caused by deviation of local policies from the state policies, but by default of teaching resources and the examination system that are historically formulated. This is the issue of *Zhongjieyu*, the language used to teach and learn English and to compile textbooks for minority pupils. Traditionally, this language has been mostly Chinese for the simple reason that most teachers of English are Chinese speakers, and textbooks are compiled by Chinese writers and use Chinese as *Zhongjieyu*. So, minority students have to depend on their second language rather than their mother tongue as *Zhongjieyu* to learn the third language. Their mother tongue hardly plays a role in the learning process. With the growth of the trilingualism and trilingual education literature, this issue has gradually attracted some attention and has been studied in recent years. Research has already shown that the use of the mother tongue as *Zhongjieyu* is more effective in helping minority students to acquire a third language (J. Xu 2000; Xiao 2003). Sunnudula and Feng (in press) also report that their interviewees agreed unanimously that the use of the mother tongue rather than the second language facilitates the thinking and learning process. However, their data show that the use of the mother tongue in high-stake exams is unusual, and minority students are disadvantaged because there are always test items that require test takers to translate sentences from English to Chinese, and vice versa. Minority groups such as Tibetans and Uyghurs have a strong desire to maintain their linguistic and cultural identities, and their mother tongues are often official languages in the regions where they live. In these regions, Sunnudula and Feng (in press) argue that when pupils' home language is used not only for classroom teaching and learning but also in high-stake examinations, they will be less disadvantaged. Pupils may feel confident in keeping their linguistic identity and become empowered through learning a third language. Without a system that fully honours their home languages, Sunnudula amd Feng state that this remains speculative.

Addressing the differences?

The discussion above demonstrates that, in this gigantic country of China, the kaleidoscopic variety of English language educational policies and practices makes the attempt for a simple typology innately problematic. The 'typical pupil' as portrayed in the first half of the paper may exist given the large learner population, but the typicality makes sense only as a benchmark for most stakeholders. The privileged and those who strive to become members of the privileged group in the society try hard to surpass the 'typical pupil' model, while the underprivileged and the marginalized have to settle for less than the 'typical'. This situation can be explained by the concept of linguistic capital, now frequently used by foreign language education theorists to refer to fluency in a prestigious language or international language used by groups who possess economic, social, cultural and political power and high status in local and global society (Morrison and Lui 2000). Economically and socio-politically privileged groups have an upper hand as they have access to the resources necessary for amassing this capital and the power to make the rules that appear that they gain it legitimately. As Bernstein (1971:202) points out, "how a society selects, classifies, distributes, transmits and evaluates the educational knowledge [the linguistic capital in this case] it considers to be public reflects both the distribution of power and the principles of social control" (insertion by the author).

Thus, it can be argued that disparities caused by socioeconomic factors are perhaps inevitable and they will exist as long as inequality in a society exists. This explains why social divisiveness and inequality in English access are commonly reported in many societies such as Hong Kong (Morrison and Lui 2000; D.C.S. Li in press) and Singapore (Tupas in press). Theoretically, therefore, it may be extremely difficult to eradicate the issues. However, it is possible for a government to make evidence-based policies to minimize the problems. The recent effort to 'fine-tune' the medium of instruction policies in Hong Kong after many years of research and debate can be seen as a step moving in this direction (Lin and Man 2009; D.C.S. Li in press). In Mainland China, research such as the study carried out by Zou and Zhang (in press) has started, but extensive research and discussion are essential to inform policy-making. In addition, as discussed above, geographic factors augment the complexity of the situation. Disparities in access to English provision between coastal and inland regions and between the urban and the rural have been historically thorny issues. It is widely reported that there have been policies made to address the differences. Admittedly, however, it is hard to imagine that, without huge investments by the central and local government and solid commitments by several generations of the country, a village school in remote regions could have similar access to quality education as a school in the Zhujiang Delta Region or Shanghai.

Turning now to disparities in terms of English provision by ethnicity, we see that the main issues are separate policies, sometime overt and sometimes hidden, for minority and majority groups practised in many regions and the issue regarding *Zhongjieyu*. These two issues are interrelated. The former is apparently attributed to the fact that minority children need to study Chinese as a second language while there is no such need for the majority counterparts. Because of this, the two groups should be treated differently. Although the consequences may be dire, there does not seem to be an alternative in the current sociopolitical context. The literature showing the difficulties the minority children face in learning the third language seems to provide evidence in support for different policies for different ethnic groups (Xiang et al. 2004; J. Yang 2005). Nevertheless, it seldom gives evidence on what factors cause the difficulties and how tri/multilingual competence can be effectively developed. Trilingualism is by no means an unusual phenomenon and it has proved to be a common occurrence in many countries in Europe, Africa and Asia. Cenoz and Genesee (1998) in an overview of the concept in relation to bilingualism remark that the latter helps the acquisition of a third language rather than hinders it. Cenoz and Jessner (2000) and Cenoz, Hufeisen and Jessner (2001) have researched the cognitive advantages and meta-linguistic awareness of bilingualism in third language acquisition from pedagogical and psycholinguistic perspectives. The theoretical discussions and case studies reported by Cenoz and colleagues and by Hoffmann and Ytsma (2004) suggest that, for meaningful and effective trilingual education, pupils' experience of acquiring a second language is crucial and, equally importantly, trilingual education programmes need to be planned and implemented with a full understanding of the educational, geographical, sociolinguistic and political dimensions.

Although models and theories developed in one context may not apply to another, they can serve as a starting point for constructing models that suit the other. With this insight, this paper argues that, for trilingual education to be effective in China, minority education policy makers and researchers need to first of all address three outstanding issues. The first is the issue of the acquisition of the first language, the mother tongue, in the learners' long journey to become trilingual. The importance of mother tongue acquisition for a child's cognitive development is well documented in the literature (Baker 2000; Benson 2005). If a child does not acquire age-appropriate language competence in at least one language, usually his/her mother tongue, the child may find it difficult to cope with any school subject. Nowadays, when minority children in China start schooling, they are either submerged in learning through the medium of Chinese or taught in their mother tongue but transited to Chinese instruction in a few years because of the nation-wide examination system (A.W. Feng 2005). Many of the minority children may have what Cummins (2000) calls the Basic Interpersonal Communication Skills (BICS) in both languages, but lack the Cognitive Academic Language Proficiency (CALP) in either to cope with school subjects. Thus, they usually lag behind their mainstream counterparts. Therefore, extensive research is needed to inform policy making and to develop models that are workable for different minority groups in different contexts.

In learning the third language, the issue of *Zhongjieyu*, as discussed before, is also under-researched. Experiments with the use of minority languages as *Zhongjieyu* in classrooms have begun to surface (J. Xu 2000; Xiao 2003), but they seem to have made little impact on policy making and practices. There is no known study into how using minority test takers' second language as *Zhongjieyu* in high-stake examinations can affect their performance and how using their mother tongue as *Zhongjieyu* in teaching, learning and assessment can improve their understanding and performance in exams and empower them. Sunnudula and Feng (in press) suggest that this is a serious issue awaiting an answer. Adamson and Feng (2009), however, point out that the seemingly linguistic question may well be a political question.

The third and perhaps the most important is the issue of whether there should be different policies for minority students and majority students. The dire consequence of such differentiation has been reported by researchers such as Tsung and Cruickshank (2009). Another important point is made by Feng and Sunnudula (2009) and Sunnudula and Feng (in press) on the basis of their research among minority tertiary students in three minority regions. They found that, against all odds, many minority students were highly motivated to learn English. This was because for most academic subjects, they were usually shown by test marks as the weaker group compared with their majority counterparts. However, they found themselves competitive in English or courses conducted in English. Many of them invested heavily in English as they took the language as linguistic capital for negotiating their identities. Sunnudula and Feng (in press) therefore argue that if minority groups are expected to be integrated into the mainstream society, which is a widely acknowledged political objective, it is then important to keep them in the system. Any policies to differentiate educational opportunities and standards by ethnicity are therefore misinformed. Those policies, once made, would not benefit the minority groups; on the contrary they would segregate them further from the mainstream society and put them on an unequal footing for life opportunities.

Conclusion

There is little doubt that China is experiencing rapid development on all fronts, including foreign language education. Foreign language education — English in particular — has undergone tremendous changes and transformations in recent decades. Policy makers and academics such as Cheng (in press), Wen and Hu (2007) and Q.D. Wu (2005) are often aware of limitations of the policy documents and theoretical issues concerning foreign language acquisition and assessment. Understandably, they often discuss such issues as at what age a child is likely to benefit most in foreign language learning, which language skills are most important for foreign language learners, in what order they can be effectively acquired, and how the competence in a foreign language can appropriately be assessed. These are important questions for policy studies, of course. However, it is hoped that this paper has provided some evidence that there is potentially a vicious cycle in which social stratification can be exacerbated by inappropriate language policies, which may result in more severe inequality in education, and in turn lead to further social and ethnic divisiveness. These can have negative consequences. These issues are vitally important for China, but are under-researched and insufficiently discussed in the literature. In combatting these issues, all stake-holders have a role to play, but the role of researchers and policy makers at various levels is undeniably crucial.

Notes

1. Mandarin Chinese is known as 'Putonghua' in China. Strictly speaking, however, Putonghua (literally 'common speech') refers to the official Chinese spoken language, the phonology of which is based on that of the capital, Beijing, while Mandarin Chinese is a category of related Chinese dialects spoken across most of northern and southwestern China. The standard written form of Chinese is referred to as Vernacular Chinese. Though some linguists and writers still make a distinction between these terms in their writings, most use 'Putonghua', 'Mandarin Chinese' and even simply 'Chinese' interchangeably to refer to both the spoken and written forms of contemporary Chinese. This paper follows the mainstream. It is also worth pointing out that, although Putonghua or Mandarin Chinese differs greatly from some 'related' languages such as Cantonese and Hakka and they are mutually unintelligible, the latter are officially defined as 'dialects' of Chinese. In the 'dialect'-speaking regions, the language used in formal domains such as the classroom should be Putonghua or Mandarin Chinese according to the Language Law of the country (*National Law* 2000).

2. 'Minority home language' in this paper refers only to a language spoken by an officially defined minority nationality (there are 55 minority nationalities altogether). It does not refer to any other language or 'dialect' of Chinese such as Cantonese. A minority home language, although it may only exist in its spoken form with some minority groups, can be used in classrooms and other formal domains by the Language Law.

3. Many Chinese scholars such as K.Q. Xu (2003) use the term 'mother tongue' to refer broadly to all varieties of Chinese spoken by the Han people, be it Putonghua, Mandarin Chinese or a 'dialect' of the language.

References

Adamson, B. (2004) *China's English: A History of English in Chinese Education*. Hong Kong: Hong Kong University Press.

Adamson, B. and A.W. Feng (2009) A comparison of trilingual education policies for ethnic minorities in China. *Compare* 39(3): 321–333.

Baetens Beardsmore, H. (ed.) (1993) *European Models of Bilingual Education*. Clevedon: Multilingual Matters Ltd.

Baker, C. (2000) *A Parents' and Teachers' Guide to Bilingualism*. Clevedon: Multilingual Matters.

Baker, C. (2001) *Foundations for Bilingualism and Bilingual Education*. Clevedon: Multilingual Matters Ltd.

Bastid-Bruguiere, M. (2001) Educational diversity in China. *China Perspectives* 36: 17–26.

Beckett, G.H. and S. MacPherson (2005) Researching the impact of English on minority and indigenous languages in non-western contexts. *TESOL Quarterly* 39(2): 299–307.

Benson, C. (2005) The importance of mother tongue-based schooling for educational quality. Paper commissioned for the *EFA Global Monitoring Report 2005, The Quality Imperative*. Retrieved on 12 November 2008 from http://unesdoc.unesco.org/images/0014/001466/146632e.pdf.

Bernstein, B. (1971) On the classification and framing of educational knowledge. In M.F.D. Young (ed.) *Knowledge and Control*, pp. 47–51. London: Collier-Macmillan.

Blachford, D.Y.R. and M. Jones (in press) Trilingual education policy ideals and realities for the Naxi in Yunnan. In A.W. Feng (ed.).

Byram, M. (1997) *Teaching and Assessing Intercultural Communicative Competence*. Clevedon: Multilingual Matters Ltd.

Byram, M. (2008) *From Foreign Language Education to Education for Intercultural Citizenship*. Clevedon: Multilingual Matters Ltd.

Cenoz, J. and F. Genesee (eds) (1998) *Beyond Bilingualism: Multilingualism and Multilingual Education*. Clevedon: Multilingual Matters Ltd.

Cenoz, J., B. Hufeisen and U. Jessner (eds) (2001) *Cross-Linguistic Influence in Third Language Acquisition*. Clevedon: Multilingual Matters Ltd.

Cenoz, J. and U. Jessner (eds) (2000) *English in Europe: The Acquisition of a Third Language*. Clevedon: Multilingual Matters Ltd.

Chen, S.X. (2002) Language law bewilders bilingual educators. *China.org*. [Translated by Chen Chao for *china.org.cn*.] Retrieved 18 August 2006 from http://www.china.org.cn/english/2002/Apr/31210.htm.

Cheng, X.T. (in press) The 'English Curriculum Standards' in China: Rationales and issues. In A.W. Feng (ed.).

Cortazzi, M. and L. Jin (1996). English teaching in China. *Language Teaching* 29: 61–80.

Cummins, J. (2000) *Language, Power, Pedagogy*. Clevedon: Multilingual Matters Ltd.

Dong, Y.F. (2003) Reading and writing should always be given priority in China's English language education. *Wai Yu Jie* [Foreign Language World] 93(1): 2–6. [In Chinese.]

Feng, A.W. (2005) Bilingualism for the minor or the major? An evaluative analysis of parallel conceptions in China. *International Journal of Bilingual Education and Bilingualism* 8: 529–551.

Feng, A.W. (ed.) (2007) *Bilingual Education in China: Policies, Practices and Concepts*. Clevedon: Multilingual Matters Ltd.

Feng, A.W. (ed.) (in press) *English Language across Greater China*. Clevedon: Multilingual Matters Ltd.

Feng, A.W. and Sunnudula M. (2009) Analysing minority language education policy process in China in its entirety. *International Journal of Bilingual Education and Bilingualism*. (iFirst, DOI: 10.1080/13670050802684396)

Feng, M. (1995) A survey of the psychological factors in learning English among students of science and engineering. *Waiyu Jiaoxue Yu Yanjiu* [Foreign Language Teaching and Research] 102(2): 54–57. [In Chinese.]

Fu, K. (1986) *History of Foreign Language Teaching in China*. Shanghai: Shanghai Foreign Language Education Press. [In Chinese.]

Gil, J. and B. Adamson (in press) The English language in China: A sociolinguistic profile. In A.W. Feng (ed.).

Harbin Ribao [Harbin Daily] (2005) English has been pushed to the Altar: Who can afford the cost? 5 December. [In Chinese.]

Hoffmann, C. and J. Ytsma (eds) (2004) *Trilingualism in Family, School and Community*. Clevedon: Multilingual Matters Ltd.

Hu, G.W. (2003) English language teaching in China: Regional differences and contributing factors. *Journal of Multilingual and Multicultural Development* 24(4): 290–318.

Hu, G.W. (2007) The juggernaut of Chinese-English bilingual education. In A.W. Feng (ed.), pp. 94–126.

Hu, G.W. (2008) The misleading academic discourse on Chinese–English bilingual education in China. *Review of Educational Research* 78(2): 195–231.

Huang, B.L. (2007) Teachers' perceptions of Chinese-English bilingual education in Guangxi. In A.W. Feng (ed.), pp. 219–239.

Huang, B.L. (in press) Economic development and the growing importance of the English language in Guangxi. In A.W. Feng (ed.).

Huang, G.Y. (1997) *Yingyu Jiaoyuxue* [On English Education]. Nanchang, China: Jiangxi Jiaoyu Chubanshe. [In Chinese.]

Jing, C.X. (2007) Take language teaching as a starting point to comprehensively implement education for cultivating talents. *Zhongguo Minzu Jiaoyu* [Chinese Minority Education] 2: 30–31. [In Chinese.]

Ju, J.N. (2000) An examination of the problems encountered in teaching beginning minority students at college. *Qinghai Minzu Yanjiu* [Nationalities Research in Qinghai] 11(3): 76–77. [In Chinese.]

Khoo, R., U. Kreher and R. Wong (eds) (1994) *Towards Global Multilingualism: European Models and Asian Realities*. Clevedon: Multilingual Matters Ltd.

Li, D.C.S. (in press) Improving the standards and promoting the use of English in Hong Kong: Issues, problems and prospects. In A.W. Feng (ed.).

Li, L.Y., Zhang, R.S. and L. Liu (1988) *A History of English Language Teaching in China*. Shanghai: Shanghai Foreign Language Education Press. [In Chinese.]

Li, Y.L. (2003) An analysis of the special characteristics of minority students in learning English. *Xinan Minzu Daxue Xuebao* [Journal of Southwest University for Nationalities] 24(8): 334–336. [In Chinese.]

Liu, R.Q. and Dai, M.C. (2004) On the reform of College English teaching in China. *CELEA Journal* 27(4): 3–8.

Lin, A.M.Y. and E.Y.F. Man (2009) *Bilingual Education: Southeast Asian Perspectives*. Hong Kong: Hong Kong University Press.

Met, M. (1998) Curriculum decision-making in content-based teaching. In Cenoz and Genesee (eds), pp. 35–63.

Ministry of Education (2001a) *Guiding Ideas to Promote English Curriculum in Primary Schools by the Ministry of Education (Document No. 2)*. Beijing: Ministry of Education. [In Chinese.]

Ministry of Education (2001b) *Standard of English Courses for 9-Year Compulsory Education and General Senior Secondary Schools (for Experiment)*. Beijing: Beijing Normal University Press. [In Chinese.]

Ministry of Education (2001c) *Guidelines for Improving the Quality of Undergraduate Teaching*. Beijing: Ministry of Education. [In Chinese.]

Ministry of Education (2007) *College English Curriculum Requirements (Document No. 3)*. Beijing: Department of Higher Education, Ministry of Education. [In Chinese.]

Morrison, K. and I. Lui (2000) Ideology, linguistic capital and the medium of instruction in Hong Kong. *Journal of Multilingual and Multicultural Development* 21(6): 471–486.

Nanfang Dushibao [Southern City Daily] (2004) The fight to protect the mother tongue: Meandering on the borders of love and pain. 16 November. [In Chinese.]

National Law on the Use of Common Language and Script (the P.R.C.) (2000) Retrieved 10 July 2009 from http://news.xinhuanet.com/legal/2003-01/21/content_699566.htm. [In Chinese.]

Olan, M. (2007) An investigation of the status quo of minority college students learning English. *Xinjiang Daxue Xuebao* [Journal of Xinjiang University] 35(2): 156–160. [In Chinese.]

Ross, H. A. (1993) *China Learns English: Language Teaching and Social Change in the People's Republic*. New Haven, CT: Yale University Press.

[The] State Council (2002) *State Council's Decision to Further Enhance and Speed Up the Reform of Minority Education*. No. 14. Document issued on 7 July 2002 by the State Council. [In Chinese.]

Sunnudula, M. and A.W. Feng (in press) English language education for the linguistic minorities: The case of Uyghurs. In A.W. Feng (ed.).

Tian, J.L. (2001) Past, today and future of trilingual education in Tibet. *Xizong Daoxue Xuebao* [Journal of Tibet University] 16(4): 49, 75–79. [In Chinese.]

Tsung, L.T.H. and K. Cruickshank (2009) Mother tongue and bilingual minority education in China. *International Journal of Bilingual Education and Bilingualism*, iFirst Article: DOI: 10.1080/13670050802209871.

Tupas, T.R.F. (in press) English-knowing bilingualism in Singapore: Economic pragmatism, ethnic management and class. In A.W. Feng (ed.).

UNESCO (The Delors Report) (1996) *Learning: The Treasures Within*. Paris: UNESCO.

Wang, B.H. (ed.) (2003) *Shuangyu Jiaoyu Yu Shuangyu Jiaoxue* [Bilingual Education and Bilingual Teaching]. Shanghai: Shanghai Jiaoyu Chubanshe. [In Chinese.]

Wang, J. (2002) Is it really true that survival in the training market depends on asking for a 'sky-high price'? *Keji Zhilang* [Scientific Think Tank] 3: 70–73. [In Chinese.]

Wang, J.J. (1991) Rectifying the relationship between the syllabus, teaching and testing and strengthening the administration of College English teaching. Special issue. *Wai Yu Jie* (Journal of the Foreign Language World] 43: 21–24. [In Chinese.]

Wang, W.Z. (2000) An analysis of positive transfer of Zhuang in English acquisition. *Zhongnan Minzu Xueyuan Xuebao* [Journal of South-Central University for Nationalities] 20(1): 122–124. [In Chinese.]

Wen, Q.F. and Hu, W.Z. (2007) History and policy of English education in Mainland China. In Choi, Y.H. and B. Spolsky (eds) *English Education in Asia*, pp. 1–32. Seoul: Asia TEFL.

Wu, Q.D. (2005) A speech at the press conference on CET 4 and CET 6 reforms. *Wai Yu Jie* [Journal of Foreign Languages] 106(2): 2–4. [In Chinese.]

Wu, Y.M. (2002) An analysis of the barriers to learning College English encountered by minority students in Yunnan. *Yunnan Caijing Xueyuan Xuebao* [Journal of Yunnan University of Finance and Economics] 18(6): 116–120. [In Chinese.]

Wu, Y. (2008) A Study of Disparities of English Provision between Urban and Rural Schools in Shiyan and Its Balancing Strategies. MA dissertation, Huazhong Normal University, China.

Xiang, X.H., Du, H.P., Jia, N. and Chen, J.M. (2004) The status quo and suggestion for English language teaching in Tibetan regions. *Xinan Minzu Daxue Xuebao* [Journal of Southeast University for Nationalities] 25(2): 374–376. [In Chinese.]

Xiao, X. (2003) An investigation of Yi-English bilingual teaching at the Xichang School for Nationalities. *Minzu Jiaoyu Yanjiu* [Research on Education for Ethnic Minorities] 14(2): 58–65. [In Chinese.]

Xu, J. (2000) Obstacles of Zhuang students learning English and their solutions. *Minzu Jiaoyu Yanjiu* [Research in Ethnic Education] 2: 72–75. [In Chinese.]

Xu, K.Q. (2003) Beware of the loss of Chinese culture in the fervour of 'bilingual schooling'. *Waiyu Jiaoxue* [Foreign Language Education] 25(3): 86–89. [In Chinese.]

Yang, H.Z. (2003) 15 years of the CET and its impact on teaching. *Waiguoyu* [Journal of Foreign Languages] 245(3): 21–29. [In Chinese.]

Yang, J. (2005) English as a third language among China's ethnic minorities. *International Journal of Bilingual Education and Bilingualism* 8(6): 552–567.

Yuan, G.R. (2005) The phenomenon of stressing foreign languages and weakening mother tongue should be rectified. *Kejiao Wenhui* [Journal of Scientific Education] 5: 24. [In Chinese.]

Zhang, Y.X. (2008) General guidelines for reforming CET 4 and CET 4. *Wai Yu Jie* [Journal of Foreign Languages] 128(5): 2–4. [In Chinese.]

Zhongguo Jiaoyubao [Chinese Education Daily] (2003) Shuangyu jiaoyu yu minzu jingsheng [Bilingual education and national spirit], Section 7. 11 March.

Zou, W.C. and Zhang, S.L. (in press) Family background and English learning at compulsory stage in Shanghai. In A.W. Feng (ed.).

The teaching of English as an International Language in Japan

An answer to the dilemma of indigenous values and global needs in the Expanding Circle*

Nobuyuki Hino
Osaka University

This paper explores the ambivalent nature of Japanese attitudes toward English vis-à-vis the Japanese language, followed by a discussion of Japanese efforts in incorporating the concept of English as an International Language (EIL) into their educational system and teaching practice as a solution to this dilemma. While the Japanese have an indigenous language used for all purposes including academic discourse, in this age of globalization they seem to find it to their disadvantage. The recent move in Japan in both public and private sectors is to promote the use of English even among Japanese people, often at the expense of their native language. One practical approach to a solution or a mitigation of this dilemma is the teaching of EIL or de-Anglo-Americanized English as a means of expressing indigenous values in international communication. Although Japanese teachers of English have not really gone beyond the World Englishes paradigm, which describes the Expanding Circle Englishes including Japanese English as basically exonormative, efforts have been underway in Japan to put the idea of EIL into practice. The teaching of EIL in place of Anglo-American English provides a chance of reconciliation between the use of internal and external language resources.

Introduction

With the increasing number of foreign residents which mounts to over two million (Yamamoto 2007: 1; Ministry of Justice 2008), Japan is faced internally with the task of embracing multicultural and multilingual diversity. In addition to Koreans whose presence in the country stemmed from Japanese colonialism before and during World War II, Japan now accepts long-term residents from such countries as Brazil, China, Taiwan, and the Philippines, among others. Public services for such a variety of linguistic backgrounds, including school education, are being developed at local levels, though quite slowly (cf. Kawahara and Noyama 2007).

In spite of the growing need for multilingualism, linguistic life in Japan is still heavily dependent on the native language of the majority group, known simply as Japanese. Indeed, due to the lack of colonization by Western powers, Japan escaped a possible setback in the public use of their indigenous language. The Japanese language is dominantly used for almost all domains of Japanese life, from family conversation to court procedures. Although some change is perceived which will be discussed later, the language of instruction from elementary schools to universities is basically

AILA Review 22 (2009), 103–119. DOI 10.1075/aila.22.08hin
ISSN 1461–0213 / E-ISSN 1570–5595 © John Benjamins Publishing Company

Japanese, with the exception of the reading assignment at the graduate level where the use of English is not rare.

The dominance of the Japanese language actually presents various domestic sociopolitical problems. Japan has indigenous languages other than Japanese, notably Okinawan (Ryukyuan) and Ainu, but the maintenance of these languages has won very little governmental support, with especially the latter being nearly extinct as a result. Japan has allowed practically no room for the minority native languages in public domains. Linguistic handicaps for the increasing number of foreigners, alluded to above, are also becoming serious social problems. This is evident in the lack of court interpreters for many languages, which makes it difficult to protect the human rights of foreigners involved in court cases.

Unlike some countries in the Kachruvian Outer Circle, where English plays a significant role as a lingua franca between their nationals with different native languages, an intra-national use of English is generally not considered to be a solution for this newly arising diversity of foreign residents in Japan. In view of the fact that these foreign workers, mostly from Latin America and Asia, do not necessarily understand English, such use of English in Japan would create another linguistic divide. The Japanese in general are not proficient in English either. Moreover, as mentioned again below, introducing an internal use of English with no such historical background would indeed be sociolinguistically difficult.

Although it is wrong to regard Japan as a monolingual country, a common misconception traditionally held by the Japanese leadership, it is also true that the Japanese language enjoys an overwhelmingly dominant status intra-nationally. As long as one lives inside of Japan, Japanese is the only language one needs. A recent symbolic example for this is physicist Toshihide Masukawa, a Nobel prize winner in 2008, who is capable of speaking very little English. In spite of his extremely limited oral skills in English, Masukawa was able to achieve the highest position as a scientist.

In contrast to the nearly exclusive use of their native language in domestic situations, the Japanese today are facing a global demand to accommodate themselves to international means of communication, which de facto is English in most cases. As a country belonging to the Expanding Circle in the World Englishes paradigm (B. Kachru 1985), for whom English is a foreign language rather than an internal means of communication, the global need for learning English presents a challenging task for the Japanese at least in two important aspects. Firstly, as a language linguistically unrelated to the Japanese language, English is not an easy language for the Japanese to learn. Otani (2007: 35–47) points out that one of the basic reasons for the notoriously poor performance by Japanese examinees on the TOEFL is the linguistic distance between English and their native language, a stronger factor than the mode of their English language education which is usually held responsible. In view of the fact that few Japanese have ever even tried to learn Korean, which is a language with close linguistic kinship to Japanese, it is ironic that the Japanese now find themselves in a position where their international survival may depend on the learning of this 'alien' language. Secondly, the global use of English means that Japanese people face a formidable task of expressing, in a language embedded in the Anglo-American culture including the Judeo-Christian tradition, their indigenous values which have historically been formulated through the mixture of East Asian influence and their original culture.

In short, the Japanese nowadays seem to be somewhat lost in a limbo between English and their native language. A clue for them to get out of this situation lies in the learning and teaching of English from EIL perspectives, which will be discussed in this paper.

Increasing presence of English in Japan

In response to the global need for the use of English, a trend is perceived in Japan today of incorporating this foreign language in those domains of Japanese life affected by the tide of globalization. The most drastic and controversial of these moves was a proposal by a government-affiliated policy council in 2000 that it should be worth considering designating English as "the second official language" of Japan (*Nijuisseiki Nihon no Koso Kondankai* 2000). Simply put, this idea was, in my interpretation, an attempt to remodel the whole nation into a gigantic English language school which would provide all Japanese with opportunities to acquire the language in their daily lives. Although criticisms voiced by some Japanese that such a proposal would lead to an erosion of their 'national language' may be questionable, it is also uncertain whether it would be sociolinguistically realistic to try to artificially relocate Japan from the Expanding Circle to the Outer Circle where English is used as a second language. However, this proposal by a major government-authorized committee still serves as a salient example of an urge among Japanese today to integrate themselves into English-speaking environment.

In 2003, the Ministry of Education issued a proposal known as "The Action Plan to Cultivate 'Japanese with English abilities'", which further promoted the presence of English in educational contexts. For example, although considerably slow compared to their Asian neighbours such as Korea and China, it was decided by the Education Ministry in 2008 that the teaching of English should start at elementary school instead of at junior high school. These English lessons at elementary school will at least at the outset be limited to only one hour a week, and just for fifth and sixth graders. Still, this new curriculum has not been free from objections, some of which were voiced by leading Japanese teachers of English themselves. In addition to relatively convincing criticism that elementary school teachers have not been provided with the necessary training for teaching English, a controversial claim has been made by some teacher-scholars to the effect that the teaching of English at elementary schools will be tantamount to a reduction of learning opportunities for the native language (e.g. Y. Saito 2005).

As to higher education in Japan, we see an increase in the number of graduate schools, especially in the field of science and technology, where students can pursue their advanced degrees with no knowledge of Japanese as long as they are proficient in English. Not only are the students allowed to write their dissertations in English, which has not been uncommon even in the conventional system, but the classes are taught in English, and discussions are carried out in English. The international programme of frontier biotechnology at Osaka University, as an example, offers such a curriculum. In fact, according to admission information for this five-year course for master's and doctoral degrees, sponsored by the Japanese Government, the only language requirement for prospective students is to have "a good command of English," with no mention of their ability in Japanese (Osaka University 2009a). The establishment of the international graduate programmes, pioneered by the graduate school of technology at Tokyo University in 1989, suggests that the Japanese education system, which has traditionally been monolingual, is under pressure to respond to the need for English as an international language.

Further exploring the case of Osaka University, one of the major national institutions of higher education in Japan, the university leadership has recently been urging their schools and departments, both at the graduate and undergraduate levels, to promote the number of classes taught in English, even in regular programmes. One recent example is a workshop for its faculty members entitled "Communicate and learn with the world: For effective teaching and learning in English," held in July 2009 (Osaka University 2009b), which is aimed at helping the professors, in various fields including human, social and natural sciences, to teach their classes in English.

The purposes of offering the academic courses in English at this university are two-fold. One is to attract more students from abroad, and cater to their linguistic needs, in accordance with the Education Ministry's policy to increase the number of foreign students in this country. The other aim, which is more interesting, is to provide the Japanese students with opportunities to practise English. Although this university policy is not the one that has been proposed by language teaching specialists, this method of learning English could be taken as a form of content-based approach.

In terms of the pressure to use English even inside of Japan where globalization is relevant, the academic circles of applied linguistics are not an exception. For example, for the first time since their foundation over 40 years ago, the Japan Association of College English Teachers (JACET), an affiliate of AILA, recently issued a notice in the call for papers for their annual convention, as an answer to the tide of globalization, that the presentations should in principle be given in English (JACET 2009). It may be added here that the majority of presentations and discussions in most academic conferences in the country, including even those of English language teaching, have traditionally been carried out in Japanese. This fact illustrates the strong tradition of scholarship in the native language of this country, which has been in practice for more than a thousand years (Hino 1992). This new policy by the JACET has stirred some controversy among its members. Some have claimed that it would be much more efficient and natural to present and discuss in Japanese, given the reality that most of the participants at their conferences are Japanese.

All these moves for the use of English even inside of Japan in a way present an ironic picture. The status of English as a second language is a legacy of the colonial past in many countries in Asia and Africa. With the proposal for authorizing English as a second language in Japan, it almost looks as if the Japanese now regret that they have never been colonized by Britain or the USA. In fact, Otani (2007:83–98) equates this proposal with other 'pro-Western' movements in the history of Japan, such as the claims made by political leaders Arinori Mori in 1873 and Yukio Ozaki in 1950, to designate English as the national language in place of Japanese. Likewise, teaching subject matter in English instead of Japanese may seem like returning to the rather primitive teaching practice more than a hundred years ago, where most of the academic subjects had to be taught with textbooks written in English, simply because teaching materials in Japanese were not yet available.

There have been harsh criticisms against the increasing presence of English among the Japanese, no less strong than the well-known arguments on 'linguistic imperialism' such as by Phillipson (1992). Most notable is the one by Tsuda (e.g. 2003), who warns against the menace of "the hegemony of English" for Japan. He argues that the pressure to use English, such as the aforementioned teaching of English at elementary schools, will lead to an erosion of the Japanese culture, or even some mind-control. This criticism is debatable on the basis of the fact that English nowadays is a tool of multicultural communication rather than a means of expressing Anglo-American culture.

Teaching English as a de-Anglo-Americanized language of self-expression

With respect to this dichotomous conflict between English and Japanese, or globalization vs. indigenous values, then, what should be and will be the course Japan is heading for?

First of all, it may be pointed out that a conspicuous sociohistorical pattern of this country is that it does not directly absorb foreign cultures but takes them in through its domestic filters. Things that are foreign to Japan are accepted only after they go through an indigenization process. Although indigenization or nativization is essentially a universal phenomenon, this tendency is often considered to be especially strong in Japan, as analyzed by many Japanese scholars, such as noted economist Iwao Nakatani (2006). In my observation, this cultural template is symbolized, for instance, in the Japanese interpretation of baseball, in which the runners are expected to steal as many bases as they can even when their win is already certain, an act criticized for being unfair in the original American version. Another example, which is closely related to our field of expertise, is the *yakudoku* tradition (Hino 1992) by which foreign language texts are considered read only after they have been translated into the native language. The *yakudoku* method is a deeply rooted sociolinguistic convention in Japan, which dates back to over a thousand years ago when Japanese started studying Chinese, and is still alive and well in the teaching of English in Japan today. Anglo-American values, or varieties of values represented in World Englishes nowadays, are not directly imposed on Japanese readers of English, but are accepted via their own local interpretation. Putting aside an argument as to whether the *yakudoku* method is an appropriate approach to the learning of English today, this Japanese attitude towards foreign cultures seems to indicate that the fear for invasion of indigenous values by English might be a little bit of an overreaction, as far as the reception of English is concerned. It should be noted, however, that the issue of production models of English could be quite another matter, as discussed below.

A solution, or at least mitigation, for the dilemma of English as a global language and Japanese as an expression of indigenous values is the teaching of English as a de-Anglo-Americanized international language. This form of English language education deals with Englishes that are based not solely on the values of the native speakers but on a diversity of values including those of Japanese culture. As for the production of English by the Japanese, this position means to "speak English with Japanese mind" (Nishiyama 1995). There is recently a growing interest in this idea among educators of English in Japan.

Japan has in fact a relatively long history of seeking its own models of English, essentially independent of the major schools of thought such as EIL (Smith 1976, in its early form), World Englishes (B. Kachru 1985), and English as a Lingua Franca (ELF) (Jenkins 2000). As early as 1928, lexicographer Hidezaburo Saito expressed his hope for an English of Japan's own in the preface of his Japanese-English dictionary:

> The mastery of a language has for its final object the expression of the exact light and shade of meaning conceived by the speaker. In a word, the Japanese speaker of English should be original … In short, the English of the Japanese must, in a certain sense, be Japanized. (H. Saito 1928: Preface)

Around 1970, when the Japanese were faced with the growing need for a tool of expressing themselves in international communication, some Japanese scholars pointed out that English could be used as a means of expressing Japanese values rather than Anglo-American culture. Masao Kunihiro, with his proposal for "*eigo no datsu-eibeika*" (de-Anglo-Americanization of English), is the one who first used the word *kokusai-eigo* (International English) in Japanese, making him an EIL pioneer largely unknown outside of Japan. His observation was as follows:

> It seems possible to say that de-Anglo-Americanized English, rather than the one deeply embedded in the Anglo-American culture, more efficiently communicates our own feelings and our original patterns of thought. (Kunihiro 1970: 262, translation mine)

This work by Kunihiro has not only been read by academics and language professionals but also by a great many learners of English in Japan, with its sale of approximately 750,000 copies. With view to the fact that it was not until the mid-1970s that the concept of de-Anglo-Americanization of English became a hotly debated subject in the academic circles at the world level (B. Kachru 1976; Smith 1976), it is remarkable that the Japanese public were already intensely discussing this idea in 1970. This also shows how strong the Japanese sentiment is towards English as an international means of expressing themselves.

Another pioneer thinker in EIL for the Japanese is Takao Suzuki, who expressed the following views approximately at the same time as Kunihiro:

> It would be strange, as we come to use English more extensively, if the features of Japanese English were not internationally recognized. When Japanese people begin to make full use of English, it is

inevitable that the English they use will be 'Japlish' which is influenced by the Japanese language. (Suzuki 1971: 224, translation mine)

This stance by Suzuki may not be readily accepted by scholars of World Englishes. In the World Englishes paradigm, it is generally believed that indigenization of English occurs only when the language is used intra-nationally. However, among the proponents of EIL in Japan, it is assumed that indigenization of English could take place through its international use. This position was reiterated, for example, by Takesato Watanabe:

As Japanese people use English actively, without regarding the Anglo-American English as the only model, an original means of international communication for themselves will emerge. (Watanabe 1983: 9, translation mine)

This claim leads us to the controversial issue of models of English for the Expanding Circle including Japan, which is discussed in the next section.

It must be pointed out that some confusion is observable in the above discourses by the proponents of Japanese English between two seemingly independent factors, that is, the 'linguistic features' of Japanese English and the 'cultural content' expressed in Japanese English. However, it is my position that these two are not really separable. Adequate expression of a certain cultural values requires linguistic features, including phonological, grammatical, lexical, discoursal and pragmatic aspects, to come with it, just as Singapore English functions as a vehicle of Singaporean culture with linguistic features of its own.

However, it needs to be admitted that Japan has so far been largely unsuccessful in identifying their original production models in terms of specific linguistic features. As the abovementioned EIL philosopher Kunihiro put it in several of his lectures around the year 2000, "there are many samples, but no models". Indeed, Japan has a number of skilled users of English whom learners can turn to as a reference, but at the moment there are still no systematic and comprehensive production models available for them.

Feasibility of an indigenous model of English for the Japanese

According to the Kachruvian Three Circles framework, Englishes in the Expanding Circle such as Japanese English are regarded as "norm-dependent," or reliant on external norms, unlike the "norm-developing" varieties in the Outer Circle such as Indian English (B. Kachru 1985: 17). This view of Expanding Circle varieties has constantly been repeated by World Englishes scholars. Below are two such examples:

A speaker of English in the Outer Circle will be careful to speak English in a way that will make his or her cultural identity clear. In the Expanding Circle, on the other hand, the ideal goal is to imitate the native speaker of the standard language as closely as possible. … Keeping a native standard in the Expanding Circle does not seem to present problems. (Andreasson 1994: 401–402)

The question of a model is often discussed with reference to spoken English and it is usual to make a distinction between EFL and ESL situations. For the former, it is usual to advocate a native model, but for the latter, enlightened opinion will support the need to use a non-native model. (Bamgbose 1998: 8)

It is true that Expanding Circle users of English, unlike their Outer Circle counterparts, hardly find it necessary to express their indigenous values in English in domestic situations, but they obviously need to do so in their communication with the outer world. The fact that Expanding Circle users normally do not speak English among their fellow country people, which is often emphasized in the WE theory in denying the need for local models of English for the Expanding Circle including Japan (e.g. B. Kachru 1976:235; Mufwene 2008), would not be considered to be directly relevant, in the eyes of the Japanese advocates of EIL such as Suzuki and Watanabe mentioned above, to the issue of models of English for expressing oneself in international settings.

One of the recent approaches to the teaching of English for international communication, which seems to have the potential of serving as a theoretical basis for Japanese English, is ELF (English as a Lingua Franca) proposed by Jenkins (e.g. 2000, 2007). The concept of ELF, though highly controversial in many respects, centres around the Lingua Franca Core which is meant to ensure international intelligibility, with an emphasis on the need for interactions between non-native speakers. Although ELF studies are often believed to be limited to the areas of phonology, a number of research projects from ELF perspectives have been undertaken recently in various other domains, such as lexico-grammatical, discoursal, sociolinguistic and pragmatic aspects (cf. Seidlhofer 2009:241).

In seeking original models of English for the Japanese, ELF seems to be especially significant on two counts. One is that ELF makes no discrimination between Englishes in the Outer Circle and the Expanding Circle. By exploiting 'non-core' features to express their identities, speakers in both circles can equally enjoy their own varieties of English. In fact, as Jenkins herself put it, ELF is "an attempt to extend to Expanding Circle members the rights that have always been enjoyed in the Inner Circle and to an increasing extent in the Outer" (Jenkins 2006:38). In my interpretation, the other salient characteristic of ELF is that this approach would not necessarily presuppose 'national' varieties. Under the ELF paradigm, users of English would be free to speak their individual varieties as long as they hold on to the core features to ensure international intelligibility. If this is the case, ELF gives the Expanding Circle a major advantage, since a lot of the current discrimination between the Outer Circle and the Expanding Circle comes from the view that the former consists of established national varieties unlike the latter.

On the other hand, ELF seems to have its own limitations. For example, a careful look at the Lingua Franca Core reveals that all the core features (e.g. Jenkins 2002:96–97) in ELF are still based on native speaker English. That is, ELF is, at least in its current form, may not be exactly free from native-speaker centredness.

It is not easy to predict at the moment how promising the ELF approach will be in terms of the Japanese quest for their own models of English. However, it surely has some important implications for the construction of a new framework for EIL, of which Expanding Circle varieties are a part along with Outer Circle varieties.

Based on available studies combined with my own experiences in the use of EIL, I have proposed, in Hino (2008:21–24), a tentative production model of Japanese English for international communication, which describes some linguistic, sociolinguistic and paralinguistic features. The list is far from comprehensive, but is hopefully a meaningful start for devising an educational model of Japanese English which is intended to be capable of expressing Japanese values and also be internationally comprehensible. As for phonology, for example, I argue that syllable-timed rhythm, with few elisions, linking, assimilation and reduction, should be recommendable. Here, syllable-timed rhythm, a natural rhythm for Japanese users of English, is regarded as an identity marker for the Japanese, which is also often more intelligible than stress-timed rhythm in EIL communication involving non-native interlocutors (Jenkins 2000; Deterding and Kirkpatrick 2006).

With regard to the grammar of Japanese English, I suggest that we should accept the Japanese interpretation of present perfect, definite/indefinite articles (Komiya 2007), singular/plural forms, etc. The Japanese usages of those grammatical items differ in a subtle manner from those of native speaker English, reflecting the Japanese world views shaped through their cultural experiences.

As for expressions, idioms that are deeply embedded in the Anglo-American culture are not recommended, such as "It's not cricket." which hardly makes sense to the Japanese. On the other hand, expressions which convey indigenous Japanese values are encouraged as long as they are comprehensible, such as "in a forward-looking manner". Another example is the Japanese custom of always distinguishing older and younger siblings. For the Japanese who have been raised to be conscious of seniority, one cannot be just a "brother" or a "sister", so to speak. In their conceptual framework, it has to be clearly stated if he or she is an "older brother/sister" or a "younger brother/sister", even when Americans perceive no need to make a distinction between these two.

Concerning discourse features, I propose that a transfer of Japanese text organization to English writing should be acceptable, as a reflection of Japanese thought patterns. Thus, the writing style that Hinds (1990:98) calls "delayed introduction of purpose", which is also often characterized by non-assertiveness with an emphasis on harmony (Y. Kachru 1997:58–59), is permissible as an option for Japanese learners of English. In conversational discourses, Japanese characteristics such as frequent back-channel cues are allowed to be retained, which is a sign of respect for others that is highly valued in the Japanese society.

In this model of Japanese English for international communication, sociolinguistic rules are also relativized vis-à-vis native speaker norms. For instance, in contrast to the usual practice in English conversation classes taught by American teachers, where students are so often encouraged to call each other by their first names regardless of seniority, first-name calling is not considered a norm even among close friends in this educational model. Also in non-verbal domains, Japanese bowing instead of handshakes, for example, is presented as a possible form of greeting, depending on some situational factors.

This pedagogical model of Japanese English — though some of its features still need to be tested for international intelligibility — is what I have been applying to my classrooms with the IPTEIL method discussed later in this paper. It is hoped that this idea will be further developed into a more comprehensive form so that it can fully serve as an educational alternative to the conventional American or British models.

EIL philosophy in the public school system in Japan

The conflict for learners of English between indigenous values and Anglo-American values is especially evident in the cultural content of teaching materials. I discuss in Hino (1988) that the cultural components of English textbooks in Japan had been changing like the swing of a pendulum between the two extremes, until some balance was achieved. During World War II, in which Japan fought against the Allied Forces including Britain and the USA, the one and only official English textbook for the public school system in Japan those days was filled with indigenous Japanese values by deliberately excluding Anglo-American cultures under the censorship by the Ministry of Education. In terms of cultural content, this may look like an EIL textbook on the surface. However, its exhibition of Japanese nationalism was so strongly ethnocentric that the basic idea of this book was obviously incompatible with the cause of English for international communication today. Below is an example:

> When we get up, it is still dark. We stand in a line, turn towards the Imperial Palace and bow. We thank our soldiers and sailors for their brave deeds. We pray for our success in war.
>
> (*Eigo*, reprinted in Kawasumi 1978)

After the war, in turn, the cultural content of English textbooks, written in accordance with the course of study set by the Ministry of Education, came to reflect Anglo-American values in an overwhelming manner. Even in the 1960s, Anglo-American culture was still predominantly represented in junior high school textbooks. A typical example is as follows:

Uncle: It's half past two now. Where shall we go next?
Roy: I want to see the British Museum.
Uncle: All right. I often go there to read.
Roy: Is it a library?
Uncle: Yes, it is. It's a museum, too. You'll find a great many books there. Many people go there to study the fine arts, too. It's the biggest museum in the world. I have a friend there.
                                                                                  (*New Prince Readers* 2, 1968: 42)

Junior high school English textbooks in those days mostly centred around the life of American students, describing American culture and American values. As shown in the example above, even when the leading character went abroad, Britain was chosen to be most appropriate for cultural description in the English textbook. It was also a norm that interactions should take place between native speakers of English. In short, English was regarded as nothing but a means of expressing Anglo-American culture. Japanese learners of English were expected to talk, think, and act like Americans.

In contrast, English textbooks nowadays deal with non-native English speaking cultures including that of Japan. Below is an excerpt from a recent junior high school textbook:

Ryo: Was Hong Kong always a big city like today?
Jing: No, it wasn't. It was a very small village once.
         But now, it is famous for business and sightseeing.
Ryo: Which places are good for sightseeing?
Jing: Well, let's see … I like Victoria Peak. The night view from there is beautiful.
                                                                                  (*Total English* 2, 2002: 16)

Ryo is one of the leading characters in this textbook, a Japanese junior high school student just like its intended readers. This textbook is aimed at expressing the student's own values rather than those of native speakers of English. Another character is Jing, a non-native speaker of English from Hong Kong, who talks about her own culture. In fact, the cultural content of today's junior high school textbooks is not restricted to Anglo-American components, but it represents a diversity including both native and non-native English speaking cultures. Presenting interactions between non-native speakers as in the example above, which was unimaginable 40 years ago, is also quite normal in textbooks these days. It is clear, at least as far as the cultural content of textbooks is concerned, that English language education in Japan today reflects the concept of English as an International Language (EIL) or that of World Englishes.

The Courses of Study set by the Ministry of Education, which includes guidelines for the content of textbooks for primary and secondary education, has legal binding force for textbook writers. That is, the selection of cultural components of textbooks described above is based on the national policies of the Japanese government. After going through a number of revisions after the war, the current Courses of Study for junior and senior high schools states that teaching materials should deal with matters such as "the daily lives, customs and habits, stories, geography, and history of people of the world, especially those who use English, and the Japanese". As to the selection of materials, the Courses of Study cites the importance of helping the students deepen their understanding of the lives and cultures of "the world and our own country". In other words, it is a governmental policy to understand not only native but also non-native English-speaking cultures through English and to express Japanese values in English. In this respect, the concept of EIL is clearly a national policy of Japan.

On the other hand, the Ministry of Education has not made their position very clear in regard to the issue of production models. For a senior high school EFL class called "Oral Communication", the current Courses of Study states that "Language materials, in principle, should be based on the present-day standard Englishes. However, it should also be taken into consideration that varieties of English are used as a global means of communication" (translation mine). With this regulation, tolerance of the diversity of English is encouraged, according to an official notation of the Courses of Study given by the Ministry of Education (1999: 27–28). However, the meaning of "the present-day standard Englishes" is rather ambiguous. I have translated it here as plural "Englishes", in reference to the above notation by the Ministry of Education which describes it as "not monolithic, and representing a diversity in various respects, especially in such areas as pronunciation and lexicons" (translation mine). Yet, the Education Ministry goes on to say in the same explanation that "this regulation does not require that varieties of English be given to the students as the models of learning" (translation mine). Although certainly progressive compared to the conventional stance of ELT, this official interpretation of the Courses of Study in practice seems to be leading the textbook writers and the teachers to the same old American or British English after all, at least for the production models.

The recent diffusion of EIL philosophy in Japan is observable also in the employment of Assistant Language Teachers (ALTs) for English in the public school system. In 1989, as was reported in the Yomiuri newspaper, there was only one non-native English speaking ALT in Japan for the subject of English (then called AET), who was from the Philippines. I interviewed her on a radio English education programme for which I served as the host. Asked what she thought of the reality that all the AETs but herself are native speakers of English, this AET from the Philippines appealed to the Japanese listeners as follows:

> So, I think Japan should also open their minds, you know, not to close their minds, you know, thinking that the right English is only American or British English. It's really quite unfair. (*English for Millions*, broadcast on 5 January 1990)

It still took Japan more than several years before her vision began to come true. Until 1996, as ALTs for English, the Japanese government only hired applicants from the US, Britain, Australia, New Zealand, Canada, and Ireland, reflecting the traditional notion that only native speakers can provide appropriate language models for learners. In 1997, the Japanese government finally opened the JET programme (ALT programme) to non-native speakers of English. In 2008, Japan had 99 ALTs from South Africa, 17 from India, 48 from Singapore, 46 from Jamaica, etc. (JET Programme 2009). They are still a minority in the total of over 4,000 ALTs, but their presence is gradually getting to be accepted in public schools in Japan.

Tagawa (2008) reports on the case of a public junior high school in Hyogo Prefecture, where an ALT from India is naturally received by both students and colleagues, with no one questioning her credentials as a model speaker of English. Moreover, outside the JET program sponsored by the central government, these days we quite frequently encounter non-native English-speaking ALTs employed at local levels. In a public elementary school in the Kyoto area, where the teaching of English is already regularly practised for the 5th and 6th graders in accordance with the policy set by the local city board of education, I was able to observe recently (in June 2009) that an ALT from Russia was also positively received by the students and Japanese teachers as a model speaker of English. The fact that she comes from the Expanding Circle was not considered to be a negative factor in any respect.

In sum, non-native speakers of English are in the process of gradual integration into the English teaching staff in public schools in Japan. It could be expected that the presence of non-native English-speaking ALTs with their own varieties of English would help Japanese students realize the positive value of Japanese English of their own.

Classroom practice in English as an International Language

The teaching of EIL, for expressing Japanese values in English and for understanding a diversity of cultures through English, is gradually beginning to be practised at various educational settings in Japan.

The aforementioned radio programme *English for Millions*, a major English education programme broadcast all over Japan for which the present writer was the lecturer from 1989 to 1992, can probably be called a forerunner for such educational practice in EIL. In a series of programmes aired once a week from 1989 to 1990, I invited non-native English-speaking guests from various countries, namely, Malaysia, Hong Kong, Bangladesh, the Philippines, Sri Lanka, and France. Using my Japanese English, I discussed a range of topics including environment, education, human rights, politics and economy with these speakers of English from a diversity of linguistic and cultural backgrounds (Hino 1989–1990).

I had three primary purposes for this radio venture twenty years ago. One was to expose Japanese learners of English to varieties of English. As Smith and Bisazza (1982) found, experience in exposure is one of the keys to international understanding. Another aim was to show examples of NNS/NNS interactions in English, which was becoming increasingly common in actual international communication and yet whose significance was hardly recognized by teachers and learners of English those days. Still another purpose was to give a certain confidence to Japanese learners of English by demonstrating that Japanese English, my own variety of English, is internationally communicative, capable of expressing indigenous values while maintaining international intelligibility.

Although English teaching programmes on the radio and TV are abundant in Japan, it had been unimaginable before then to have regular talk-show programs with non-native speakers of English. As most other phases of English language education in Japan, radio and TV programmes for teaching English in Japan were largely based on the traditional premise that both productive and receptive models of English should be those of native speakers. This new radio project was only made possible by my luck of having a director and a producer for this programme who were both open to innovative ideas. In deciding on the selection of speakers, I made a point of inviting guests not only from the Outer Circle (Malaysia, Hong Kong, Bangladesh, the Philippines, and Sri Lanka, in this case) but also from the Expanding Circle (France, in this case) to make my stance clear that I do not discriminate between Englishes in the Outer Circle and the Expanding Circle.

The responses I received from the listeners of this radio programme were mostly positive, which included comments such as "This programme, which gives us opportunities to listen to varieties of English, is really rare and valuable." and "I was surprised to find that non-native varieties of English are often easier to listen to than native-speaker English." There was only one letter which expressed a clearly negative opinion, which said "I don't want to listen to such strange English as Filipino English", but this response actually further convinced me of the importance of this education programme which was intended to help the listeners eliminate such prejudice against non-native varieties of English.

An example from this radio talk which stimulated a lot of responses from the listeners concerns the English expressions used by the guest from Bangladesh in response to my invitation for his radio appearance. Although this conversation was not recorded, we took it up in our radio talk (broadcast on 10 November 1989) since his reply, based on his Islamic faith, was an ideal example of non-Anglo-American cultural expression in EIL. The original dialogue was as follows:

> Japanese host: Could you come to the studio next Wednesday?
> Bangladeshi guest: Well, maybe.
> Japanese host: I beg your pardon?
> Bangladeshi guest: I don't know, but I will try.

This university student from Bangladesh explained on the radio that it would constitute a blasphemy to God (Allah) if he made a future promise to humans, because he believed that the future is in the hands of Allah. Indeed, in accordance with his religious faith, "Maybe" and "I don't know, but I will try" must have been the most appropriate expressions, which are in effect tantamount to "Sure" or "Certainly" in native-speaker English. In other words, he was performing the speech act of agreeing in a way which conformed to his important cultural values. Imposing American or British expressions such as "Sure" or "Certainly" on this student, which had been taken for granted in conventional ELT, would be a serious invasion of human rights for him. Anglo-American English has been largely formed upon the Judeo-Christian tradition, and is not always appropriate for expressing Islamic values. As the host for this programme, I called on the Japanese audience to follow the example of this Bangladeshi youngster in his worthy attempt to express his own cultural values in English rather than using American ways of thinking.

Twenty years after this radio programme, in my university EFL classes in Japan for first and second year students, I use a method which I call IPTEIL, or the Integrated Practice in Teaching English as an International Language (Hino 2006, 2007). This method, which is a type of content-based language instruction, is an integrated approach in several aspects, especially in the sense that it attempts to integrate the notion of EIL with multiple pedagogical concepts including Global Education, Media Literacy Education, and Legitimate Peripheral Participation, among others.

Teaching materials for IPTEIL are authentic materials, i.e. a variety of web newspapers that are read in class real-time, combined with satellite TV news videotaped on the morning of the class day. In class, we start by watching the TV news, such as *Channel NewsAsia* (Singapore), *ATV* (Hong Kong), *ABS-CBN* (Philippines), *CNN* (US), and *BBC* (UK). *Channel NewsAsia*, for example, covers daily news which mainly involve speakers of Asian varieties of English. It also provides a lot of authentic NNS/NNS interactions, such as international exchanges between Singaporean anchors and reporters from such areas as India, Sri Lanka, Hong Kong, Thailand, and Japan. In this way, my students witness living examples of the reconciliation of indigenous values and English as a global language. After watching the TV news, taking advantage of the CALL room connected to the internet, I lead the students to read about the same news topic on the web newspapers, integrating listening and reading skills. In order to train Media Literacy based on Critical Thinking, we compare and contrast newspapers around the world which differ in their perspectives, such as *CNN* (US), *BBC* (UK), *Channel NewsAsia* (Singapore), *Al Jazeera* (Qatar), *The Jerusalem Post* (Israel), *IRNA* (Iran), *The News* (Pakistan), *Bangkok Post* (Thailand), *The Standard* (Hong Kong), *People's Daily* (China), *The Korea Herald* (Korea), *The Standard* (Kenya), and *NHK* (Japan), among many others. Across these news media all over the world, syntactic differences are limited, but they present a wide variety of cultural values, reflecting the diversity of EIL or World Englishes. For example, we compared the following articles by *CNN* and *Al Jazeera* on the new Pope's inauguration sermon:

> During his homily, the new pontiff said he wished to reach out to Jews and "believers and nonbelievers alike" and asked for prayers from the St. Peter's Square onlookers as he assumed "this enormous task". (*CNN* 24 April 2005)

> In his inaugural ceremony, the new pope has praised Christianity's common heritage with Jews but has taken no notice of Islam. (*Al Jazeera* 24 April 2005)

From the *CNN* coverage, readers get the feeling that the new Pope spoke to the whole world beyond religious differences, while the *Al Jazeera* article gives the impression that the Pope simply ignored Muslims who do not share the Judeo-Christian tradition. Students are surprised to find that the same event, the same speech in the above case, can be interpreted and reported even in the opposite ways, depending on the viewpoints of each media. They learn a diversity of cultural values represented in Englishes in the world.

IPTEIL is basically an attempt to provide the learners with opportunities for Legitimate Peripheral Participation in the community of practice (Lave and Wenger 1991) in EIL. I try to make this possible with a task that is commonly shared by any user of EIL, which is to watch, read, and talk about daily news. Through real-time news on the Internet, I invite my students to join me in the real world of EIL.

When there are foreign students in addition to local Japanese students, the IPTEIL class takes on a clearer nature of the "community of practice in EIL" (Hino 2003). Native English-speaking students are normally exempted from EFL classes, but I welcome those Inner Circle users of English to stay in my IPTEIL class. In fact, it is an important principle of EIL that its learners include native speakers of English as well as non-native speakers (Smith 1978; Kubota 2001). For example, a student from New Zealand has expressed to me that he enjoyed learning about the varieties of viewpoints in this class. We have also had foreign students, though still limited in number, from countries such as Malaysia, China, Taiwan, Korea, Vietnam, and Thailand. It is hoped, with the increase of international students, that the IPTEIL class will be a true realization of the community of practice in EIL, where local Japanese students, international students regardless of their native languages, and also the teacher as their leader will share their views and experiences so as to learn from each other (Hino 2003).

A fact that may prove the value of IPTEIL is that an award known as "Osaka University Award for Outstanding Contributions to General Education" was given eight times to the teaching with this method during the period 2002 to 2008. This would be a rare example world-wide of an official award for classroom teaching in EIL or World Englishes. This award, decided upon every semester on the basis of the students' evaluation questionnaire and reviews by the faculty committee, is a highly competitive award, yielding the competition rate of approximately 1% every time. At the most recent occasion (fall 2008), for example, only 12 teachers were chosen out of the 1,187 teachers of this large national university. The reasons for giving the award to IPTEIL, officially cited by Osaka University (2009c), include the following, which shows that EIL aspects of this method are highly evaluated:

> Gained recommendation from overwhelmingly many students, by introducing them to varieties of English and leading them to analyze world events from multiple perspectives, through activities such as comparing the viewpoints of various news media real-time. (For Spring Semester, 2008; translation mine)

"Varieties of English" and "multiple perspectives," found in the above evaluation, are key concepts of EIL and World Englishes. This is an example in which a major institution of higher education in Japan is beginning to appreciate a new type of English language teaching that is founded on the recognition of varieties of English with a diversity of cultural values. The fact that this approach has proved to be very popular among students also looks promising for the future development of EIL education.

There are of course teaching practices other than IPTEIL which are successful at the university level. In the current IPTEIL practice described above, personal and direct contact with other users of EIL from different cultural backgrounds are still rather limited. Waseda University offers such opportunities with the technology of TV conferences, an approach known as Cross-Cultural Distance Learning (CCDL). In an example reported by Ueda et al. (2005), 20 students from Waseda University in Tokyo engage in discussions via TV conference with 20 counterparts from Korea University in Seoul. Ueda et al. explain one of the aims of this project as follows:

> Students who have been exposed in person to the styles of English communication by Chinese or Koreans, which are influenced by their cultures, would be in an advantageous position to better understand their English, compared with those who have not had such chances. This activity should be also meaningful as an effort to help Chinese and Korean people become familiar with the styles of communication in Japanese English. (Ueda et al. 2005: 171. translation mine)

This educational project at Waseda University could be viewed as an attempt to create a community of practice, a constructivist notion mentioned earlier, in which participants learn from each other through interactions. CCDL is a suggestive example in terms of future prospects for the teaching of EIL.

Chukyo University, with its college of World Englishes, has also been holding TV conferences for the purpose of teaching EIL through authentic interactions. Most recently in 2009, for example, undergraduate students at Chukyo University had two talk sessions, one with Chinese diplomats and the other with Indonesian military officers, both of whom were studying at RELC in Singapore. The development of information technology is indeed opening new possibilities of EIL education.

Conclusions

The conflict between indigenous and foreign values has been a problem in the language attitudes of the Japanese, which is becoming even more serious with the tide of globalization today. One way to ease this tension, if not the final solution, is to employ the teaching of EIL, or de-Anglo-Americanized English for multicultural expression. In fact, Japanese users of English have long been struggling to express their own values in English for international communication. The concept of EIL is also exerting increasing influence on traditionally EFL classrooms in Japan.

The fact that the world's first independent college of World Englishes and also the first autonomous graduate school of World Englishes were founded in this country, in 2002 and 2006 respectively at Chukyo University, is a salient example to show the keen interest among Japanese users of English in expressing indigenous values through English. The Chukyo leadership has stated on several occasions, such as at the Chubu Chapter meeting of JACET in December 2008, that they would like to see Japanese English with its own norms, rather than to settle with the classic definition of 'exonormative' Expanding Circle varieties of English in the World Englishes paradigm. In this sense, the Chukyo position may be, despite their school name, actually closer to what I define as EIL (Hino 2001, cf. Tupas 2006: 174, 180–181) than to World Englishes. Chukyo University has recently even opened an EIL course for their affiliated senior high school as a test case. At the moment, they are running a short-term course, in which senior high students are introduced to the concept of EIL and also given chances to engage in EIL communication.

On the other hand, although Japan has been quick to adopt a diversity of cultures including their own as the content of teaching materials in English, they have not been able to come up so far with a comprehensive production model with specific linguistic features, which remains a difficult job in EIL education in this country.

It is true that Japan is faced with many other serious problems in language policy today. It should make a last-minute effort to maintain aboriginal languages like Ainu. Japan must also ensure language services for foreign residents, such as Portuguese and Spanish for those from Latin America. Developing and diffusing EIL education is just one of the tasks that Japan must tackle in regard to the urgent sociolinguistic need that it is facing. However, it cannot be denied that English for international communication is an indispensable linguistic skill for the Japanese in this age of globalization. The Japanese need to understand a diversity of values expressed in both native and non-native varieties of English, and also to express their own thoughts, rather than Anglo-American values, in English. The teaching of English as an International Language is an answer, if not the panacea, to the dilemma of indigenous values and global needs.

Notes
* This research is partially funded by the Japan Society for the Promotion of Science, Grants-in-Aid for Scientific Research (C) 20520548, 2008–2010. I am thankful to my colleagues in AILA, IAWE, JACET and JAFAE for their academic support. I am also grateful to the two anonymous reviewers for their constructive and useful comments.

References
Andreasson, A. (1994) Norm as a pedagogical paradigm. *World Englishes* 13(3): 395–409.
Bamgbose, A. (1998) Torn between the norms: Innovations in world Englishes. *World Englishes*, 17(1): 1–14.
Deterding, D. and A. Kirkpatrick (2006). Emerging South-East Asian Englishes and intelligibility. *World Englishes* 25(3–4): 391–409.
Hinds, J. (1990) Inductive, deductive, quasi-inductive: Expository writing in Japanese, Korean, Chinese, and Thai. In U. Connor and A.M. Johns (eds) *Coherence in Writing: Research and Pedagogical Perspectives*, pp. 89–109. Alexandria, VA: Teachers of English to Speakers of Other Languages.
Hino, N. (1988) Nationalism and English as an international language: The history of English textbooks in Japan. *World Englishes* 7(3): 309–314.
Hino, N. (1989–1990) Let's Read & Think. *English for Millions* (Monthly textbook) July 1989-March 1990.
Hino, N. (1992) The Yakudoku tradition of foreign language literacy in Japan. In F. Dubin and N.A. Kuhlman (eds) *Cross-Cultural Literacy: Global Perspectives on Reading and Writing*, pp. 99–111. Englewood Cliffs, NJ: Regents/Prentice Hall.
Hino, N. (2001) Organizing EIL studies: Toward a paradigm. *Asian Englishes* 4(1): 34–65.
Hino, N. (2003) Teaching EIL in Japan. *Proceedings: First Conference on World Englishes in the Classroom*, pp. 67–78. Chukyo University.
Hino, N. (2006). Reflective teaching in EIL. 12th Annual Conference of the International Association for World Englishes (Featured Speaker). Chukyo University, Nagoya, Japan, 7 October.
Hino, N. (2007) Togoteki kokusai-eigo kyojuho (IPTEIL) no kaihatsu to jissen [The development and implementation of Integrated Practice in Teaching English as an International Language]. In *Gengo to Bunka no Tembo [Perspectives on Language and Culture]*, pp. 113–128. Tokyo: Eihosha.
Hino, N. (2008) Kokusai-eigo [English as an International Language]. In S. Kotera and H. Yoshida (eds) *Supesharisuto ni Yoru Eigo-Kyoiku no Riron to Oyo [Theories and Practice of English Language Teaching by Specialists]*, pp. 15–32. Tokyo: Shohakusha.
Horiguchi, T. et al. (2002) *Total English 2*. Tokyo: Gakko Tosho.
Inamura, M. et al. (1968) *New Prince Readers 2*. Tokyo: Kairyudo
JACET (2009) Retrieved 30 May 2009 from http://www.jacet.org/2009convention/call_for_papers_j.pdf
Jenkins, J. (2000) *The Phonology of English as an International Language*. Oxford: Oxford University Press.
Jenkins, J. (2002). A sociolinguistically based, empirically researched pronunciation syllabus for English as an International Language. *Applied Linguistics* 23(1): 83–103.
Jenkins, J. (2006). Global intelligibility and local diversity: Possibility or paradox? In R. Rubdy and M. Saraceni (eds) *English in the World: Global Rules, Global Roles*, pp. 32–39. London: Continuum.
Jenkins, J. (2007). *English as a Lingua Franca: Attitude and Identity*. Oxford: Oxford University Press.
JET Programme (2009) Retrieved 13 May 2009 from http://www.jetprogramme.org/documents/stats/2008-2009/2008sanka_ninzu_kunibetsu.pdf.
Kachru, B.B. (1976) Models of English for the Third World: White man's linguistic burden or language pragmatics. *TESOL Quarterly* 10(2): 221–239.
Kachru, B.B. (1985) Standards, codification and sociolinguistic realism: The English language in the Outer Circle. In R. Quirk and H.G. Widdowson (eds) *English in the World: Teaching and Learning the Language and Literatures*, pp. 11–30. Cambridge: Cambridge University Press.
Kachru, Y. (1997). Culture and argumentative writing in World Englishes. In L.E. Smith and M.L. Forman (eds) *World Englishes 2000*, pp. 48–67. Honolulu: University of Hawaii Press.

Kawahara, T. and H. Noyama (eds) (2007) *Gaikokujin-Jumin eno Gengo-Sabisu [Language Services for Foreign Residents]*. Tokyo: Akashi Shoten.

Kawasumi, T. (ed.) (1978) *Shiryo Nihon-Eigakushi 2: Eigokyoiku-Ronsoshi [Collection of Primary Sources on the History of English Studies 2: Controversies on English Language Teaching]*. Tokyo: Taishukan Shoten.

Komiya, T. (2007) Nihonjin-eigo ni okeru teikanshi no tokucho to antei-ka ni tsuite [On possible stabilization of the definite article in Japanese English]. *Asian English Studies* 9: 7–24.

Kubota, R. (2001) Teaching World Englishes to native speakers of English in the USA. *World Englishes* 20(1): 47–64.

Kunihiro, M. (1970) *Eigo no Hanashikata [English Works for You]*. Tokyo: Simul Press.

Lave, J. and E. Wenger (1991) *Situated Learning: Legitimate Peripheral Participation*. Oxford: Oxford University Press.

Ministry of Education, Science, Sports and Culture (1999) *Kotogakko Gakushu Shidoyoryo Kaisetsu [A Commentary on the Courses of Study for Senior High Schools]*. Tokyo: Kairyudo.

Ministry of Justice (2008) Retrieved 6 July 2009 from http://www.moj.go.jp/PRESS/080601-1.pdf.

Mufwene, S.S. (2008) Does Japan need a separate English norm? Symposium on What is global English communicative competence?: Models, standards, and pedagogy for the teaching of English in Japan. Annual Convention of Japan Association of College English Teachers, 13 September.

Nakatani, I. (2006) "Jomon-bunka" koso nihon no kisou-bunka da [The Jomon culture is the basic culture of Japan]. *PHP Business Review*, July & August issues. Retrieved 14 July 2009 from http://www.murc.jp/nakatani/articles/php/bunmei/200607.html

Nijuisseiki Nihon no Koso Kondankai [The Prime Minister's Commission on Japan's Goals in the 21st Century] (2000) *Nihon no Furontia wa Nihon no Naka ni Aru [The Frontier Within]*. Tokyo: Kodansha.

Nishiyama, S. (1995) Speaking English with a Japanese mind. *World Englishes* 14(1): 27–36.

Osaka University (2009a) Retrieved 11 May 2009 from http://www.mls.eng.osaka-u.ac.jp/FB_inter_prog/FB_inter_prog.html

Osaka University (2009b) Retrieved 13 July 2009 from http://www.osaka-u.ac.jp/en/seminar/info/2009/07/536

Osaka University (2009c) Retrieved 9 July 2009 from http://www.cep.osaka-u.ac.jp/modules/fd/index.php?content_id=33

Otani, Y. (2007) *Nihonjin ni totte Eigo towa Nanika [What does the English Language Mean to the Japanese?]*. Tokyo: Taishukan Shoten.

Phillipson, R. (1992) *Linguistic Imperialism*. Oxford: Oxford University Press.

Saito, H. (1928) *Saito's Japanese-English Dictionary*. Tokyo: Nichieisha. (Reprinted in 2002. Tokyo: Nichigai Associates.)

Saito, Y. (2005) Shogakkoeigo hisshuka no giron ni hisomu otoshiana [Pitfalls hidden behind the arguments on designating English as a compulsory subject in elementary school]. In Y. Otsu (ed.) *Shogakko deno Eigokyoiku wa Hitsuyonai! [We don't Need English Language Teaching in Elementary School!]*, pp. 19–36. Tokyo: Keio University Press.

Seidlhofer, B. (2009) Common ground and different realities: World Englishes and English as a lingua franca. *World Englishes* 28(2): 236–245.

Smith, L.E. (1976) English as an international auxiliary language. *RELC Journal* 7(2): 38–53. Also in L.E. Smith (ed.) (1983) *Readings in English as an International Language*, pp. 1–5. Oxford: Pergamon Press.

Smith, L.E. (1978) Some distinctive features of EIIL vs. ESOL in English language education. *The Culture Learning Institute Report*, June, 5–7 & 10–11. Also in L.E. Smith (ed.) (1983) *Readings in English as an International Language*, pp. 13–20. Oxford: Pergamon Press.

Smith, L.E. and J.A. Bisazza (1982) The comprehensibility of three varieties of English for college students in seven countries. *Language Learning* 32(2): 259–269. Also in L.E. Smith (ed.) (1983) *Readings in English as an International Language*, pp. 59–67. Oxford: Pergamon Press.

Suzuki, T. (1971) *Tozasareta Gengo, Nihongo no Sekai [A Closed Language: The World of Japanese]*. Tokyo: Shinchosha.

Tagawa, Y. (2008) Chugakko-Eigokyoiku ni okeru Kokusaieigo-Kyoiku no Teian (A Proposal on the Teaching of English as an International Language in Junior High School). Master's dissertation, Graduate School of Language and Culture, Osaka University.

Tsuda, Y. (2003) *Eigoshihai towa Nanika [What is the Hegemony of English?]*. Tokyo: Akashi Shoten.

Tupas, T.R.F. (2006) Standard Englishes, pedagogical paradigms, and their conditions of (im)possibility. In R. Rubdy and M. Saraceni (eds) *English in the World: Global Rules, Global Roles*, pp. 169–185. London: Continuum.

Ueda, N., K. Owada, M. Oya and E. Tsutsui (2005) Shakai e tsunageru daigaku-eigokyoiku [University English language education in social contexts]. In M. Nakano (ed.) *Eigokyoiku Gurobaru Dezain [Global Design for English Language Teaching]*, pp. 135–173. Tokyo: Gakubunsha.

Yamamoto, K. (2007) Maegaki [Preface]. In K. Yamamoto and T. Kawahara (eds.) *Sekai no Gengoseisaku [Language Policies around the World]*, pp. 1–5. Tokyo: Kuroshio Shuppan.

Watanabe, T. (1983) *Japalish no Susume [An Invitation to Japalish]*. Tokyo: Asahi Shimbunsha.

Multilingual Asia

Looking back, looking across, looking forward

Paul Bruthiaux

Asian University, Chonburi, Thailand

Introduction

In°any discussion of multilingual Asia, caution is in order, for two reasons. One is that Asia is a vast land mass connecting variegated peoples cartographically but not sociologically. By convention, Asia includes Lebanon, a country much like nearby EU-member Cyprus especially in terms of its history and uneasy combination of Muslim and Christian value systems. Kazakhstan, meanwhile, a country that shares a (short) border with Mongolia in a part of the Asian land mass that lies to the east of Bhutan, has managed to join a number of European groupings including UEFA (Union of European Football Associations) and OSCE (Organization for Security and Cooperation in Europe). The present volume alone covers a league of nations that includes towering China (Feng) and ambiguous Hong Kong (Li), fast aging Japan (Hino), the fractious Philippines (Tupas), race-sensitive Malaysia (Azirah Hashim), planned Singapore (Lim), and rising but unruly India and bitterly divided (though hopefully recovering) Sri Lanka (Canagarajah). Commentators, therefore, would be well advised not to look too hard for Asian commonalities over such a vast and disparate continent.

Second, describing and accounting for the sociolinguistic complexities of Asia (or anywhere else, for that matter) is history in the making in that, just like populations themselves, languages and the social factors they affect and are affected by are highly fluid. Because events have a knack for occurring just as a meticulously researched submission is being sent off to a journal, few sociolinguistic analyses of the type contained in this volume remain entirely valid for long. In some cases, an event occurs and accidentally confirms an analysis that had hitherto been only tentative. In other cases, an unforeseen event suddenly invalidates an analysis based on a state of affairs that had appeared permanent. In July 2009, for example, even as I read Feng's contribution to this volume and in particular his argument that neglect of minority languages on the fringes of China may result in widening social divisions in the country, the city of Urumqi (in the far-western province of Xinjiang) exploded, leaving over 180 Han Chinese and Uighurs dead before a massive injection of troops restored an uneasy calm. Days later, as I read Azirah Hashim's forecast that the 2002 introduction in Malaysia of English as the medium of instruction for science and math will give rise to a new group of Malaysians with intermediate English language proficiency, slotting them halfway between those who are comfortable in English and those who know little or none, I read in the morning news that the policy will be abolished by 2012, apparently as a result of a post-Mahathir power play between those pushing for stronger support for Malay and those advocating greater balance between Malay and English (Gooch 2009). So much for carefully considered forecasts, then.

But of course, commonalities do exist, at least across the language issues and the locations considered in this volume. Among them, I discuss in this review article some that address the most fundamental or the most controversial aspects of language in the parts of contemporary Asia examined

AILA Review 22 (2009), 120–130. DOI 10.1075/aila.22.09bru
ISSN 1461–0213 / E-ISSN 1570–5595 © John Benjamins Publishing Company

in this volume. Some of these issues are methodological, including the need for useful terminologies and the advisability of forecasting sociolinguistic or educational developments. Some are geopolitical, such as the respective roles of China and India in shaping the (probable) sociolinguistic ecology of the region in the coming decades. Others are conceptual, among them theoretical models such as Kachru's Three Circles or the notion of 'bilingualism'. Overall, I aim in this article to support the more robust conclusions and policy recommendations for language education made in the contributions to this volume for specific locations in the region, and I suggest ways in which some of the discussions might be deepened and issues habitually skirted around might be more confidently and usefully addressed.

What's your good name?

Definitions have a bad name, and (for the most part) rightly so. They constrict exploration by pre-defining meaning, constructing categories and erecting firewalls between them, and creating a sense that entities were named on the basis of a set of intrinsic properties rather than as a result of an accident of nomenclature or as a convenient shorthand. Clearly, the reification of fluidity should not be interpreted as fact but only used as a mental tool that makes observation possible through artificial and temporary stabilization. If the temptation to accord that temporary stabilization of fluid processes permanent status is resisted, definitions do have the advantage of focussing debate and forcing the principal actors — especially the powerful — to reveal their meanings and their intentions. While over-defining undoubtedly restricts options and makes out-of-the-box thinking less likely, under-defining — being all meanings to all people — allows the powerful to keep everyone in a conceptual fog while a covert agenda is promoted until it is too late for the participants to dispute an unpopular or ineffective policy. To use an Asian image, if you drop a frog into boiling water, it'll jump right out. But if you drop it into warm water and then raise the temperature gradually, it'll cook without even noticing. Deliberately under-specifying water temperature makes it impossible for the frog to reach an informed decision on whether to adopt a participatory approach, until it is too late. And so it is for citizens' participation in language-related debates and policy implementation, including language education policy.

Chinese and Chineses

In this volume, the contributions by Tupas and Azirah Hashim show that language nomenclature in the region has long been used as a political tool. After all, the notion that a single language should ideally be a defining characteristic of a well-ordered nation-state has long been a key principle behind the rise of nation-states not only in Asia but also in countries such as France and even in Franco's Spain despite that country's obvious multilingualism. Today the notion is generally regarded as unacceptable (if it ever was descriptively accurate) though, as Hino (this volume) shows, the belief is alive and well in Japan. In addition, Canagarajah (this volume) shows that some types of linguistic practices defy labelling, especially what he terms 'plurilingualism', that is, the ad hoc improvization of emergent, transitory codes consisting of elements of several languages shared by all the participants.

That said, some tidying up of even the vibrant hodgepodge Canagarajah describes is at times necessary in part because language policy must be made, whether in the traditional top-down manner for nation-building purposes (see Lim, Azirah Hashim, this volume) or as Tupas (this volume) recommends, by allowing it to emerge bottom-up out of the socioeconomic needs of the most disadvantaged social groups.

A case in point is China and the nature of Chinese, or to use Bolton's (2003) term, 'Chineses'. Of course no aspect of so vast a nation and in particular the linguistic practices of so large and relatively diverse a population can ever be tidied up in, for example, the Singapore manner. But not to try at least minimally for the purpose of discussing major language-related issues including language education allows for conceptual fog to rise. Perhaps this under-specification is accidental. Or perhaps it is traditional. Or perhaps it reflects a concern for inclusivity. But most probably it points to an unwillingness to challenge politically convenient simplifications.

At the national level, the term 'Chinese' appropriately refers to the national language, the Beijing-based standard that has become the official voice of China, the language of government, and the primary medium of education. It is widespread, prestigious, and increasingly studied abroad as a foreign language. The trouble starts as soon as the focus shifts to the regions where a variant of that standard is spoken. This is especially conspicuous in Hong Kong, which, by historical accident, operated for a century and a half beyond the reach of the Beijing power base and came under pressure to take the Beijing lead only a dozen years ago after the 1997 handover of Hong Kong to China.

As Li (this volume) shows, Hong Kong is overwhelmingly a Cantonese-speaking place where by all accounts Chinese (understood as the Mainland standard) is poorly understood and rarely — if ever — used for domestic communication. In time, this may change. But for now it is sensible to regard Hong Kong speech as a variant of Chinese that is sufficiently autonomous to justify its own label of 'Cantonese' to be contrasted with the Beijing-based 'Mandarin' standard or, as it is usually called in Hong Kong, 'Putonghua'.

Inside Hong Kong classrooms, the fog thickens further. Language policy documents (in English) routinely refer to 'Chinese' as the medium of education in full knowledge that what is often used in the classrooms by students and teachers alike is in fact Cantonese. At some level, the two can be regarded as variants of each other because they share a writing system. However, this is only partially true since Hong Kong (like Taiwan) retains traditional characters whereas Mainland China uses the simplified system. Moreover, as Li (this volume) explains, many local concepts have no written representation in standard Chinese writing, requiring special combinations of characters to be created, which are comprehensible to locals only. In any case, the fact that two codes share a writing system even in large part is not a sufficient condition for regarding them as the same language. After all, written Italian and Spanish share an almost identical set of written symbols and are in part mutually intelligible (especially in written form). Yet history has long determined that the two should be seen as two languages. And of course Japanese *kanji* is essentially Chinese writing, yet no one suggests that Japanese is a dialect of Chinese.

The difficulty for Hong Kong and for Cantonese is of course political in nature. Whether modern rulers like it or not, all nation-states have roots in some kind of imperialism, that is, the gradual imposition of power by one group over neighbour after neighbour. The result is often a degree of territorial insecurity on the part of nation-states and their rulers, a weakness that needs to be periodically and forcefully addressed by the political centre not only to deal with bumptious regions as they take their chances against the centre but also to convince the population, not least through the publicly funded education of children, of the inherent indivisibility of the national territory, a long history of imperial breakups notwithstanding.

This is evident in much of the official discourse (at least in its English version), especially at times of sociopolitical crisis. As witnessed again in the official response to the recent interethnic violence in Xinjiang, the unitary nature of the Chinese state is declared 'inalienable' and the use of the term 'splittist' to tar those said to promote separation (or in the case of Taiwan, non-reunification) is one epithet inherited from Maoist days that has as yet escaped modernization. As regards language, the promotion of the Mandarin standard seems to me to parallel in a highly symbolic manner the single (Beijing) time zone imposed on a vast nation that stretches 5,200 kilometers from east to west. But just as unofficial time zones are tolerated on the western fringes, unofficial language practices are tolerated in linguistically ambiguous locations, including Hong Kong, under cover of the conveniently vague umbrella term 'Chinese'.

Matters are not helped by the occasional use in discussions of language policy in Hong Kong of the term 'mother tongue' without it being made clear what this code might consist of or how it relates to Chinese, Mandarin/Putonghua, or Cantonese. To an outsider, this suggests diffidence on the part of Hong Kong citizens and in particular educators and language policy makers. Perhaps the terminological fudge is expedient because it saves having to come to terms with what Hong Kong's primary language really is and what Hong Kong's best option for a medium of instruction should therefore be. Postcolonial Hong Kong, it seems, continues to deny its primary linguistic identity as if, like Hino's Japan, it wished it were English-speaking and English really were the primary medium of instruction not because this is supposed to be the optimal option for purposes of globalization or modernization but because most students are comfortable in it.

But what this fudge may also permit is the gradual insertion of Mandarin, by the back door, as it were, as happened in Southern China and elsewhere in non-Mandarin-speaking parts of the country, where Mandarin was gradually introduced into schools, with the language and other subjects sometimes taught by teachers who were far from fluent in it. If so, what is the risk that a Cantonese-speaking society might not end up semi-literate in not two but three languages (Mandarin, Cantonese, and English)?

For decades, medium of instruction policy in Hong Kong has gone back and forth between promoting Chinese (without specifying what that might mean but probably with the Mandarin standard in mind) as well as English in a society where neither is spoken domestically and therefore fluently by the vast majority of the population. As regards English, and despite repeated educational failure, Hong Kong educators and language education policy makers continue to hope that as long as enough money is thrown at the problem, the teaching is efficient and the testing rigorous, and Hong Kong students can be made to sit through enough English grammar lessons, they will perform competently in English. As Li (this volume) reports, this belief appears to be in the process of being applied to Mandarin in the hope that 'trilingualism and triliteracy' might ensue. If so, this would flow not from an educational but a political agenda, namely the aim of drawing Hong Kong gradually into the Chinese fold.

Ideally, the proper response would be to at last accept the linguistic realities of Hong Kong and do the unmentionable, namely, make Cantonese (not 'Chinese') the primary medium of instruction, with English and Mandarin added gradually through the grade levels. This would require considerable political courage, starting with a clear statement of the rationale behind such as move if the advocates of national unity above all else and, not least, Hong Kong parents were to be brought on board. Regrettably, there are no signs that this scenario is being considered, and semi-literacy in three languages seems the most likely outcome for Hong Kong.

Running around in Circles

Discussions of language and language education in Asia and elsewhere often take place in just the kind of terminological fog I describe above. A case in point is the issue of what it means to be 'bilingual'.

In Bruthiaux (2003a), I take issue with the Kachru model of the Three Circles of English for being over-focussed on colonial history, thereby missing key differences including varying degrees of multilingualism in each locality leading to varying needs for English as a lingua franca. However, as a description of the presence of English worldwide, the model does capture broad (though not always fashionable) realities. In brief, in one type of setting (the Inner Circle), English is spoken by a substantial majority, often having been acquired as the sole language of the home. In another (the

Outer Circle), English is spoken for domestic communication to a high degree of proficiency by a minority, as an additional language and to varying degrees of proficiency by many, and little or not at all by the rest of the population. In a third (the Expanding Circle), English is studied extensively but used domestically very little, resulting in vast numbers of what Bolton (2003) calls with reference to China 'English-knowing bilinguals'.

Clearly, millions all across Asia know English or at least something about it. Indeed, given the huge sums devoted to English language education in Asia both publicly and privately over the past decades, if this were not the case, it would amount to educational failure on a shocking scale. But does knowing English amount to bilingualism? The answer, of course, is what might be understood by the term 'bilingual' so that the debate takes place on ground broadly shared by all participants. In response, a personal anecdote may be revealing.

I grew up in a monolingual home in an overwhelmingly monolingual town in a country (France) that was in the final stages of wiping out its minority languages (Catalan, Basque, Breton, Flemish, German, etc.) before it began to acquire new ones through immigration (Arabic, Turkish, Portuguese, etc.). The language of home was French, and from about the age of ten I was familiarized with my first additional language when I started studying Latin in school. Study consisted of memorizing morphological paradigms, discussing the intricacies of Latin syntax in French, and translating in both directions, thereby — incidentally — picking up valuable dictionary skills. I was reasonably proficient at it and I learned early on that any school subject could be motivating as long as the content was of interest to a 14-year-old boy (Caesar's military campaigns were a special favourite), but could also induce profound stupor (readily diagnosed by teachers as laziness) when the content consisted of odes to Etruscan orchards (Virgil) or disquisitions on the virtues of republican government (Cicero). Obviously, communication was never envisaged, but through weekly church attendance I probably had more contact with Latin as an additional language outside of the classroom than millions of Asian students have with English in settings where English has little or no extracurricular presence.

Without a doubt, I was 'Latin-knowing', but to regard myself as bilingual at that point would have been absurd. Obviously, bilingualism should not be seen as the preserve of those rarely sighted beasts known as 'balanced' bilinguals. Nor should we ignore the fact that, as I said at the start, Asia is a hugely disparate continent, home to the entire gamut of mono-, bi-, multi-, and especially plurilingualisms. But at some point, going beyond one language must involve acquiring the ability to process information (also known as 'communicative competence') in all of the simultaneous or subsequent languages, however unequally. Importantly and despite a misconception widely shared among language teachers, communicative competence need not involve speaking and listening in that an engineer, say, who is reading technical material in English fluently but has little or no need for spoken communication in English qualifies as 'bilingual', in my book. But merely knowing about a language such that a test might be aced and admission to further study gained should be seen as a necessary but not sufficient characteristic of bilingualism.

Curiously, some Asian perspectives of language education (including, in this volume, both Canagarajah and Feng) look to Europe for support of policies promoting bi- and trilingual education. Much quoted — perhaps even revered — by analysts is the Council of Europe's 2000 document entitled *Common European Framework of Reference for Languages* and analyzed in some detail in Bergan (2009).

This is puzzling, for two reasons. First, while there is an obvious parallel between most European nations and countries such as China or Japan in terms of the ubiquitous presence of English in classrooms but its notable absence outside, any comparison with Europe is largely invalid in riotously multilingual countries such as India, Sri Lanka, the Philippines, Malaysia, or Singapore, where unlike in Europe, monolinguals are few and English has a strong presence outside of the classroom (at least in urban areas) because it functions as a medium of internal communication.

Second, probably as for most EU-wide public issues, language policy is framed within a highly politicized context. Typically, the aim is to reconcile the often jarring interests of nation-states that include substantial monolingual populations (at least in early life), a second language learned in school, and a third added at the insistence (mostly) of the French to ensure that English does not become the sole second language of Europeans. In other words, European language education policy reflects not second language acquisition research but highly political horse-trading among treaty writers. The result of this deal is that vast numbers of speakers of a multiplicity of L1s are also learners of two foreign languages, typically at a proficiency level far below that of their L1 and rarely coming into contact with these L2s, let alone having opportunities to communicate in them outside of the classroom: in Bolton's (2003) terms, 'L2/L3-knowing trilinguals', but in mine, monolinguals with some knowledge of two foreign languages.

This distinction matters not because some conventional association between the term 'bilingual' and a specific meaning must be respected. Meaning evolves as social preoccupations come and go and usage shifts. For a social contract over meaning to be effective, meanings need to be flexible but also reasonably constrained. Yet in some discussions of language education, the term 'bilingual' is used to refer to any state of knowledge of two languages on a continuum, where at one end both are known and used equally in most domains while at the other end one language is used almost exclusively in most domains and the other rarely or not at all because it is only known about and in any case hardly ever needed. At this point, the term ceases to function as a tool for communication over matters of language.

To pick up the personal narrative a few decades later, I now boast substantial communicative competence in two languages: French and (I hope) English. Largely through watching *futbol* on Hispanic TV stations, I acquired moderate communicative competence in Spanish, somewhat less in Portuguese. Several dreary years of study made me German-knowing, and I have picked up limited Japanese and Thai. Adding Latin to the mix makes me octolingual. And come to think of it, I do have a smattering of Malay, so perhaps I should make that nine. Or not, depending on where the line is drawn. For draw a line we must, I suggest, if the debate is not to turn into a recitation of relativistic pieties.

It is widely believed throughout Asia (except perhaps in North Korea) that everyone must have English. Hino (this volume) even reports that voices are now heard in Japan bemoaning the fact that the country had the misfortune not to be colonized by Britain or the US since colonization would most likely have bequeathed Japan an English on par with, say, the Philippines variety. The most common justification for this belief is that English is essential to international trade, hence modernization and economic development. Of course this ignores the fact that absence of English did not prevent Japan from going from post-WW2 annihilation to first world status in just three decades even as the nation with English (the Philippines) struggled (and continues to struggle) to emerge from poverty.

In Bruthiaux (2008), I outline a rationale for doubting that developing countries in Southeast Asia should embark on expensive policies aiming (implausibly) at equipping every one of their citizens with communicative competence in English. In effect, I caution against the inroads currently made by English as medium of instruction in both postcolonial and non-postcolonial Asian settings. This is meant to counter the widespread belief that globalization involves everyone — or at least everyone's children — and that the process will benefit those who can join in thanks to English and leave those who cannot mired in poverty. This belief, I argue, is based more in faith than in evidence because it has not been demonstrated that the future livelihood of every student across the region will soon depend on communicating in English on a daily basis.

An additional misconception in postcolonial, post-Kachru Asia is not just that everyone must have English but that every nation must have **an** English. To put it crudely, once I have spotted the latest top-of-the-range model in my neighbour's driveway, I must have one too regardless of how unsuited to my needs or my pocketbook the acquisition might be. Call it 'English envy', perhaps. To the extent that English is perceived as a mark of modernity, and aspirations to modernity play a significant role in driving efforts by populations to rise out of poverty, this is to be welcome. But wishing for an English does not by itself provide evidence that such as thing has come into being.

For an Asian country to transition from Kachru's Expanding to Outer Circle would require that those decades of English language study finally begin to bear fruit. At that point, Asians would have become truly bilingual in the sense that they would have added English to their linguistic repertoire to the point where they communicate in it competently not only internationally but also internally, English-knowing Japanese, say, readily speaking English to other English-knowing Japanese much as English-knowing Indians readily speak English to other English-knowing Indians when called upon by circumstances. Until this happens — and it is very difficult to see what social reconfiguration might make it happen in countries such as Japan, China, or South Korea — English in these societies will not become endonormative beyond exhibiting local phonological features and some locally borrowed lexis (for the educational implications of this observation, see He and Li 2009).

As Li (this volume) explains, even in a former British colonial setting such as Hong Kong English never found a substantial internal role beyond a few niches such as the law and higher education (at least in theory). This is because Hong Kong has a remained an overwhelmingly largely monolingual, Cantonese-speaking society where English did not grow deep roots because — unlike in Singapore, to which it is often compared — English was never called upon to serve as a local lingua franca. This suggests that despite widely-shared aspirations — with educational budgets to match — to institutionalized bilingualism, non-postcolonial societies such as China and Japan but also South Korea, Indonesia, or Thailand are likely to be disappointed in their quest for an English. Nor should we imagine that, as Hino (this volume) advocates, merely introducing English in local classrooms via local, culturally appropriate content (a welcome development in itself) is tantamount to witnessing the rise of another English. In practice, there is little evidence that countries such as Japan, China, or South Korea are transitioning from Kachru's Expanding to Outer Circle. For now and for the foreseeable future, Kachru's original characterization of Expanding Circle locations remains valid.

Do predictions have a future?

Ever since the sage of baseball Yogi Berra pointed it out, it has been widely recognized that it's tough to make predictions, especially about the future. In systems as complex as modern countries, making predictions on the basis of past trends is often necessary but highly unstable because of the permanent risk of sudden interference by what Taleb (2007) calls a 'Black Swan', that is, a highly improbable but not entirely impossible event that, when it occurs, is of such magnitude that it invalidates neat descriptions of past or present conditions (such as bell curves, for example) as well as rational, linear predictions of future trends.

Of course, countries do not come any larger than China in terms of population and — before too long — in economic clout either. Among recent expositions of China's emergence to global supremacy, Jacques (2009) is especially sanguine in forecasting — among other upheavals — that Shanghai will overshadow New York and London as a centre of global finance, the thoughts of Confucius will be as familiar to students worldwide as those of Plato, and Mandarin will have supplanted English as the language of choice for international communication. At least that is the plan.

Now consider the following scenarios. Imagine that at some point in the coming decade or two, we witness the peaceful integration of Taiwan into Greater China along 'One Country, Two Systems' lines, or the converse, international confrontation as Taiwan rejects integration and neighbouring countries as well as the US are drawn into military conflict with China. Or the Kim regime in North Korea suddenly collapses, sending vast numbers of refugees south, which becomes South Korea's problem, but also north, which now becomes China's problem, possibly leading to severe social and economic destabilization in the northeast of China. Or China as a nation undergoes territorial adjustments as a result of growing separatism in western provinces (Tibet and Xinjiang), or the converse, namely, further territorial expansion into central Asia or Siberia at the expense of a waning Russia to secure access to hydrocarbons and other mineral resources.

This is not to wish calamities on the people of China. A nation that managed to raise so many of its people out of poverty in such a short time deserves admiration as well as our fervent hope that the country will continue on the path to substantial poverty reduction. However, extrapolations on the basis of 30 years of rapid development and linear predictions of more of the same over the next 30 or more are premature. In other words, watch out for black swans, and never say ever.

In Bruthiaux (2003b), I review research warning that the growing integration of most world economies widely known as 'globalization' should not be taken for granted. Just as an earlier process of global integration ended in sharp retreat — and for many, in severe impoverishment — as the devastations of WWI were followed by those of the Great Depression of the 1930s, early 21st century trends toward greater economic and cultural globalization are not inexorable. Indeed, the 2008 financial crisis led to immediate falls not just in the paper value of investments but also to real incomes for many, especially for the very poor, and to sharp and immediate falls in economic output, international trade, and exchanges, including travel. While a prolonged downturn accompanied by significant protectionism is highly undesirable because it would inevitably return many in Asia to the poverty they escaped only recently, at the time of writing (July 2009) it remains a distinct possibility despite some recent sightings of 'green shoots'. Were this to happen, the recent debate (including much of the content of this volume) on the effect of globalization on the language ecology of Asia may become moot.

In fact, history suggests caution. Few at the end of the US civil war in 1865 imagined that a war-ravaged, relatively isolated, largely agrarian country was destined to become a world power within a few short decades. Conversely at the start of the 20th century, Argentina was one of the ten wealthiest nations in the world (Tanzi 2007) but in 2008 ranked 81st in per capita GDP (CIA 2009). As recently as the 1970s, the Soviet Union was heralded as a model of rapid and equitable economic development and widely copied especially in newly independent nations in Africa and elsewhere. Today the model is widely seen as a historical oddity, and mostly unlamented.

It is also useful to remember that predictions of inexorable growth and imminent supremacy similar to those being heard about China were made regarding Japan as recently as the 1980s, when the export-oriented Japanese economy was expanding rapidly and Japanese financial interests were purchasing US cultural icons including a major Hollywood studio and some very tall buildings in Manhattan (Morton and Olenik 2004). By the end of the decade, Japanese controlled 1% of total US property values. In 1988, seven of the ten largest banks and six of the ten richest men in the world were Japanese. So inexorable was the march of Japanese economic power that a raft of alarmist books came out lamenting the state of terminal decline afflicting the US economy and confidently predicting that the 21st century would be the 'Japanese Century'. Two decades of stagnation and deflation later, Japan has a long-ruling monopolistic single political party (the LDP) seemingly in terminal decline as well as the (not unrelated) largest ratio of public debt to GDP among wealthy nations, which can only be exacerbated by a shrinking population and a rapidly growing 'dependency ratio' (the percentage of people aged 65 and over who depend on those of working age for their welfare). Looking back, world domination by Japan and the attendant rise of the Japanese language as the dominant medium of international communication simply failed to materialize.

What is clear is that whether Mandarin Chinese becomes a major language for international communication — perhaps **the** major language — depends in large part on economic factors and especially on the extent to which China succeeds not only at growing its overall economy — which, after all, given the huge size of the country, cannot help being very large — but also on the country's ability to close the wealth gap being experienced by its own citizens. In this respect it is sobering to recall that in 2008, China remained 132nd in the world in terms of per capita GDP, still substantially behind Thailand (116th) and little more than a quarter of the way to matching South Korea (52nd) (CIA 2009). Until this disparity is reduced and the benefits of rapid economic development and its attendant effects in terms of opportunities for global communication are felt by most, Mandarin, though probably growing in international use and recognition, will likely continue to function overwhelmingly as the medium of national communication for those inside China who have it as a mother tongue and as the medium of instruction for those who do not.

An additional sobering factor is the fact that China continues to do poorly in terms of wealth distribution as measured by the Gini coefficient, a gauge of income disparity where 1 equals 100% of total income going to one person and 0 equals total income shared equally by all, with country coefficients normally multiplied by 100 to range between 0 and 100. While Japan (24.9) has the least unequal distribution in Asia, China is very much at the high end (46.9), far in excess of much poorer Indonesia (34.3), for example (UNDP 2009). A gap of this magnitude will not be narrowed simply as a result of China's economy experiencing another decade or two of rapid economic development, making the risk of social instability — one of the blackest of Black Swans — a confounding variable that invalidates all neatly linear projections regarding the country and the future welfare of its people.

However, probably the only component of forecasting in social policy making that is inherently stable and therefore predictable (apart from death and taxes) is demographics. After all, except in rare cases of pandemics, warfare, or genocide, populations do not normally shrink dramatically over a short period of time, and given the huge size of China's population, it would take near-apocalyptic events — whether natural or man-made — to significantly alter current demographic trends in the country. A peculiarly modern consequence of this predictability is what is sometimes called a 'demographic time bomb', a concept familiar to social policy analysts as well as ordinary citizens, especially in Japan, Russia, and most of Western Europe.

Rapid increases in longevity have become a feature of many societies. This is creating a challenge never before faced by humanity, namely, how to ensure the welfare in old age of large numbers of citizens likely to live far longer than they could have imagined earlier in life. Whether this welfare is provided through taxation (as is the norm in many Western societies) or directly within the extended family (as is the practice in most of Asia), this implies a transfer of wealth from the younger and more active to the older and less active members of society. China is no exception, but the problem for China is about to be exacerbated by the unintended consequences of the 'One-Child Policy' introduced in 1979. Although mostly successful in the short term, the policy has also created a severe imbalance between those born after the policy came into effect (the under-30s) and the two generations before them, who for the most part were born in much larger families.

In practical terms, this means that the number of elderly people as a share of those of working age (the dependency ratio) will rise sharply in many countries including China over the next three to four decades. The biggest absolute increase will be in Japan, where the dependency ratio is already the world's highest (35%) and where it will more than double (to 73%) by mid-century (Eurostat 2009). This will direct an increasing share of the national wealth toward providing welfare for the relatively unproductive elderly and most likely further weaken the geopolitical influence of Japan. Although the rise in the dependency ratio in China will be less severe, the number of older citizens relying on the younger generation for their well-being will rise from 12% today to 39% by 2050. This will be on par with rapidly depopulating Russia, but higher than in the UK and especially the US, assuming that the latter continues to welcome immigrants. By contrast, the ratio for India is expected to rise to just over 20%. This is due to a steadily higher birth rate (2.72 per woman compared to 1.77 for China) (CIA 2009). The likely result in the short- to medium- term is not only that a larger percentage of India's population will be young, dynamic, and productive and dependency costs will be much lower than in China, but also that India's overall population will surpass that of China as early as 2020 (Mari Bhat 2000).

For China, this suggests that, unlike Japan or Germany, the country may become old before it becomes rich and therefore have too little time to make financial provisions for the oncoming demographic crunch. For India, by contrast, this points to continued growth at least a generation beyond the likely Chinese peak. It is true that India introduced reforms to its economy leading to rapid economic growth some 15 years after China, and that its per capita GDP is still less than half that of China's (CIA 2009). Moreover, while China is (and looks likely to remain) a one-party state with a tradition of top-down command that few seem inclined to challenge, India is a tumultuous democracy operating within a federal system, a combination that does not facilitate smooth decision making or efficient policy implementation.

Taken as a whole, however, this information suggests that not only China but also India will grow in global importance both economically and geopolitically but that Indian expansion is likely to outlast China's. By mid-century, Asia will feature not one but two economic, geopolitical, and cultural giants. At present China is receiving the lion's share of attention from observers including language education specialists. India, however, is factored into the linguistic equation in a manner that does not reflect its current and especially its future impact on Asian as well as global affairs.

Specifically, this suggests that discussions of the growing role of Mandarin Chinese as a regional, then global, means of communication should be moderated by the counterbalancing force likely to spring from India in terms of economic development, geopolitical clout, cultural influence, and of course language. The question is, which language or languages? While the major regional languages of India are likely to continue functioning as dominant means of communication each within its own geographic domain, even the language with by far the largest number of speakers, Hindi, is unlikely to rival Chinese because outwardly-oriented Indians for the most part already have access to English not only for the sort of international communication widely forecast to take place increasingly in Chinese but also for internal communication. This will give English of the Indian variety a vitality that it lacks in societies where it manifests itself almost exclusively in classrooms. Assuming also that US economic and geopolitical power does not shrivel into insignificance over the coming decades — a most unlikely outcome — the current combination of economically powerful nations will include India, a country that happens to have English as a substantial player among its languages. This suggests that Chinese, though undoubtedly destined to grow in international representation, will at best have to share the limelight with English as global prominence for Chinese is likely to be tempered by parallel, India-driven growth in the global role of English.

References

Bergan, S. (2009) Academic recognition: Status and challenges. *Assessment in Education: Principles, Policy & Practice* 16: 39–53.

Bolton, K. (2003) *Chinese Englishes: A Sociolinguistic Survey*. Cambridge: Cambridge University Press.

Bruthiaux, P. (2003a) Squaring the Circles: Issues in modeling English worldwide. *International Journal of Applied Linguistics* 13: 159–178.

Bruthiaux, P. (2003b) 21st century trends in language and economics. *Current Issues in Language Planning* 4: 84–90.

Bruthiaux, P. (2008) Language education, economic development, and participation across the Greater Mekong Subregion. *International Journal of Bilingual Education and Bilingualism* 11: 134–148.

CIA (Central Intelligence Agency) (2009) *The World Factbook*. Retrieved 12 July 2009 from https://www.cia.gov/library/publications/the-world-factbook

Eurostat (Statistical Office of the European Commission) (2009). Retrieved 11 July 2009 from http://epp.eurostat.ec.europa.eu/portal/page/portal/eurostat/home

Gooch, L. (2009) In Malaysia, English ban raises fears for future. *International Herald Tribune*. Retrieved 9 July 2009 from http://www.nytimes.com/2009/07/10/world/asia

He, D. and D.C.S. Li (2009) Language attitudes and linguistic features in the "China English" debate. *World Englishes* 28: 70–89.

Jacques, M. (2009) *When China Rules the World: The Rise of the Middle Kingdom and the End of the Western World*. London: Allen Lane.

Mari Bhat, P.N. (2000) *Indian Demographic Scenario 2025*. New Delhi: Institute of Economic Growth.

Morton, W.S. and J.K. Olenik (2004) *Japan: Its History and Culture,* 4th ed. New York: McGraw-Hill.

Taleb, N.N. (2007). *The Black Swan: The Impact of the Highly Improbable*. New York: Random House.

Tanzi, V. (2007) *Argentina: An Economic Chronicle*. New York: Jorge Pinto Books.

UNDP (United Nations Development Programme) (2009) *Annual Report 2009: Living up to Commitments*. UNDP. Retrieved 12 July 2009 from http://www.undp.org/publications/annualreport2009

Access to online full text

ıngenta *connect*

John Benjamins Publishing Company's journals are available in online full-text format as of the volume published in 2000. Some of our journals have additional (multi-media) information available that is referred to in the articles.

Access to the electronic edition of a volume is included in your subscription. We offer a pay-per-view service per article for those journals and volumes to which you did not subscribe.

Full text is provided in PDF. In order to read these documents you will need Adobe Acrobat Reader, which is freely available from **www.adobe.com/products/ acrobat/readstep2.html**

You can access the electronic edition through the gateways of major subscription agents (SwetsWise, EBSCO EJS, Maruzen) or directly through IngentaConnect.

If you currently use **www.ingenta.com** or **www.ingentaselect.com** (formely, Catchword) to access your subscriptions, these rights have been carried over to **www. ingentaconnect.com**, the new, fully merged service. All bookmarked pages will also be diverted to the relevant pages on **www.ingentaconnect.com**.

If you have not yet set up access to the electronic version of the journal at IngentaConnect, please follow these instructions:

If you are a personal subscriber:
- Register free at **www.ingentaconnect.com**. This is a one-time process, that provides IngentaConnect with the information they need to be able to match your data with the subscription data provide by the publisher. Your registration also allows you to use the e-mail alerting services.
- Select *Personal subscriptions.*
- Select the publication title and enter your subscription number. Your subscription number can be found on the shipping label with the print journal, and on the invoice/renewal invitation.
- You will be notified by email once your online access has been activated.

If you are an institutional subscriber:
- Register free at **www.ingentaconnect.com** by selecting the registration link and following the link to institutional registration.
- Select *Set up subscriptions.*
- Select the publication title and enter your subscription number. Your subscription number can be found on the shipping label with the print journal, and on the invoice/renewal invitation.
- You will be notified by email once your online access has been activated.
If you purchase subscriptions via a subscription agent they will be able to set up subscriptions on IngentaConnect on your behalf – simply pass them your IngentaConnect ID, sent to you at registration.

If you would like further information or assistance with your registration, please contact **help@ingentaconnect.com**.

For information on our journals, please visit **www.benjamins.com**

New in Applied Linguistics

Connected Words

Word associations and second language vocabulary acquisition

Paul Meara

Swansea University

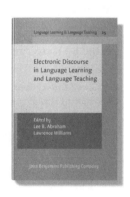

What words come into your head when you think of SUN?
For native English speakers, the most common responses
are MOON, SHINE and HOT, and about half of all native
speaker responses to SUN are covered by these three words.
L2 English speakers are much less obliging, and produce
patterns of association that are markedly different from those
produced by native speakers. Why? What does this tell us about the way L2 speakers'
vocabularies grow and develop? This volume provides a user-friendly introduction to
a research technique which has the potential to answer some long-standing puzzles
about L2 vocabulary. The method is easy to use, even for inexperienced researchers,
but it produces immensely rich data, which can be analysed on many different levels.
The book explores how word association data can be used to probe the development of
vocabulary depth, productive vocabulary skills and lexical organisation in L2 speakers.

[Language Learning & Language Teaching, 24] 2009. xvii, 174 pp.

HB 978 90 272 1986 2 EUR 95.00 / USD 143.00
PB 978 90 272 1987 9 EUR 33.00 / USD 49.95

Electronic Discourse in Language Learning and Language Teaching

Edited by Lee B. Abraham and Lawrence Williams

Villanova University / University of North Texas

New technologies are constantly transforming traditional
notions of language use and literacy in online communication
environments. While previous research has provided a foundation
for understanding the use of new technologies in instructed
second language environments, few studies have investigated new
literacies and electronic discourse beyond the classroom setting.
This volume seeks to address this gap by providing corpus-based
and empirical studies of electronic discourse analyzing social and linguistic variation as
well as communicative practices in chat, discussion forums, blogs, and podcasts. Several
chapters also examine the assessment and integration of new literacies. This volume
will serve as a valuable resource for researchers, teachers, and students interested in
exploring electronic discourse and new literacies in language learning and teaching.

[Language Learning & Language Teaching, 25] 2009. x, 346 pp.

HB 978 90 272 1988 6 EUR 95.00 / USD 143.00

For full title information see *www.benjamins.com*

New in Applied Linguistics

The Exploration of Multilingualism
Development of research on L3, multilingualism and multiple language acquisition

Edited by Larissa Aronin and Britta Hufeisen
University of Haifa / Technical University of Darmstadt

This volume offers an ontogenetic perspective on research on L3, multilingualism and multiple languages acquisition and a conceptually updated picture of multilingualism studies and third/multiple language acquisition studies. The contributions by prominent scholars of multilingualism present state-of-the-art accounts of the significant aspects in this field. This unique collection of articles adopts a broad-spectrum and synthesized view on the topic. The volume, largely theoretical and classificatory, features main theories, prominent researchers and important research trends. The articles also contain factual and historical material from previous and current decades of research and offer practical information on research resources. For lecturers, students, educators, researchers, and social workers operating in multilingual contexts, *The Exploration of Multilingualism* is manifestly relevant.

[AILA Applied Linguistics Series, 6] 2009. vii, 158 pp. + index
HB 978 90 272 0522 3 EUR 85.00 / USD 128.00

Task-Based Language Teaching
A reader

Edited by Kris Van den Branden, Martin Bygate and John M. Norris
Katholieke Universiteit Leuven / University of Lancaster / University of Hawai'i at Manoa

Over the past two decades, task-based language teaching (TBLT) has gained considerable momentum in the field of language education. This volume presents a collection of 20 reprinted articles and chapters representative of work that appeared during that period. It introduces readers – graduate students, researchers, teachers – to foundational ideas and themes that have marked the emergence of TBLT. The editors provide a first chapter that locates TBLT within broader discourses of educational practice and research on language learning and teaching. The book then features four sections consisting of important, often difficult to find, writings on major themes: fundamental ideas, approaches, and definitions in TBLT; curriculum, syllabus, and task design; variables affecting task-based language learning and performance; and task-based assessment. In a concluding chapter, the editors challenge simplistic notions of TBLT by reflecting on how this body of work has initiated the possibility of a truly researched language pedagogy, and they highlight critical directions in TBLT research and practice for the future.

[Task-Based Language Teaching: Issues, Research and Practice, 1] 2009. ix, 512 pp.
HB 978 90 272 0717 3 EUR 110.00 / USD 165.00
PB 978 90 272 0718 0 EUR 36.00 / USD 54.00

For full title information see *www.benjamins.com*

New in Applied Linguistics

Bilingualism and Identity
Spanish at the crossroads with other languages

Edited by Mercedes Niño-Murcia and Jason Rothman
The University of Iowa

Sociolinguists have been pursuing connections between language and identity for several decades. But how are language and identity related in bilingualism and multilingualism? Mobilizing the most current methodology, this collection presents new research on language identity and bilingualism in three regions where Spanish coexists with other languages. The cases are Spanish-English contact in the United States, Spanish-indigenous language contact in Latin America, and Spanish-regional language contact in Spain. This is the first comparativist book to examine language and identity construction among bi- or multilingual speakers while keeping one of the languages constant. The sociolinguistic standing of Spanish varies among the three regions depending whether or not it is a language of prestige. Comparisons therefore afford a strong constructivist perspective on how linguistic ideologies affect bi/multilingual identity formation.

[Studies in Bilingualism, 37] 2008. vii, 365 pp.
PB 978 90 272 4179 5 EUR 33.00 / USD 49.95

Incomplete Acquisition in Bilingualism
Re-examining the Age Factor

Silvina A. Montrul
University of Illinois at Urbana-Champaign

Age effects have played a particularly prominent role in some theoretical perspectives on second language acquisition. This book takes an entirely new perspective on this issue by re-examining these theories in light of the existence of apparently similar non-native outcomes in adult heritage speakers who, unlike adult second language learners, acquired two or more languages in childhood. Despite having been exposed to their family language early in life, many of these speakers never fully acquire, or later lose, aspects of their first language sometime in childhood. The book examines the structural characteristics of "incomplete" grammatical states and highlights how age of acquisition is related to the type of linguistic knowledge and behavior that emerges in L1 and L2 acquisition under different environmental circumstances. By underscoring age of acquisition as a unifying factor in the study of L2 acquisition and L1 attrition, it is claimed that just as there are age effects in L2 acquisition, there are also age effects, or even perhaps a critical period, in L1 attrition. The book covers adult L2 acquisition, attrition in adults and in children, and includes a comparison of adult heritage language speakers and second language learners.

[Studies in Bilingualism, 39] 2008. x, 312 pp.
PB 978 90 272 4180 1 EUR 36.00 / USD 54.00

For full title information see *www.benjamins.com*

Phraseology in Foreign Language Learning and Teaching

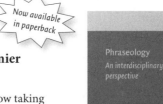

Edited by Fanny Meunier and Sylviane Granger
Université Catholique de Louvain

This book addresses the key role of phraseology in second language acquisition and instruction. It is divided into three main sections: *Extracting and Describing Phraseological Units* investigates the role played by native and learner corpora in the extraction and description of multiword units, two initial and crucial steps in informing language pedagogy; *Learning Phraseological Units* deals with the learning aspect, an oft-neglected yet essential dimension of phraseology in second/foreign language pedagogy, this section also addresses issues in new literacies; and *Recording and Exploiting Phraseological Units* focuses on pedagogical tools, notably monolingual and bilingual dictionaries and textbooks. This stimulating collection presents cutting edge research in the field and identifies major avenues for future theoretical and applied work. It is of particular relevance to researchers and teachers interested in the patterned nature of language.

2008. xi, 259 pp.

PB 978 90 272 3267 0 EUR 33.00 / USD 49.95

Phraseology
An interdisciplinary perspective

Edited by Sylviane Granger and Fanny Meunier
Université Catholique de Louvain

Long regarded as a peripheral issue, phraseology is now taking centre stage in a wide range of fields. This recent explosion of interest undoubtedly has a great deal to do with the development of corpus linguistics research, which has both demonstrated the key role of phraseological expressions in language and provided researchers with automated methods of extraction and analysis. The aim of this volume is to take stock of current research in phraseology from a variety of perspectives: theoretical, descriptive, contrastive, cultural, lexicographic and computational. It contains overview chapters by leading experts in the field and a series of case studies focusing on a wide range of multiword units: collocations, similes, idioms, routine formulae and recurrent phrases. The volume is an invitation for experienced phraseologists to look at the field with different eyes and a useful introduction for the many researchers who are intrigued by phraseology but need help in finding their way in this rich but complex domain.

2008. xxviii, 422 pp.

PB 978 90 272 3268 7 EUR 36.00 / USD 54.00

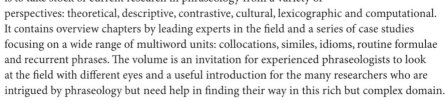

For full title information see *www.benjamins.com*